The Hungarian Pocahontas:
The Life and Times of
Laura Polanyi Stricker, 1882-1959

Judith Szapor

EAST EUROPEAN MONOGRAPHS, BOULDER, COLORADO
DISTRIBUTED BY COLUMBIA UNIVERSITY PRESS, NEW YORK
2005

EAST EUROPEAN MONOGRAPHS, NO. DCLXII

Copyright 2005 by Judith Szapor

ISBN: 0-88033-562-9

Library of Congress Control Number: 2005924342

Printed in the United States of America

Table of Contents

List of Illustrations

1. Three generations of Polanyi women: Laura, Eva, and Cecile, at their last reunion, winter of 1937, Budapest. Courtesy of Hungarian National Museum, Hungarian Photo Archive (HNM HphA).

2. The Pollacsek ancestors: Adolf and Zsofia Pollacsek, around 1850. Courtesy of Eva Zeisel.

3. A. Wohl, rabbinical scholar and assimilationist. Courtesy of Eva Zeisel.

4. The Pollacseks' living room around the turn of the century; Cecile with the portrait of the children. Reprinted from Hanák, ed. *Magyarország története*, illustration 146.

5. Andrássy út, representative of the capitalist splendour of the Hungarian capital, in 1899. The Pollacsek apartment occupied most of the third floor of the building on the left. HNM PhA, reprinted from Kontler, *Millennium in Central Europe*, illustration 21.

6. The title page of A. Wohl's *Prayer of the Jews for the Whole Year*, Vilna, 1870. Courtesy of Eva Zeisel.

7. Mihály Pollacsek (on the right) with his brother Károly in the early 1900s. Courtesy of Eva Zeisel.

8. The salon at the beginning of the 20th century. In the centre, in her trademark reclining position, Cecile. To her right, Mihály Pollacsek. Sitting on the far right, Ervin Szabó and Oszkár Jászi. Courtesy of HNM HPhA.

9. Young Laura (in the middle) with the Klatschko girls at the Klatschkos' summer house at Hinterbrühl, near Vienna, around 1900. Courtesy of HNM HPhA.

10. Title page for the 1904 edition of the *Bibliographia Economica Universalis*, edited by "Laure Pollacsek." Courtesy of Eva Zeisel.

11. Portrait of Laura from the early 1900s. Courtesy of HNM HPhA.

12. Laura and Sándor Stricker shortly after the birth of their first child. Courtesy of Eva Zeisel.

13. The young wife and mother in the summer of 1907. Courtesy of Eva Zeisel.

14. Laura with Michael and Eva, in impeccably tailored, matching outfits, around 1909. Courtesy of Eva Zeisel.

15. Laura and her children in the garden of her kindergarten under 86 Andrássy út, in 1911. Attesting to Laura's progressive pedagogical ideas, the picture was sent as a postcard to her friend, Recha Rundt in Vienna. Courtesy of Eva Zeisel.

16. "Aunt Mausi" teaching, 1911. Eva is on the right. Note the gym outfits and bare feet of the children. Courtesy of Eva Zeisel.

17. The classroom of the kindergarten. In the first row to the left is Eva Stricker, behind her in the last row is young Arthur Koestler. Courtesy of Eva Zeisel.

18. An intimate portrait of Laura with Michael and Eva, shortly after the birth of their brother George Otto in 1912. Courtesy of Eva Zeisel.

19. Karl Polanyi on leave in Vienna, with the Stricker children, around 1915. In the back: Sophie and Cecile. Courtesy of Eva Zeisel.

20. The family during World War I: Egon Szécsi, Sophie, Cecile, Adolf, Médi Vedres, and (in uniform) Karl and Michael Polanyi. Courtesy of Eva Zeisel.

21. At home on the Danube: Sándor and Laura with (from left) Gina Stricker, Eva and Michael Stricker, and unidentified children. Courtesy of HNM HPhA.

22. Laura, the only Polanyi sibling remaining in Hungary, with her husband and youngest son around 1920. Courtesy of Eva Zeisel.

23. Portrait of the young artist: Eva in the garden during the early 1920s. Courtesy of Eva Zeisel.

24. Alexander Weissberg and Eva in the Soviet Union, early 1930s. Courtesy of Eva Zeisel.

25. Laura in front of a Lenin monument, somewhere in the Soviet Union. Courtesy of HNM HPhA.

26. Laura, back from the Soviet Union. Courtesy of HNM HPhA.

27. Last visit: Cecile with Laura, Hilde, and Michelle Stricker in Budapest, end of 1938. Courtesy of HNM HPhA.

28. Family reunion in uncertain times: Michael, Adolf, and Laura Polanyi in England, spring of 1939. Courtesy of Eva Zeisel.

29. Laura in her New York apartment in the early 1950s, posing under Cecile's portrait. Laura's inscription on the back: "The thoughtful mother and her pretty little daughter." Courtesy of Eva Zeisel.

30. The last reunion of the four surviving Polanyi siblings in New York in 1954: Michael, Adolf, and Karl, with Laura lovingly looking on. Reprinted from Vezér, ed., *Irástudó Nemzedékek.*

31. One of the last pictures of Laura. Courtesy of HNM HPhA.

Acknowledgements

Almost ten years in the making, the completion of this project could not have been possible without the generous co-operation of Eva Zeisel and Jean Richards. Not only are they connected with the closest family ties, as daughter and granddaughter, respectively, to the subject of this biography, they are also the true heirs of Laura Polanyi as keepers of the Polanyi-Stricker family's history. They have provided invaluable help by devoting days to lengthy inteviews, sharing with me memories, family documents, photographs, and insights. I hope to have lived up to their trust by making this biography as complete and fair as I possibly could. I also thank other members of the family, Kari Polanyi Levitt, Barbara Stricker, Sándor Stricker, Ruth Danon and the late Hilde Striker, for granting me interviews and copies of family documents.

While I am truly grateful for all their help, I realize they might not agree with every detail of my presentation of their family's history. A thorough inquiry would reveal controversial episodes and conflicting interpretations in any ordinary family's past; this applies to a much greater extent to a family of distinguished intellectuals, determined to control their own history and legacy. But such is the historian's task, at once privileged and overwhelming: to keep a balance between the roles of confidant of family secrets, judge of character and chronicler of achievement, success, and occasional failure.

Over these years, at times struggling with the balancing act between studies, writing and family responsibilities, I relied on the endless encouragement, insight and example of Bettina Bradbury of York University. She and Yves Frenette of Glendon College and York University read previous versions of the manuscript and provided invaluable advice. Harold Troper, Paula Draper, Jeet Heer, Andrea Pető and Annie Szamosi helped with advice and friendship at various impasses. Two Andrew W. Mellon Foundation travel grants, received through the CREES of the University of Toronto helped finance initial stages of my research. A SSHRC post-doctoral fellowship, held at the Department of Theory and Policy Studies of OISE, University of Toronto made it possible to expand on the original doctoral dissertation and incorporate new research into the manuscript.

Professor Margie Mendell of Concordia University, in her role as director of the Karl Polanyi Archives in Montreal was a most generous host in every sense. The librarians at the Hungarian National Széchényi Library's Manuscript Collection, including Dr. Orsolya Karsay were generous with their time and assistance. Katalin Jalsovszky, director of the Photo Archives of the Hungarian National Museum provided expert help with locating family photographs as well as copies and copyright issues. Dr. Eva Gabor welcomed me to the journal *Polanyiana* and has been a valuable source of information on all things Polanyi.

I had encountered the Polanyi family many years before embarking on the writing of this book. I was an undergraduate student at Budapest University, searching for a thesis topic when a young professor, the late Péter Balassa suggested that I look at a freshly published collection of articles from the turn-of-the-century progressive journal called "Twentieth Century." Another helpful professor, Éva H. Balázs sent me to the editor of the volume, György Litván. At the time a political outcast, safely kept from teaching, he introduced me to the politics and culture of the golden age of the Hungarian fin-de-siècle, advised me on a dissertation topic (barely tolerated by university officials at the time) and subsequently became my unofficial supervisor. In the decades that followed, the Soviet Empire crumbled, regimes fell, and former outcasts were elevated to leading positions. But some things never change: I still consider him my most important first reader.

The list of my debts would not be complete without mentioning my closest family. Most of all, I have to thank my partner in life with whom I have also shared the adventure of building, from scratch, a new life in a new country and language. It is his unflinching support, not to mention his steady help with computers and other technical matters that had given me the confidence and energy to finish this project. As for my two children, they keep me on my toes and, as my daughter had put it so succinctly years ago, make life infinitely more interesting. Finally, I would like to think that my late mother, a pioneering lawyer and legal historian in her own time, would be thrilled to read this book about another female pioneer. She would have found much in common with her kind of gentle and considerate trailblazing.

Introduction

Three generations of women, from the left, Laura Polanyi, Eva Stricker, and Cecile Pollacsek, posed for this photograph in Budapest, in the winter of 1937-38 (Fig. 1.). The photo's careful staging and the expression of two younger women suggest that they were fully aware of the significance of the occasion. What Laura and Eva knew (and may have kept from Cecile) was the fact that it was their last visit to Budapest before their imminent emigration to the United States; what none of them could possibly foresee was that it was to be their last meeting with Cecile who died within less than two years.

The picture captured more than a memorable moment, the reunion of grandmother, mother and daughter: the three women, each remarkable and accomplished in her own right, represented three consecutive generations of the Polanyi family. As such, it provides a fitting introduction to the following biography of Laura Polanyi, located within the larger family history of the Polanyis.

By the late 1930s, the family already earned legendary status by virtue of its contributions to early-twentieth-century's Hungary's political and cultural life and was well on its way to reach the highest echelons of Western European and North American academia. A look at the Polanyis' family tree gives some indication of the staggering extent of talent in the family.[1] Two of Laura's younger brothers, Karl and Michael Polanyi, were to achieve international renown and their ideas continue to inspire and provoke to this day. Their older brother, Adolf Polanyi, along with their eldest sister, Laura, had similarly brilliant starts in the early years of 20th-century Austria-Hungary. Along with members of the extended family, among them, most notably, their mother, the Polanyi siblings made vital contributions to the progressive political and cultural scene of the period. Taking into account the family's friends and acquaintances, it would not be entirely farfetched to state that a family history of the Polanyis would amount to a veritable cultural and intellectual history of this period, noted for its extraordinary cohort of social scientists, philosophers, and modernist artists.

In addition, the family's history from the second half of the 19th century offers a valuable case study in the history of Jewish assimilation. The Polanyis exemplified one of the trajectories of the assimilating Jewish middle class, shared by many in the early-twentieth-century Hungarian intellectual elite; they arrived from the Monarchy's periphery to its political and cultural heartland, then reached the centres of European and North American culture, all within a few generations.[2]

Several family members achieved prominence in the Central-European intellectual elite during the 1920s, but the family's reputation reached almost mythical proportions in North American academic circles in the aftermath of WWII, due mainly to the rising scholarly stature of Karl and Michael Polanyi. In American scholarship devoted to the refugee intellectual wave, the Polanyis came to represent the small but remarkably talented and successful group of Hungarian émigrés who arrived in North America just before World War II, prompting scholars to investigate the "clues to the mystery of Hungarian talent."[3] Highlighting the family's significance, an important survey of the intellectual refugees in the United States devoted two pages to the Polanyis out of a five-page long chapter on Hungarians.[4]

While American scholarship acknowledged the contribution of intellectual émigrés from Hungary, it has paid little attention to their roots in turn-of-the-century Austria-Hungary.[5] The Polanyis' significance in Hungarian and Central European cultural history was only surpassed by their contribution to Western European and North American culture; the history of the family thus promised to be ideally suited to carry the legacy of this wonderfully rich and undeservedly little-known period of Hungarian history to a North American readership.

My decision to focus on the women of the family was initially motivated by the fact that compared to the thriving scholarship dedicated to the famous Polanyi men,[6] very little effort had been committed to chronicle the achievements of the women in the family.[7] True, Cecile Pollacsek, the mother of Karl and Michael Polanyi was cited as the source of the Polanyis' legendary intellectual talents.[8] As well, the role of her legendary salon in Budapest, the gathering place of the progressive young intellectuals and artists in the early years of the 20th century, has been repeatedly mentioned, along with her journalistic and pedagogical ambitions and connections with the Russian revolutionary Left.[9] As for Laura, the older sister of Karl and Michael Polanyi, she was noted as much for her legendary beauty as for her pioneering activities before WWI; among the first women to graduate with a Ph.D. from Budapest University, she was known to be a feminist and the founder of an experimental kindergarten.[10]

A closer look at these accomplishments, often mentioned but never before explored as well as at the women's role in the family dynamics, revealed highly unique qualities about each of the three women. Cecile's ease of moving between countries, languages and cultures, from Vilna through Vienna to Budapest and Weimar Berlin, in the course of a few decades between the 1880s and the 1920s, was simply spectacular. In her unerring instinct for new intellectual trends and disregard for bourgeois conventions, she was more original and rebellious than her ever-cautious daughter Laura. As for Eva, not only she inherited the rebellious spirit of Cecile and became an artist of international renown but was also a consummate professional, something her mother never managed to achieve.

Yet even in comparison with her remarkable mother and daughter, Laura Polanyi emerged as not only pivotal to the family's history but also as the most complex and fascinating subject of the three. During a long and productive life, Laura Polanyi amassed a stellar list of accomplishments. From her early achievements as an educator, historian, and politician in Hungary, to her late contribution to American historiography, she earned a place in the vanguard of women pioneers in politics and the professions. Her life allows us to ponder the "possibilities and impossibilities" faced by educated professional women of her generation, born in the last decades of the 19th century. Moreover, as a member of the refugee wave from Hitler's Europe to North America, she made a successful transition, all the more remarkable because achieved relatively late in life. Finally, by assembling and preserving a family archive, she became the custodian of her family's history, as if calling future historians to the task.

To capture a life that spanned historical periods, cultures and continents, called for an approach that went beyond fixed paradigms and methodologies. Most importantly, it resulted in bridging hitherto separate bodies of literature, most notably, connecting the social and intellectual history of the Hungarian turn of the century with the scholarship on the intellectual refugees to North America. In addition, Laura Polanyi's role as a feminist activist and politician in the early-20th-century Austro-Hungarian Monarchy called for confronting two distinct narratives of the bourgeois women's rights movement in Austria-Hungary, one told by the North American scholarship of women's history, the other, emerging, embedded in local social and intellectual history. Combined with her late professional success in the United States, it also offered Laura Polanyi as the potential subject for a study in transnationalism.[11]

The retelling of this life entailed piecing together archival documents with secondary and literary sources as well as interviews and photographs, and, finally, sifting it all through layers of family myths.

Of all these bodies of literature, Hungarian scholarship on the social and intellectual history of the early twentieth century is the most important backdrop to the history of the Polanyis, and the least familiar to the North American reader. It is also a relatively recent field of inquiry. While the collective achievement of the literary and artistic avant-garde of the period (the poet Endre Ady, the poets and writers of the revue *Nyugat*, the artists' group "The Eights," the music of Bartók and Kodály) had been a long-accepted part of the Hungarian national canon, the work of the progressive group of sociologists and philosophers, gathered around the journal *Huszadik Század*[12] and the Sociological Society, were just as long banished from it. This small group, led by Oszkár Jászi and named after their flagship journal "The circle of the Twentieth Century," single-handedly introduced modern social science in Hungary. In the twenty volumes of the series "The Library of Social Science" they translated and published the works of Darwin, Spencer, Durkheim, Loria, Bergson, and Marx, to mention just a few. At the same time, they mapped out the obstacles hindering Hungary's modernization and proposed a comprehensive programme to bring Hungary's political and social structure in line with the Western European democracies.[13]

The journal and the debating society provided the basis for a broad-based coalition of progressive political and intellectual movements, encompassing the artistic and literary avant-garde, Georg Lukács' Sunday Society, the Social Democrats, and the progressive student organizations. In addition, the circle created a wide web of institutions, including their journal, publishing house, the Free School for Social Sciences, an open university and workers' education courses, along with a multitude of civic associations. Members of the circle even founded their own free-mason lodges and, from 1914, their political party, the Hungarian Bourgeois Radical Party. These institutions allowed the circle to function as a "progressive counter-culture," independent from the official political system and its nationalistic culture.[14] During the political crisis of 1905-6 the circle was confronted with the choice between the politics of national independence or democratic progress. Jászi and his friends' unequivocal decision to opt for the latter proved to be fatal. First, it resulted in the dissolution of the circle's original coalition of newly assimilated Jewish intellectuals with the most progressive elements of the traditional middle-class intelligentsia and limited its membership, almost exclusively, to young Jewish intellectuals.[15] In the long run, it provided the pretext for the ideology of the right-wing regime of the afterwar period to declare the circle of the Twentieth Century the scapegoat for Hungary's defeat and dismemberment in the Peace Treaty.

To the Communist regime of the post-WWII era, the legacy of the circle evoked bourgeois and liberal-democratic values and political tolerance, and was equally unacceptable. It was only in the late 1970s, with the Hungarian democratic political opposition searching for its own tradition, that the circle of the Twentieth Century was rediscovered.[16] While the democratic counter-culture of the early century provided its late twentieth-century equivalent with a sense of continuity and tradition, the achievements of the circle in sociology, political science, and economics, infused the social thought of the 1970s and 1980 with a new energy.

Historical scholarship was among the primary beneficiaries of this process. The volumes of correspondences of the period's leading figures, Mihály Károlyi, Ervin Szabó, and Oszkár Jászi, were followed by re-editions of their historical and political writings and were partially responsible for the re-evaluation of the social and cultural history of the entire period between 1867 and 1918. The late Péter Hanák led the charge to modify the accepted dogmatic Marxist interpretation of the period and to move away from political to economic, social, and intellectual history.[17] By the mid-1980s, Hanák and his younger colleagues ventured into uncharted waters and explored the issues of modernization and the emergence of urban society as well as Jewish assimilation and identity.[18] Finally, they explored the space where this modernization took place; the scenes of an emerging urban lifestyle and family life.[19]

This biography contributes to these scholarships in two main areas. My account of the family's rise to the intellectual elite of turn-of-the-century Hungary joints the biographical narrative to the social history of the assimilating Jewish middle class in Austria-Hungary. Important previous studies provided examples of the rise of the Jewish entrepreneurial class[20] and the magisterial biography of Ervin Szabó by György Litván examined the life of one of the leaders of the progressive counter-culture (and a Polanyi-cousin).[21] As well, autobiographies by eminent artists and writers of the Hungarian turn-of-the-century provided multigenerational accounts of their own families' assimilation and rise to prominence.[22] This is, however, the first attempt to combine the biographical and social historical approaches in a multi-generational study of a single family.

My focus on the Polanyi women, and Laura and Cecile in particular, helps to fill a missing dimension of early-twentieth-century Hungary's social history in general and the history of the progressive counter-culture in particular. Recent works pointed to the first signs of modern marriage and family patterns[23] as well as the emergence of a new, modern type of the educated, emancipated woman within this counter-culture.[24] This is, however, the first study to offer a comprehensive examination, through the lives of Cecile and Laura Polanyi, of the concrete details and stages of women's emancipation in this period and the dilemmas and choices this "new woman" faced both within the small community of the counter-culture and the broader social context of turn-of-the-century Austria-Hungary.

Relying on the emerging Hungarian scholarship of women's history as well as my own previous contribution to the history of women's rights movement in Hungary,[25] here, as before, I attempt to combine the strengths of Hungarian and North American scholarships; the attention to the complex layers of social and intellectual history of the former and the ability to cut through detail in order to articulate important theoretical questions of the latter.

The organization of the chapters alternates between the chronological and the thematic. The title of Chapter 1, Literate Generations, pays homage to the family's first historian.[26] It provides a narrative of the family's rise from its origins in Vilna and the Northern edge of Hungary to Vienna and Budapest, and weaves this narrative into the economic and social fabric of the dual Monarchy. It documents the main events in the life of the first and second generations of the Polanyis as well as their commitment to the progressive political and cultural movements of the period. The account of Laura Polanyi's choices as a representative of this new type of educated, emancipated woman is presented in the context of the "trends, possibilities and impossibilities" facing middle-class, educated women of the pre-war era.

Chapter 2 stops the narrative and revisits the options of Cecile and Laura in terms of political and public activities. The chapter begins with an illustration of the limitations of applying the paradigms and terminology of Western women's history to the history of East-Central European women. Accounts of the role of Cecile's salon and Laura's feminist and pacifist activities before and during the war are followed with an analysis of Laura's political role during the 1918 democratic revolution.

Based on the material advanced in the first two chapters, I argue that the progressive counter-culture offered an extensive range of public and professional roles as well as a supporting environment for a small cohort of university educated women. Laura's wide-ranging family connections in this community provide partial explanation for her ease in moving between the various sub-groups and institutions of the progressive counter-culture, whether feminist, radical, socialist or academic. She was part of a group of professional women and led them during the political crisis of 1918 when they reciprocated this support by breaking with the bourgeois feminists and pledging allegiance to their male allies, the bourgeois radicals.

Chapter 3 continues the narrative and follows the itinerary of Laura's immediate family from the fall of 1919 to the spring of 1938. It also addresses the gap of professional activities in Laura's life between 1919 and the 1950s. Laura's personal and professional life in the interwar period was overshadowed by the emergence of a right-wing political regime in Hungary, resulting in the destruction of the Polanyis' pre-war social and intellectual community and the emigration of all her siblings. The emergence of a new generation of Polanyis, that of Laura's children adds a new layer to the family's narrative. Their cosmopolitan upbringing and their experiences of studying and working in Vienna, Weimar Berlin and the Soviet Union resulted in a weakened commitment to Hungarian politics and culture, compared to the previous generation of the family.

Chapter 4 completes the narrative of the emigration of Laura's immediate family to the U.S. North American scholarship on the intellectual refugees has devoted very little attention to the Hungarian contingent. The Polanyis' case can serve to fill some of this gap and add to our understanding of the influence on American academia and intellectual life in general, and the often cited success of the Hungarians in this cohort in particular. On a personal level, the heroic—and largely successful—efforts of rescuing friends and relatives from Hitler's Europe resulted in a shift in Laura's priorities and an affirmation of her place in the family's dynamics. On a general level, they highlight little-explored aspects of the refugee intellectual scholarship such as agency and the particular experiences of the women among their ranks. Finally, in Chapter 5, I bring the narrative of Laura's last years to its conclusion as well as take a step back to assess the legacy of Laura Polanyi, the historian and educator. Following her scholarly and pedagogical achievements in the early years of the century, she came full circle in the last years of her life, making a contribution to American historiography. Her belated yet seamless adjustment to the new academic environment has important ramifications for the study of intellectual émigrés in the United States. In addition, the two last chapters demonstrate that in their social as well as professional adjustment, the Polanyis successfully transplanted the same values that had helped them achieve their prominence in Hungarian and Central European culture.

Chapter 1:
Literate Generations

A photograph of the Pollacsek family's apartment from the late 1890s was reproduced in *The History of Hungary*.[1] In a series of historical photos, illustrating the living conditions of various socia l strata, the Pollacseks' sitting room, overflowing with draperies, Persian rugs, potted palms, throws and knickknacks, exemplified the decorating tastes of the emerging entrepreneurial bourgeoisie at the turn of the century. The lady of the house, Cecile Pollacsek, is seen at the centre of the picture, reclining on a bearskin-covered sofa. But the centrepiece of the room is an imposingly large painting on the wall. From it, the five children of the house, Laura, Adolf, Karl, Sophie, and Mihály are looking at the photographer, as if they were actually present in the room. The painting is no longer in existence, making the photograph the sole visual evidence, preserving the moment when the Pollacsek family reached the pinnacle of its social and financial standing. Indeed, the erstwhile existence of such a painting is indication of the family's financial and social success at the time; while the commissioning of family portraits had been customary among the aristocracy and the gentry, in the 1890s it had only recently been taken up by the upper-middle class.

Equally telling of the family's standing is the geographical location of their home. The spacious flat was under no. 2 of "Sugárút" (literally: boulevard, later named Andrássy Avenue), at the top of the recently constructed, tree-lined avenue that linked the rapidly developing downtown core of Budapest with City Park. Modeled after the Parisian grand boulevards, it was built between 1871 and 1884. Complete with the Continent's first subway line, it became one of the showpieces of Hungary's millennial celebrations in 1896 and a symbol of the unparalleled economic growth Hungary and especially its capital experienced.[2]

The father of the children was the railway engineer and contractor Mihály Pollacsek, whose profession epitomized Hungary's industrial boom. His own professional and financial rise, along with his family's social standing and lifestyle were at this point very much in line with Hungary's economic development and the emergence of its overwhelmingly Jewish entrepreneurial bourgeoisie and professional middle class. Likewise, successive generations of the family illustrate one of the dominant patterns of Jewish assimilation in Eastern and Central Europe; the geographical move from the peripheries of two

9

empires, the Austro-Hungarian Monarchy and Russia, to their centres, and the astonishing pace of upward social mobility in the course of a mere three generations.

In the following account of the life of the young Laura Polanyi from 1882 to 1919, I will attempt to find a balance between the personally significant and the sociologically relevant by identifying the important events and experiences in her life against the backdrop of her larger environment. In extending concentric circles, these include her family, her peers and friends, her social circle, and the political and cultural developments of the country in which she had been born and raised, the Austro-Hungarian Monarchy between 1882 and 1919.

Laura Matild Polanyi was born on 16 February 1882 in Vienna, the eldest child of Mihály Pollacsek (1848-1905) and Cecile Wohl (1861-1939).[3] On the maternal side, we know relatively little of the ancestors, and much of what we do know rests on anecdotal rather than archival evidence.[4] Cecile's father, Assir or Ascher Wohl (he has been variously identified as Alex or Andzrej; he preferred to sign his letters as A. Wohl.) was born in 1836 and by 1860 was a professor at Vilna's Rabbinical Seminar.[5] Vilna's role in the Jewish religious and cultural revival of the nineteenth century and in fertilizing Jewish life in the United States and Western Europe in the first half of the twentieth century has been extensively documented.[6] Recent research has pointed out Vilna's rise as an important centre in the administration of Russian Jews during the 1860s, at a time when the Czarist government temporarily embraced (and eventually abandoned) a policy of relative liberalization in its handling of the "Jewish question." As such, Vilna offered rare government positions for Jews in the educational bureaucracy and the censorship office. There is evidence that A. Wohl served in both and represented a moderately assimilationist position in the public debate on the pages of *Vilenskii Vestnik* on the best approach to educate the Jews in the spirit of officially sanctioned Russification.[7]

Wohl's works: *The Influence of the Talmud on Christianity, The History of the Jews from BC. 586 to AD. 640* and *The Prayer of the Jews for the Whole Year*, the first Hebrew-Russian prayer book, were all published in Russian-Hebrew bilingual editions. In addition to provide Russian translations of the Hebrew originals for the Jewish reader, these also served the purpose of educating the Russian public about Jewish cultural and religious customs and traditions. As such, they demonstrated Wohl's continuous support of governmental policy and earned him the Anna and Stanislaus orders.[8]

There were other signs of the Wohl family's gravitation toward the imperial centres; A. Wohl's son, Lazar, worked for the Moscow and St.

Petersburg branches of the International Commerce Bank and A. Wohl eventually followed his daughter to Budapest and he died there in 1905.[9] Throughout, he had claimed an important role in the grandchildren's education, in a manner that confirmed his assimilationist reputation. In their extensive correspondence he used Russian and German with his daughter and encouraged the use of German and French, even Latin with his grandchildren. Yet while there was no academic or medical matter small enough to escape his grandfatherly attention, there was not a single reference to religion or Jewish tradition in his numerous letters.

Information concerning Cecile's mother is even more patchy; in the family documents and correspondence there is virtually no sign of her, apart from the obligatory ending of each of grandfather Wohl's letters: "grandmother/" Mamasha"/my wife joins me in sending her love."[10]

Cecile, the Wohls' only daughter enrolled at the Mariinskii Higher Girls' School in Vilna at age ten in 1871. Her high-school years coincided with the period when, following the establishment of the first girls' gymnasium in Russia in 1858, Russian women were making unprecedented gains in their access to higher education. A government statute of 1867 authorized publicly funded university-level establishments and the first of these opened in St. Petersburg in 1878, the very year Cecile Wohl graduated from high school. It was followed by similar institutions in Moscow, Kiev and Kazan. By the early 1880s, the abrupt end of the reform era resulted in a reversal of this policy as well; for the next fifteen years, Russian women were left with the St. Petersburg institution of higher education as their only alternative to studying abroad, in Zurich.[11]

In the end Cecile was sent to Vienna, accompanied by a friend, Anna Lvovna. Perhaps the Wohls could not afford to send her to Switzerland or Cecile was not ready for the adventure shared by a courageous vanguard of young Russian women. Family legend has another version, according to which a change of scenery was needed to remove the rebellious Cecile from the revolutionary youth circles of Vilna; Vienna and its cosmopolitan cultural life provided the necessary change. The two young women may have stayed with relatives or friends while Cecile worked as an apprentice at a jewellery shop. Within a year, they were both married.

Shortly after her arrival in Vienna, Cecile Wohl met a Hungarian engineer, Mihály Pollacsek; they married in Warsaw on 21 February 1881.[12] The young couple was a true representative of the imperial capital's Jewish population for the majority of Jewish immigrants to Vienna during the 1880s came from the peripheries of the empire, the majority from Hungary.[13] In statistical terms, the

Pollacseks' stay in Vienna proved to be relatively short and transient; they moved on to Budapest in the early 1890s. In terms of their long-term ties to Vienna, however, the range of their social, economic and personal ties mirrored those between the two capitals of the Monarchy and the family maintained close links with the imperial capital even in the third generation.

Mihály Pollacsek's contribution to the building of several local railway lines must have created a sense of belonging, along with the fact that four of his children were born and spent their early years in Vienna. As for Cecile, the Viennese artistic and intellectual scene in the turn of the century seemed a much better match for her restless intellect than either Vilna or Budapest, still parochial in the late 19th century.

The single most decisive factor in the Pollacseks' lasting attachment to Vienna, however, had been the continuing friendship between Cecile and Anna, eventually extended to their husbands, children, relatives and family friends. It was maintained through correspondence, frequent visits and shared annual vacations even after the Pollacseks' move to Budapest. "Aunt Nunia" and her family became a surrogate family for the Pollacseks, and her eldest daughter, Aline (Lina), born in 1883, a sister-like friend to the young Laura and Adolf. But it was Anna's husband who had the most lasting influence on the Pollacsek family.

Samuel (Semyon) Lvovich Klatschko (1850-1914), as Cecile, also came from a rabbinical family in Vilna and there are indications that the family connections between the Wohls and the Klatsckos originated there.[14] He represented yet another alternative of Jewish assimilation, the one through participation in the revolutionary movements. His early adventures and personality come to life in the colourful description written by Karl Polanyi's future wife.

> Samuel Klatschko, already a twenty-year resident of Vienna at the turn of the century, was a confidante above and beyond fractions of the Russian underground parties and movements, the embodiment of the "red Red Cross." In 1865, the fourteen-year old high-school student and populist activist ran away from the paternal rabbinical house in Vilna and somehow managed to get to America. He became a member of the Utopian communistic community of the so-called Chaikovtsi (named after their leader, N. V. Chaikovskii). When, like many of the similar experiments, this too collapsed, Klatschko became a cattle herder and, allegedly, herded several thousand animals to Chicago. With the money he had earned, he made his way back to Europe and settled in Paris as a photographer. During his stay he became familiar not only with the populist and Marxist literature but also with many leaders of the early Russian revolutionary movement, Plechanov, Axelrod, Leo Deutsch. In Vienna, he worked as a translator for a patent office, eventually becoming one of its directors, then its co-

owner. Most of the increased income went to the movement, to support the revolutionaries escaping from Russia and the underground activists, regardless of their party affiliation.[15]

The one name Duczynska curiously ommited from the above list of Russian revolutionaries is Trotsky's, who provided an equally warm portrait of Klatschko, the Trotskys' closest friend during their years in Vienna. It depicts the Klatschko family as "a centre of political and intellectual interests, of love of music, of four European languages, of various European connections."[16] Finally, we have a description that fills in the missing early years, of the 18-year-old Klatschko, the revolutionary from Vilna. After his graduation from the local Russian gymnasium, he enrolled at Moscow University's Medical faculty, quickly rose to the leadership of the Moscow circle of the Chaikovtsy, only to be arrested in 1872. After his release a year later, young Klatschko was expelled from the circle and sent abroad, apparently over his "immoral conduct of courting a woman of 'bad reputation.'" [17]

Perhaps as a result of these early experiences of infights and petty squabbles, in Vienna Klatchko created a unique position for himself: as a financially independent entrepreneur he stood above the still bickering Russian socialist factions, providing support to all Russian revolutionary activists, regardless of their allegiances.

To the sheltered Pollacsek children staying with the Klatschkos, the Russian revolutionaries, young men and women, passing through the Klatschkos' house on their way to exile or illegally returning to Russia, must have carried the aura of extraordinary courage. The Klatschko-household, a second home to them, offered instant political and moral lessons and proof that it was possible to have it all: the comforts of bourgeois lifestyle, full-hearted participation in the artistic offerings of Vienna and the moral integrity of actively supporting, if not living, revolutionary activism.

The Pollacseks' move to Budapest was primarily a business decision, motivated by Mihály Pollacsek's desire to partake in the Hungarian building boom of the 1890s as a railway contractor. It was also a homecoming: while Mihály had never actually lived in Budapest before, the family had been established in Hungary for at least a century.

The ancestors of Mihály Pollacsek had settled in the northeastern parts of Hungary as far back as the 18th century. The earliest written document that mentions the family name is the Jewish census of 1794 which lists an Enoch

Polatsek as resident of Ungvár (today Uz'horod in the Ukraine), and lessee of all the taverns and breweries in Árva county.[18] Although the evidence is far from conclusive—the name after all was quite common in the area—this Polatsek has been regarded as the first known forefather by the family. It was probably his son, a Michael Pollacsek who lived approximately between 1780 and 1850 who became the first owner/lessee of the lands and vineyards in Ungvár.[19]

Unfortunately, no more than a couple of pages were completed of the notes Laura Polanyi titled "Some facts and hear-says about our family, recorded as remembered." Keenly aware of her own role as the link between the family's past in East-Central Europe and its present and future in America, Laura was likely the last one who could recall the family stories and memories of ancestors heard in her childhood.

In these reminiscences, the family's chronicler sometimes gave way to the social observer and historian, commenting on the various patterns of assimilation in the family.

> The portrait of our great-grandfather and [sic!] with his intellectual, energetic traces shows a strong individuality and strangely gives the pattern of seeing and dominating his world of his son and grandson: our father. Mme Pollacsek looks very stately, wears her costly dress well, she links the family with the Glasner family. [...] These parents had two sons: Vilmos and Adolf, born about 1815. The first showed all the traits of having been born, reared and educated in and for the country. He had the vigorous ways of the earthbound landholder who lives and works on and of his vineyards and knows and appreciates its fruits. His language was idiomatic country Hungarian, he wore a shortcut round beard, known as Kossuth-beard and was surely as original a type of a middle-class, not too educated vine grower as any of his neighbours. I say middle-class because in Northern Hungary, where Ungvar is the lower classes spoke Slovak, Russin or Jewish [!], the upper classes the language of the court German and French and only the middle class (in Hungary the 'gentry') spoke Hungarian.
>
> I do not know whom he married, but it must have been somebody of the same Hungarian middle class as their children spoke a lovely idiomatic Hungarian and hardly any German, in this respect I mainly think of their very sweet daughter aunt Laura.
>
> These Pollacseks the children of Vilmos Pollacsek, were part of the family, the Ungvár clan. The family policy always included them and their children. When students our father included them into a gang with his nephews housing them and providing them with a never-ending rod of salami in the quarters he let them have. Besides this he of course gave them starts into life to follow up or leave as they grew up. All this although the distinct difference in views on life, in the technics to deal [with] the problems of life, education and social integration remained as outspoken as in the two grandfathers [sic] personalities, through all these generations.[20]

From this portrait of the Pollacsek ancestors emerges a family well on its way towards assimilation, markedly Hungarian in its language, culture and lifestyle by as early as the mid-19th century. They represent two distinct patterns of assimilation; one preserving the ties to the land and emulating the lifestyle and values of the Hungarian gentry, the other, including Laura's grandfather, following a path leading toward Western European bourgeois values through education and the professions.

Adolf Pollacsek, Laura's grandfather, died in 1871. He left his widow, Zsófia Pollacsek, as the guardian of their minor children, two boys, Mihály and Károly and three girls, Lujza, Teréz and Vilma; Clementine, the eldest, must have been an adult by then. The widow continued to rent from the Crown the local steam mill, brewery, distillery and agricultural lands, and in 1871 even founded a new company, the Steam-Mill Co. of Ungvár that continued to provide a living for her children well into the 1890s.[21]

While the four girls married and stayed in the area, where their husbands managed the properties and the business, the two Pollacsek boys used their income to become the first professionals in the family. Out of law and medicine, the typical choices of upwardly mobile, assimilating Jews, the elder brother, Károly (born 1845?) took law. Mihály Pollacsek (born on 21 March 1848) followed a less predictable path. He enrolled at the *Eidgenossische Technische Hochschule* in Zurich, perhaps the most prestigious technical university in Europe at the time. After his graduation as a railway-building engineer, he worked for the Swiss State Railways.[22] By 1876 he was promoted to department head and supervised the construction of the Seebach-Zurich railway line. In 1877, the company sent him to Edinburgh to study the more developed British methods of building railway lines across city centres. In the early 1880s he moved to Vienna where he designed local lines for the Viennese State Railway Co. He also published a study on the competitiveness of the local state-built railways.[23] To this impressive professional record more than 1,000 km of railways, built in Hungary, were to be added.[24]

At the time of the Pollacsek family's move to Budapest in 1892, Laura already had three brothers and a sister born in Vienna: Adolf was born in 1883, Karl in 1886, Sophie in 1888, and Mihály in 1891. The Pollacseks had one more son, Pál-Paul, whose short life remained in the shadow. He was born mentally handicapped and died young, we cannot be sure when and at what age.

The transition to life in Budapest must have been eased by the proximity of relatives; for Mihály Pollacsek's only brother, Károly, had by then established a successful law practice in Budapest. "Uncle" Károly and his wife, Irma, remained a reliable presence in the life of the Pollacsek offspring, providing emotional and at times financial support. Their summer residence on the outskirts of Budapest (the "März-villa" under 7 Széchenyi Emlékút [Memorial Road], on Schwabenberg) and the country house near the Danube were to become favourite hangouts for the younger generation and their friends.[25]

In her last years, Zsófia Pollacsek, Mihály's widowed mother lived with the family until her death in 1898. Around school holidays, Christmas and Easter—these were also the holidays celebrated in the family rather than the Jewish ones[26]—frequent visits were exchanged with the "Ungvár cousins." The Pollacsek sisters still lived in the Ungvár area, managing the family mill and other properties, in varied circumstances. Vilma who had three daughters as well as a son and Teréz with a daughter and a son were relatively comfortable. The widow Lujza, with her seven children, was at times almost desperate as she struggled with the fallout of her husband's business failure and suicide.[27]

Hungary in the 1890s was by all accounts the place to be for an enterprising railway engineer. Following the 1873 financial crisis and the subsequent period of economic depression, the long decade between 1887 and 1898 was an unparalleled era of economic boom, aided by the similarly good years of the Austrian and German economies. Investments and the net capital of credit institutions grew threefold, production of coal, steel and pig iron twofold. The growth rate of industrial production reached an unprecedented annual 7%.[28]

Railway building became one of the leading sectors of the economy, in turn stimulating the growth of the heavy and light industries as well as the agricultural production. The density of railway network approximated that of the Western European countries and surpassed the Southern and South-Eastern European countries.29 Between 1890 and 1914 almost 11,000 km of new lines were built; within this period the years between 1882 and 1899 represented the peak, with an annual average of 541 km built.[30] The railway became an integral and crucial part of government economic policy. In 1889-91 the Hungarian government bought more than 3,000 km of the lines previously in private hands thus transforming 85% of the main lines into state-owned property and soon controlled 83% and 89% of the passenger and commercial transport, respectively.[31]

The industrial and building boom was even more marked in the capital, reaching its peak in the years leading up to Hungary's millennial celebration in 1896. Representative public buildings such as the monumental neo-gothic Parliament, the new wing of the Royal Castle, the Fishermen's Bastion, as well as grand urban designs such as a system of boulevards were just the most visible projects. Much of the old Pest centre was leveled and replaced by new apartment buildings, along with new communication, sanitation, and public health systems and commercial infrastructure.[32]

As an upwardly mobile Jewish professional and entrepreneur rolled into one, Mihály Pollacsek seemed to embody the social group most active in Hungary's modernization process. The author of a study of the Hungarian Jewish capitalist elite at the turn of the century suggests that more than half of this elite became ennobled, which in most cases included conversion and Magyarization of the family name. Many more chose the two last options, even if they did not apply for nobility or did not succeed in obtaining it.[33]

Even if these estimates are exaggerated, the fact remains that these steps could be routinely taken up by many professionals outside the financial and entrepreneurial elite, for a variety of personal and professional reasons, and were socially widely accepted in that time of progress and secularization. Neither of these steps, however, were ever considered by Mihály Pollacsek, making him a highly atypical example of the successful entrepreneur in his time and day. Part of the explanation was his highly developed moral integrity: his most lasting legacy according to his children's memories. Another reason, paradoxically, may have been his family's long history and rootedness in the northern part of Hungary. As the family had been living in Hungary for generations and was already thoroughly assimilated in its culture and lifestyle, he did not feel obligated to prove his Hungarianness with the outward symbols of gentrification, so keenly taken up by the newly ennobled bourgeoisie.[34]

Photographs of Mihály Pollacsek show not only a conspicuous lack of any outwardly sign of Jewishness (Western European dress was by then the rule rather than the exception among Hungary's assimilated urban Jews) but an even more striking lack of the attributes of gentrification, such as the Hungarian-style formal outfit, so proudly displayed by the elite, whether Hungarian gentry or freshly assimilated German, Slavic or Jewish.

The Kossuth-beard of the youth (named after the legendary leader of the 1848 Hungarian revolution, the beard became not only a fashion but a political statement after the defeat of the Hungarian War of Independence) was in due time exchanged for the fuller beard of the serious young professional. In his last years, the entrepreneur sported a Nietzsche-mustache popular among the younger set and wore his hair at an almost bohemian length. Moreover, in this era of carefully staged and retouched photographs, his pictures were always relaxed and informal, often taken outdoors. His children inherited his high forehead, chiseled features, expressive eyes, and gentle smile.

According to her pictures, Cecile's appearance was even more unconventional. She was short and stocky, constantly struggling with a weight problem[35] and her strong features, piercing eyes, and rare smile did not in the least conform to the contemporary idea of feminine beauty. To emulate this ideal would have been of course the last thing Cecile aspired to do; her appearance with the crudely cropped short hair, the perpetual cigarette and body language—on her photographs, she invariably appeared reclining on a sofa—signaled a calculated rejection of middle-class conformity, inspired perhaps by the rebellious lifestyle of young Russians in Western Europe.

During the 1890s the family's life was centred around their home at 2 Andrássy ut and the father's Budapest office, at one point across the street, under no. 1. Since the 1890s, the building underwent so many changes that we can only speculate on the apartment's size and layout at that time.[36] The family also owned a summer residence under 18 Lóránt Street on Schwabenberg-Svábhegy, a hill on the outskirts of the city where the wealthy had only recently started to build elegant alpine-style villas. Summer holidays were spent there or at the village house the Klatschkos rented at Hinterbrühl, near Vienna. Cecile and, on occasion, the older children accompanied the father on his business trips to London and other European capitals.

The children's life was rigorously organized; according to one source, their daily schedule consisted of a cold shower, followed by simple breakfast, calisthenics, and private lessons provided by tutors.[37] After their tenth birthday, they were judged old enough to take institutionalized education in stride, an opinion shared by many of the upper middle class. Accordingly, by the late 1890s the three oldest attended gymnasium which started at grade five. The children's education also included learning French and English from governesses and private teachers. German was the first language at home because Cecile never learned Hungarian well. Hungarian was spoken at school, with friends and company. They may not have learned Russian but were likely to be exposed to it through Cecile and their grandfather. And while a typical middle-class upbringing included German, and French, along with Latin and Greek, was taught at the Gymnasium, only aristocrats would have learned English from a very early age. The number of languages and the children's early exposure to them would prove to be a tremendous asset in later years.

A letter of the 16-year-old Adolf Polanyi to his sister Laura in 1899 provides a rare insight into the family's life at this stage; it was written during an outbreak of scarlet fever, when normal family life was suspended, yet still reflects the everyday habits and reactions of family members.[38] Laura was sent to Vienna to stay with the Klatschkos and Karl was staying with friends to avoid contact with Mihaly who was quarantined, perhaps in a hospital. Adolf was clearly of the opinion that the arrangement was unfair since it forced him to continue to attend school despite his potential exposure to the disease. Meanwhile, he shared his plans with his sister for a short Easter vacation in Vienna. Adolf was wondering if he could make do for four days on his allowance if he stayed in his father's Viennese office and spent the days and meals at the Klatschkos, which seems to indicate that regardless of the family's wealth, the children were taught to manage on a strict budget.

Despite his frequent trips abroad the father seemed to be the parent most involved with the children's education. The maternal grandfather also kept up a busy correspondence with his grandchildren, encouraging them to write in German and French. Much of what we know about their early education in fact comes from this correspondence, in which grandfather Wohl patiently explains the uses of trigonometry, calligraphy, and piano lessons and reminds the children to be considerate with their tutors and governesses.[39]

From the time the family moved to Budapest, Laura continued her studies at the Lutheran Boys' Gymnasium as a private student. One of the best high schools in Hungary at the time, it accepted a disproportionate number of Jewish students in exchange for a higher tuition fee. For boys, successful graduation from gymnasium was a necessary stepping stone to the faculties, a career in the lower ranks of the civil service or military training as an officer. It was still rare but not entirely unusual for academically inclined daughters of the upper middle class to attend a gymnasium as special students: they could study privately without actually attending the classes and take the final exams every year but would not necessarily aspire to continue at university.

Post-secondary education for women had only just began to open up; only a handful of women were granted permission to attend the medical and philosophical faculties until 1895. At the end of that year, a ministerial decree opened the faculties of medicine and arts to women at the Budapest University. The decree also allowed for the founding of a girls' high school with the right to provide its students with the finishing exam and thus access to the faculties. From grade 5 (high schools had 8 grades at the time), Laura had been in the first graduating class of the Girls' Gymnasium of the National Association for Women's Education. This substantial step in both the history of Hungarian women's education and Laura's own will be the subject of a separate chapter;

here, it will suffice to say that, as expected, she sailed through school both
socially and academically. She was jokingly addressed as "the pride of the
school" in a letter from an Ungvár relative.[40] Halfway through her graduation
year, the same relative congratulated her on her "fabulous, even epic" first-term
report card.[41] The overall result of her final examinations, the dreaded *matura*
which she sat in June 1900, was less spectacular: only "good," the equivalent of
B.[42] The examinations were notoriously exacting, perhaps even more so in the
case of the first ever all-girl graduating class. Then again, Laura's less-than-
stellar final grades may have had something to do with the sudden changes in her
family's fortunes between December 1899 and the spring of 1900.

In December 1899 Hungary's unprecedented economic growth period,
experienced through the 1880s and 1890s, came to a sudden halt. The first
warning signs of a recession in the agricultural and industrial production were
followed by a full-fledged credit crisis which in turn reached the heavy industry
and put a stop to construction and railway-building. The business of Mihály
Pollacsek that had so spectacularly benefited from the late-nineteenth-century
boom, was now equally influenced by its sudden end. The crisis affected the
Ungvár relatives as well; the family-owned mill, symbol of the family's
bourgeois rise and provider of the Pollacsek sisters' livelihood, also went
bankrupt and had to be sold.[43]

Family legend has it that the financial disaster could have been avoided
were it not for Mihály Pollacsek's insistence on paying off all his debtors in
full.[44] The 1899 bankruptcy of the father's business resulted in a major shift in the
family's lifestyle. Family members and friends alike remember the event as a
watershed, a veritable "disaster;"[45] it makes one wonder about the dimensions of
their previous wealth since the new lifestyle was far from destitute, merely
middle-class. The most painfully felt change may have been that Mihály
Pollacsek had to take on contracts abroad and spend even more time away from
his children. Many of the upper-class attributes of their previous life also had to
be sacrificed. The summer residence was sold[46] and the family moved into much
more modest quarters. The new apartment was at 9 Ferenciek tere (Franciscans'
Square), the heart of the old Pest city centre, a considerable step down from the
palatial elegance of the previous flat, yet still a "good" address, and conveniently
close to schools.

The tutors and governesses of the younger children were let go and the
older siblings took on tutoring jobs themselves while also teaching the younger
ones. Their schooling arrangements however did not drastically change; in
September 1900 Laura started university as planned and Adolf his graduation

year at the Trefort Street Gymnasium. Karl and soon the youngest boy, Mihály, followed him, both on scholarships.

The events of this traumatic year left their mark on Laura's personality. Although her widely admired beauty and social skills made her ideally suited for the role of the wealthy socialite, the family's expectations as well as her own intellectual ambitions made this a very unlikely choice, notwithstanding the sudden change in the family's fortunes. For the time being, with the father's prolonged absences and a mother not known for her practical and organizational skills, Laura took on the role of the responsible eldest daughter. It was during these years that she first realized her ability to deal with complicated situations and acquired the practical skills that proved invaluable in more serious crises to come.

The changes produced perhaps the most unexpected effect on Cecile. As her future daughter-in-law, Ilona Duczynska remarked, the loss of the large upper-middle-class household may have actually come as a relief, for Cecile was never the model housewife. In any case, it was during this period that Cecile Pollacsek established a salon that soon became a fixture on the Budapest intellectual scene and served as her most lasting legacy.

To keep a salon at the turn of the century may not seem a particularly advanced idea; after all, the institution's high point preceded the French Revolution in France and, in Berlin, did not survive the Napoleonic wars. For women of Cecile's generation, however, there were not many outlets available for public activity aside from the existing charitable associations, strictly aligned along social and religious lines and in any case too dull for her restless intellect. The salon soon acquired a distinctly radical and socialist flavour and Cecile was instrumental in drawing her young intellectual charges under the influence of Marx and Nietzsche. Quick to detect the newest intellectual and artistic trends, Cecile was to become involved in the psychoanalytical movement. To be discussed in more detail, here let me just mention that in 1910 she underwent analysis in Birchner-Brenner's clinic in Zurich and consequently tried her hand at analysis herself.[47] Attempts to convey her insights into journalistic genres, although not unsuccessful, seemed to confirm the general opinion that her talents were best expressed in the art of the conversation.

For the Pollacsek children, the salon was a natural extension of their family life, providing a connection between the broader family circle, cousins, school friends and the society at large. Ervin Szabó, their cousin and one-time tutor now attended as a promising social scientist. He was one of the guiding lights of

Huszadik Század [Twentieth Century], the first scholarly journal of sociology and political science in Hungary, founded in 1900. In its first years, the periodical, effectively edited by Szabó and Oszkár Jászi (also a frequent visitor in the salon) introduced virtually all the major trends of contemporary Western political and social thought to Hungarian readers. At the same time, the debates of its sister organization, the Sociological Society (Társadalomtudományi Társaság), explored the applications of Western theories to the Hungarian political and social problems, industrial and cultural backwardness, lack of political democracy, the latifundia, the problem of nationalities. From 1903, this small group of young intellectuals, later called the "circle of the *Twentieth Century*," organized its first courses for workers, soon followed by a full-scale open university.[48] For nearly two decades, this circle, along with representatives of the emerging modernist literary and artistic movements, came to represent the core of a new, democratic Hungarian culture and social thought. Guided by Cecile's unerring instinct, Saturday afternoons at the Pollacseks invariably included a cross-section of "the best society" in terms of artistic and intellectual talent and future prospects.

From time to time, foreign visitors also dropped by if wishing to inquire about the city's newest intellectual fads.[49] As an entirely different kind of foreign connection, from time to time Russian messengers and shipments of underground press and mail appeared, sent by way of Samuel Klatschko and received by Cecile herself or, increasingly, by Ervin Szabó, who also became a close friend of the Klatschkos.[50]

For a few years, Szabó served as a sort of *eminence grise* for the Social Democratic Party, much in need of intellectual leadership. Adolf Polanyi relied on his cousin's connections and mentorship when in 1902 he founded the Socialist Students' Circle. It had two main objectives: to counter the nationalistic student body at the Faculty of Law where he was enrolled from 1901, and to provide legal advice and general courses for the socialist workers' unions. In 1903, following a radical anti-nationalistic speech on the anniversary of the 1848 revolution, Adolf was expelled from the university. He finished his studies at the Academy of Commerce. In 1904, unable to cope with what he felt were unrealistic parental expectations and, perhaps, sibling-competition, he departed on a Transatlantic journey and took up a scholarship in Japan for a few years. On his return, he married Frida Szécsi, the sister of Sophie's future husband, Egon, his comrade from the days of the Socialist Students.

Karl Polanyi, a law student from 1904, would invite his best friend, Leó Popper, the future art critic and Popper's best friend, Georg Lukács, to the salon.

It was there that Lukács met the great love of his youth, the painter Irma Seidler, one of the Ungvár cousins. Guests of the salon represented a cross-section of generations, ranging from the founding fathers of the avant-garde to the younger champions of progressive social science, to university students. In addition, the Pollacsek salon provided a quasi-public and socially acceptable setting for young women at the time when the coffeehouse, the most popular public meeting place of intellectuals was still off-limits to "proper" women.

In September 1900, Laura, or Mausi, as she was called by family and close friends, enrolled at the Faculty of Arts of Budapest University; according to her university transcripts, she took most of her courses in history and Hungarian literature.[51] Her choice of subjects, none of them leading to any sort of "practical" profession, suggests that she was considered brilliant enough to be geared for an academic career. The dilemma between an uncertain and, for women, unprecedented academic career on the one hand and a prosperous marriage on the other must have crossed her mind; after all, she was a celebrated beauty and some of her school friends were already married.[52]

In the first year of her university studies, Laura experienced this dilemma through what seems to have been her first "serious" love affair, a semi-secret engagement to Géza Molnár. From a series of passionate love letters written by Molnár and preserved in Laura Polanyi's correspondence, a seemingly banal story emerges.[53] The young scientist was at the beginning of his career (yet probably much older than the nineteen-year-old Laura) and courted her for the better part of 1900. The courtship, consisting of long walks and conversations, lasted until he left for an extended sabbatical in Venice. The long separation led to mutual confessions of love in the correspondence and Laura's assumption that they were *de facto* engaged. The young man frequently referred to their future life together but preferred to keep their plans secret. Upon hearing that Laura had made the news of their engagement public, he suddenly felt the obligation too stifling for his career and broke up with her.

The whole affair, with its melodramatic overtones—at one point papa Pollacsek became involved, demanding an explanation from the young man—underscores the confusion over the new type of women Laura represented. Clearly, the established social code had no clause for young, available women pursuing academic and professional careers. While young intellectuals celebrated the new woman and the promise of an intellectual partnership in marriage, they were equally confused by its possible ramifications. In his letter, breaking up the engagement, Molnár gave voice to the pressures and anxieties this new kind of relationship entailed: "I begin to understand new, great philosophies; the loves of Voltaire and Petrarca toward intellectually inferior women who may be without personality and colour and that is exactly why one can develop all his colours by their side."[54] These problems may have been exaggerated, even imaginary on the young man's part, but they reflected an entirely real clash between his encounter with one of the new, emancipated women and his previous experiences with women. From the young woman's perspective, the incident demonstrated how a professional or academic career was potentially limiting for her chances to marry and have a family.

Laura was fortunate to have a large, supportive family and a loyal circle of friends to counterbalance these unexpected effects of emancipation. At university, she was part of a small but growing vanguard of young women, a likely source of peer support. Within the family, Laura's cousins, the Seidler sisters also enrolled at university as did her best childhood friend, Aline Klatschko in Vienna. In her social circle, a few young women, students of medicine, as well as artists and writers, were admired and accepted as equals. Newly fashionable co-ed outdoor activities, such as tennis, rowing, swimming and hiking provided an alternative backdrop for the building of a new kind of relationship between these young men and women, at once rebels and properly bourgeois.

However, what mostly kept her feet on the ground was work. In order to subsidize her studies and contribute to household expenses, Laura took on a variety of voluntary and paid jobs, a very sharp departure from her former carefree life. Because of her excellent grades and her financial situation she paid either half of the tuition fee (76 crowns per term) or none at all.[55] She continued to serve on the board of her old high school, taking part in fundraising activities as well as the decisions on scholarships and burseries.[60]

Her cousin, Ervin Szabó, one of Laura's closest friends in the years between 1900 and 1904, edited a yearly bibliography of current international publications in economics and social studies, first published in Hungarian in the *Közgazdasági Szemle* (Economic Review) then, from 1902 as *Bibliographia Economica Universalis*, a publication of the Brussels-based *Institut International de Bibliographie*, in French, English, German, Austrian, Italian, and Hungarian editions. In these, Szabó used the new decimal system, eventually modified when he became the founding director of the Budapest Municipal Library, Hungary's first public library system.[57] Following the project's success in its first year, Szabó hired his cousin Laura in 1902 as a part-time assistant, at the time a second-year student at the university, for 20 forints a month. They produced the

1903 edition together, but Laura completed the 1904 edition largely on her own as Szabó was in Italy on an extended medical leave, and gave only occasional advice.[58] Szabó also recommended her for an assistant librarian position at the Central Statistical Institute for the summer of 1903.[59]

The same friends stood by her when a young lawyer, Sámuel Glöckner (a member of Adolf's Socialist Students' circle), who was apparently hopelessly in love with her, committed suicide at the end of 1903.[60] Repeatedly assured by all concerned that she had nothing to blame herself for, Laura was still naturally effected, and, as Jászi reported to Szabó in Italy, only gradually started to "regain her old, brave cheerfulness."[61] Her own letters to Szabó in July 1903 display a lot of introspection and only a touch of self-pity.

"First of all I have to tell you that physically-mentally, I feel if not well but not bad either. I had a couple of terrible days but all together the cheerful, happy climate at Aunt Irma's and my many assignments make me calm. [...] I forgot to mention that you should not feel sorry for me for leaving the work to me. It is very good for me and I am glad to do it."[62] A week later she was back to her usual, teasing and self-deprecating tone:

> About myself. Well, I am about all right. It seems I was put on this Earth so that one day I could be exhibited at the City Park as the Mentally Strong Woman. There will be someone—Oszi [Oszkár Jászi] would be good at it—at the gate announcing in a strong, melodical tone to the crowd that they should come and see the woman who can hold a grand piano on her little finger—sorry, a hundred pains on one heart, a thousand worries on one head—and still smile. That will bring in a good profit. And after all, I honestly deserve it. Yet sometimes I feel I am too satisfied with myself just because I was accidentally hurt and dealt with it more or less, and now I begin to cast myself into gold while still alive.[63]

A few months later, the fourth-year university student related her detailed long-term plans to Szabó.[64] She was going to take her fourth-year exams early, to save on tuition fees and to concentrate on the *Bibliography*. Furthermore, she informed Szabó of the hopeful news of a full-time position in the newly founded Social Museum. She had been warmly recommended for a position—exactly what kind of position is difficult to tell—by the economist Gyula Mandello, who, as the editor of the *Economic Review*, had been also her supervisor at the *Bibliography*. The Social Museum was founded by the government as an institution of liberal social policy, to provide resources and publications on questions of social medicine and workers' welfare. Laura's prospects seemed hopeful with the appointment of a new, progressive-minded minister. In January

1904, after she had been officially recommended to the outgoing director of the Museum, Ákos Navratil, Szabó playfully urged her to go and see him: "In any case, go and conquer Navratil; it should not be difficult since he is already married [...] Remember, the Museum is entirely his creation. Make him feel as if he had full authority in choosing his successor. Of course, for the time being, you do not aspire to be his successor, only a humble deputy or assistant".[65] These plans obviously reflected aspirations going beyond her previous assignments as a poorly paid assistant editor or assistant librarian; and they promised, at least in the long run, a decently paid, full-time, prestigious position, for which she had valuable previous experience and recommendations to show.

Considering all these plans, it must have come as a shock to her friends when in August 1904 she announced her engagement and imminent marriage to the businessman Sándor Stricker, an outsider to her circle. There is some indication, echoed by family gossip, that the decision was preceded by a romance with Szabó. Over the last few years they developed a close working relationship and a friendship, that, at least on Szabó's side, may have gone beyond that.[66] It was almost inconceivable, however, that Laura would seriously consider marriage with a first cousin. The Pollacseks had their share of endogamic marriages, accepted practice in the small and isolated Jewish communities of the eighteenth and nineteenth centuries. However, in the growing eugenic consciousness of the early 20th century, the negative effects of this practice began to be widely recognized. Several of Szabó's sisters and brothers showed signs of hereditary mental problems and Laura's immediate family produced a mentally disabled child, all telltale signs of centuries of inbreeding. In any case, the letter, announcing her marriage to Szabó could not be more matter-of-fact and provides a characteristically objective and sober description of the circumstances.

> Dear Ervin,
>   I'm truly sorry that you have learned from Oszkár and not myself the news of my engagement. When I told him, I had not only written to you already, but also asked him emphatically to keep the secret for one more day, lest by accident he should precede me. A strange kid, to be so unable to keep silent. My dear boy, Ervin, *apart from this*, everything is very, very well.
>   Not only do I marry the man who has loved and loves me in the best, boldest and most manly manner in my life but a man whose serious, manly, pure life I will enrich and deepen with the content of my being and life with the utmost happiness and purpose. [...]
>   The secondary circumstances are just as agreeable. I count that his family (his father, his three sisters, two brothers and others) received me in the most pleasant, warm manner, and they are very kind, noble people. [...] As far as my relations to academia is concerned, it is the following. The doctorate, whose non-completion was

the only request, I will not complete. However, I will have the 8th term signed. I have insisted on the Bibliography, and will keep it. After all, I do have the time, and I like it so much that I will not drop it now when it is halfway completed.[67]

The courtship must have been either very short, very secretive or both, as the news took even the immediate family members by surprise. "Dear Sándor," wrote Karl Polanyi, Laura's younger brother, from the Austrian spa Ischl, "feeling a bit strange not knowing whether you are fair or dark, tall or short, while otherwise I should know you as well as my pocket, I hope you will not find it offending if I ask for a spare photograph of yours."[68] Perhaps because it was announced during the summer holiday season when most people were away and even the Saturday sessions of Cecile's salon were in recess, friends reacted with a uniformly pleasant but definite surprise. From the long list of congratulations, preserved in Laura Polanyi's correspondence, I will quote only two more, equally characteristic but conflicting reactions.

The letter of her professor, the eminent historian Henrik Marczali underscores the general expectation that marriage was incompatible with further professional plans. "True, with your new 'career choice' I will lose a dear student but will hopefully keep a dear friend..."[69] Another congratulatory note came from a school friend, the musician Margit Kunwald (the future mother of the musician Antal Doráti) who, after the obligatory best wishes, quickly came to the point. "When I imagine you in your future lifestyle, I think of your activities, e.g. the bibliography, and wonder if you will continue them, or because of your new circumstances you will abandon them. I had already mentioned to you how attractive I find this profession. And so I decided to ask you, if you give it up, and if it is possible for me to continue it, I would love to take over!"[70] The request betrays the deep ambiguity toward women's work in academia, prevalent even among the women themselves; the friend praises the job's intellectual value but assumes that now that Laura does not need the money, she will not continue with it. It is not simply the assumption that a married woman should not work—the friend was also married—rather the combination of a shortage of supply of intellectually worthwhile jobs for women and the growing demand by qualified women.

The real question on everyone's mind must have been: why would Laura marry an outsider, a non-intellectual, a businessman thirteen years her senior who asked her to give up her academic career? After all, there were examples of successful marriages of intellectually equal partners among her close friends and relatives.[71] Was this not a betrayal of her goals and ambitions?

The above-cited letter to Szabó is crucial in evaluating her decision. We can see her future husband's "only request" to abandon her studies as an indication, on his part, to curtail her independence, and, on hers, to relinquish her ambitions; and at the time it was likely to be taken as such, as expressed by the congratulatory notes of many of the well-wishers. But there is another possible explanation; that the decision was to postpone rather than to give up her professional plans in order to start a family; and in this light, her view of the transition to married life as unproblematic, expressed in her letter to Szabó, may have been optimistic but not unrealistic.

By all measures, the marriage was the culmination of a genuine love affair; the photographs and love letters are testimony to the mutual attraction. When asked about her parents' marriage, Laura's daughter would exclaim: "but he was such a dashing fellow!"[72] Apart from physical compatibility, Laura must have considered Sándor Stricker's family as a suitable "gene pool." The Strickers, like the Pollacseks, had their roots in the northern parts of Hungary and lived there for the better part of the 19th century. In terms of their Jewishness, they were more traditional and religious than the Pollacseks while also had their share of successful professionals and artists.[73] At the time the marriage may have seemed an intellectual mésalliance on the bride's part, but, in retrospect, the Strickers produced an almost equally high number of luminaries in the arts, literature and academia than the Polanyis.

In the final analysis, the young but singularly mature and intelligent Laura Polanyi chose her life-partner wisely; intellectually, the marriage may not have been a partnership of equals, yet it succeeded in providing her with emotional and financial security, and, soon, a doting father for their children.

In January 1905 Mihály Pollacsek, at fifty-seven relatively young and healthy, suddenly died. Apart from the emotional trauma—the children clearly lost the parent closer to them—the family had to deal with yet another financial disaster. They had neither savings nor any disposable income to support the household of Cecile, the two youngest, Michael and Sophie, still in school, the mentally disabled little Pal, and grandfather Wohl, with Adolf working in Japan and Karl still a law student. Adolf's letter to Laura from Osaka describes the emotional and financial "aftershocks."

> Despite all her illnesses and weaknesses, Mother seems to cope miraculously. Yet, I can't deny I am very very worried when I think of the family. Mother, Grandfather, Misi, Pali, Zsófi—enormous *état*—and absolutely no positive income. Tell me, when you have the time, what you think of all this with your practical

intelligence. [...] After all, for a year or two Uncle Karoly could step in but he cannot be asked to take the burden of such a huge family forever. [...] If we can survive for the next four years then everything will be fine. Karli and I can underwrite everything by then. I want or rather wish that Karli join Uncle Károly's office[74]—in 3-4 years' time he will not only make but will be worth his 250-300 forints. By then I will be worth the same and either will have stay here or gone home. Miska will be a student 'who does not cost,' Zsofka, Pali and Mother will be provided for nicely.[75]

The particulars of the initial arrangement may have changed over the years but, as Károly Pollacsek's letter to Laura from twelve years later indicates, he continued to carry the financial burden of his brother's family for much longer than anticipated. (He also generously supported his sister, Teréz and her family, living in Italy.) Uncle Károly referred to an agreement from three years earlier when they had agreed on their monthly contributions to Cecile's expenses: Mausi and Sándor, 150 crown, himself 200 crown, Adolf 100 crown, Egon 50 crown.[76] At the time, in 1917, Adolf was still experimenting with various business ideas, Karl served at the Galician front, as did Sophie's husband, the lawyer Egon Szécsi.[77] Considering the "entirely positive changes" in the Strickers' financial situation, Uncle Károly suggested that a change of the above ratio was overdue.[78]

With the marriage, Laura acquired a lifestyle that returned her to the upper-class standards of her childhood. The young couple moved back to Andrássy ut, to number 83, further down the road where the leafy neighbourhood of the upper-middle-class apartment buildings spread toward City Park. There was a summer house on the hilly side of the city, and, in addition to the customary maid and cook, the young mother employed a nurse and a governess. Frequent and lengthy holidays took them to Italy and the Dalmatian coastline, often without Sándor whose prospering textile business kept him away from the family, but with enough help to enable the young mother to entertain visitors in style.[79] Photographs from these years show the proud parents of Mihály, born on 5 September 1905 and Eva, born on 13 November 1906. Later ones show the third child, born on 11 November 1913, György Ottó. These photos, with the children dressed in impeccably tailored matching outfits and the young mother the picture of bourgeois propriety, revealed a side of Laura that very much enjoyed the everyday comforts and rewards of wealth. Some of the later photographs, however, are much less formal and show her on the beach, in bathing suit, with the children naked at her side, signaling that there was another, less conventional side to the wealthy housewife.

The first signs that she was ready to take steps to balance her family life with her reawakening intellectual ambitions, appeared in 1907. In January of that year, Laura Polanyi published a short article on "Women of the Intellectual Middle Class."[80] It appeared in *Szabad Gondolat* ("Free Thought"), the magazine of the liberal *Budapesti Napló* as part of a series discussing the "Problems of the Intellectual Middle Class." Other contributors included Cecile Pollacsek, writing about "The Tragedy of the Home"[81] and the sociologist Ede Harkányi on "The Bankruptcy of Marriage."[82]

In December 1907 Laura Polanyi obtained the official certificate attesting to the completion of her university courses, one of the prerequisites for a doctoral degree.[83] Having fulfilled the other requirements, a dissertation and an examination in three subjects, she was awarded a doctorate in May 1909. According to her doctoral diploma, the subjects were: Hungarian History (major), Aesthetics and English Literature (minors).[84] The dissertation, entitled "The economic policy of Charles VI" was published in the journal *Közgazdasági Szemle* [Economic Review] later in the same year.[85] It was a relatively slim (79 pages plus appendix) but solid work; not only did it put to good use Laura's expertise acquired as co-editor of the *Bibliographia Economica Universalis*, but also ventured into the relatively new field of economic history at a time when constitutional and political history ruled unchallenged.

In the 1950s, looking back on her professional life, Laura Polanyi remarked that were it not for the "decision of the University in 1909 to disallow the habilitation [the qualifying examination required for a professorship] of women,"[86] she would have been destined for a professorship. Considering the university's standing as a stronghold of conservative-nationalistic ideology, barely tolerating professors with progressive leanings, and despite the enormous gains women made during the first decade of the century, the chances of appointing a woman (let alone a Jewish woman and a mother of two) were extremely slim. Nevertheless, the years between 1909 and 1913 turned out to be Laura Polanyi's most balanced and productive period when she seemed to "have it all:" family bliss coupled with professional recognition and a wide range of public activities.

The access to higher education and the process of accepting women in academia was a crucial scene in the battle for women's emancipation and I had already indicated some aspects of this battle. By the middle of the first decade of the twentieth century the official bastions of education and culture reluctantly lowered their defenses or—as in the case of the Faculty of Arts, reacting to the sudden rise in the number of women students—reinforced them. At around the same time, Hungarian women asserted their claims to access the political sphere with the founding of the Association of Feminists at the end of 1904[87] and, as the growing number of women artists and writers showed, to the arts and literature.[88]

In order to assess the significance of these developments and their impact on women's emancipation, we have to consider the larger changes affecting the entire political and cultural climate. One of the changes by the mid-1900s was an explosive growth in the variety and membership of the institutions catering to the progressive intelligentsia. Its flagships were the Sociological Society and the journal *Twentieth Century*. Initially, both encompassed a relatively wide political and ideological range, from the moderate conservative through the liberal to the socialist. The breach between these strains was inevitable and was only accelerated by the 1905-6 political crisis during which the Austrian leadership— in the best Habsburg tradition of *divide et impera*—threw into the constitutional turmoil the bait of universal manhood suffrage.

Despite the constitutional façade, Hungarian parliament and its parties represented less than 6% of the population. For the extra-parliamentarian left-wing parties and political movements such as the Social Democrats along with Jaszi and his circle, it was a logical step to support the pro-Austrian caretaker-government as their best chance to achieve universal suffrage, the cornerstone of their program of democratization. The promise was eventually withdrawn (and universal manhood suffrage was introduced in 1906 in the Austrian half of the Monarchy), after it had succeeded in dividing the Hungarian political opposition. The crisis ended with the triumph of the nationalist reaction, and effectively polarized the political landscape, leaving lasting divisions between the nationalist and the progressive camps.

A similar confrontation had played out earlier within the editorial board of the *Huszadik Század* [Twentieth Century] and, in the wake of the political crisis, in the membership of the Sociological Society. This battle, between the conservative nationalists on one side and the radicals and socialists on the other, ended with a reversed result: it reinforced the leadership of Jászi and his democratic socialist-radical direction.[89]

Whereas the first years of the "circle of the Twentieth Century" were characterized by a feverish effort to bring Hungarian social thought in line with the newest developments in Western sociology and political science, the years following the 1905-6 crisis increasingly focused on bridging theory and political activism. In the remaining years prior to the war, Jászi and his circle, by now overwhelmingly consisting of assimilated Jewish middle-class intellectuals, laid the groundwork for a comprehensive program of modernization and democratization. "Hungary's bourgeois transformation" proposed solutions for the most pressing political and social ills: the lack of political democracy and the limited suffrage, the system of *latifundia*, the destitution of the landless agrarian proletariat, and the explosive nationalities' issue. With some changes, the circle and the program survived the political battles of the pre-war period and World War I and reemerged as the Bourgeois Radical Party in 1917, one of the leading forces in the 1918 bourgeois democratic revolution.

Culture and education were integral parts of this full-scale reform programme; and by 1906 one of the main instruments of its implementation, the Free School for Social Science had become an institution incorporating a full range of workers' and higher courses. The curriculum offered basic courses in science, history, literature and the arts as well as overviews of the most recent developments in social sciences and philosophy.[90]

Unexpected support came from the ranks of modernist writers, poets and artists. The revolutionary forms and spirit of the poetry of Endre Ady and other poets and writers who gathered around the literary journal *Nyugat* [West], founded in 1908, the music of Bartók, the constructivist vision of the modernist artists of "The Eights," came to represent a progressive alternative to the national-romantic literary and artistic traditions. Moreover, literary and artistic modernism created a division in the public that ran as deep as the political one. Every area of education and culture became a contested ground between the institutions of official ideology and culture on the one hand and representatives of the political opposition and artistic modernism on the other.

Universal suffrage remained one of the key issues of the political life and the common ground for co-operation between the Radicals and the Social Democrats. As in other Western and Central European countries in the same period, it also provided a source of tension between these two progressive political forces and the bourgeois feminists.[91] Despite the tensions and the important differences in ideology and strategy, there was an underlying system of commonly held values and aspirations for progress, modernization and democracy, on which developed a comprehensive, progressive counter-culture.

It is in the context of this progressive counter-culture that we should look at the gains of women's emancipation and Laura Polanyi's activities during this period. Her major public engagements included a talk on "How can women participate in the work of social welfare?" at the Masonic lodge "Könyves Kálmán"[92] in 1908, a lecture on "Feminism and Marriage" at one of the country branches of the Association of Feminists,[93] and another lecture at the Miskolc branch of the Sociological Society in 1911.[94] She was elected to the executive of the National League for Public Education in 1908,[95] participated at the 1911 pedagogical conference of the Feminists with a lecture on young children's physical and mental development,[96] and the list could go on.[97] During the same period, Cecile Pollacsek also gave several lectures, including one "On the origins of the Russian Revolution."[98]

After 1911, pedagogy took on a primary place among Laura's interests. Following an intensive advertising campaign, in September 1911 she opened a kindergarten designed for five and six-year old children. She defined her main objective as providing "secular moral education"[99] based on the principles of Freud and named her school, with a hint of wordplay, "Co-operative Private Education." Not to be outdone, Cecile at the same time advertised the opening of her own "Women's Lyceum," a sort of open university for women, where a wide range of subjects was to be taught by experts in each field.[100]

What was the personal motivation of Laura Polanyi in starting an experimental kindergarten? Arthur Koestler, who was one of her pupils, provided a characteristically skeptical explanation in his memoirs.

> When I was five, I was sent for a few months to an experimental, *avant-garde* kindergarten in Budapest. It was run by a young lady belonging to a very erudite family, whose members now occupy some half a dozen chairs at various English and American universities. Mrs. Lolly (which isn't her real name) had committed an intellectual mésalliance by marrying a successful businessman and, feeling frustrated, had opened the kindergarten for five-and-six-years olds, where she put into practice some extremely advanced and, I suspect, somewhat confused pedagogical ideas.[101]

Koestler had the benefit of hindsight; it was easy for him, fifty years later, to mock the early century's zeal for experimental pedagogy. The reliability of his memories notwithstanding—and in a later chapter I will re-examine the value of his testimony in this context—he also felt particularly territorial about Freudism.

Yet from Laura's perspective and in light of her professional life up to this point, the kindergarten made sense as the perfect combination of her academic and personal interests and an outlet for her considerable energies. It also provided a practical solution for the pre-school education of her own two children, who were in 1911 five and six years old, respectively. Finally, it gave her a chance to try her hand at the practical application of her theoretical interests, feminism, psychoanalysis, and education.

In the coming chapters I will revisit the significance of Laura's and Cecile's pedagogical endeavours and their contribution to women's emancipation.

Here, the founding of the kindergarten serves as yet another point underscoring my argument that the progressive counter-culture and the urban middle class that created and supported it, offered an extensive range of public roles and an unprecedented level of professional recognition for women of Laura Polanyi's background. She was by no means the only one to take advantage of these openings; among the women artists, writers or feminists there were quite a few others with similar or more exposure. What made her position unique was the ease with which she moved between various groups and institutions, whether feminist, radical, socialist or strictly academic. To a large extent this was due to her close ties to the sub-groups of this community through family members and friends.

In addition to the "regulars" of Cecile's Saturday gatherings who by now had become the leaders of the democratic opposition and the artistic revolution, immediate family members were gaining prominence as well. Karl Polanyi was quickly becoming the leader of the progressive student movement; in 1908 he co-founded and became the first president of their organization, the Galileo Circle, and in 1914, the first secretary of the Bourgeois Radical Party. The first issue of the journal of the Galileo Circle in May 1911 published Laura's article,[102] introducing and advertising her new experimental school. The cover was designed by Károly Kernstok, a leading modernist artist and the future brother-in-law of Laura Polanyi,[103] highlighting again both the opportunities these family ties provided and the slightly incestuous nature of this counter-culture.

When the war interrupted and, ultimately, destroyed whatever chances a democratic bourgeois model may have had in Hungary, Laura Polanyi and her immediate family had already made a decision; following the business interests of Sándor Stricker, they moved to Vienna in 1913.

The move in itself should not have been a traumatic change for the family; Laura, after all, was born and raised in Vienna, and her husband's business connections had brought them to Austria frequently before. The children spoke German as fluently as Hungarian and her youngest sister, Sophie had been living in Vienna with her family. They had old friends, the Klatschkos, the Adlers (Alfred Adler, the psychotherapist was the family's physician in Vienna[104]), and the very few surviving letters from this period describe a lively social life there.[105] Yet it effectively ended Laura's involvement with the school as well as her other activities on the progressive Budapest scene.

The sole documentary evidence of any public role from the Vienna years is an undated invitation to a lecture given by Dr. Laura Stricker (it seems that in Vienna she did not deem it necessary to use the Polanyi name, or wnet by her married name) on "Women's Rights in Austria and Hungary" at the Viennese section of the Austrian Women's Rights Committee.[106] According to her Curriculum Vitae from 1957, she also participated at the 1917 conferences of the International Women's League for Peace and Freedom in Stockholm, Copenhagen and Oslo as a delegate for Austria.[107]

The final days of the war saw Laura and her family move back to Budapest, perhaps to be closer to the family in the chaotic days of the Monarchy's break-up. The Strickers' new house on the Buda hills, at 11 Istenhegyi ut, provided fresh air for the children and a safe distance from the tumultuous events in the city. The large garden was even used to keep pigs, hens and ducks during the months of food shortages.[108]

In October 1918, the government of Count Károlyi took over and its program of a democratic bourgeois revolution, declared on the ruins of the Dual Monarchy, united much of the pre-war democratic opposition with Károlyi's liberal nationalists. For a few short weeks, members of the pre-war democratic coalition, from the feminists to the socialists and the radicals rallied around the Károlyi-government. Laura drafted the program for the women's section of the Bourgeois Radical Party, whose leader, Oszkár Jászi was now cabinet minister in charge of nationality affairs. A list of women candidates was drawn up, among them Laura Polanyi, who were to run in the first election based on the newly declared universal suffrage, scheduled for April 1919.[109] A closer analysis of the programme, including its critique of the Feminists' performance will be the subject of the next chapter. Here, it figures as an example of the disintegration of the democratic alliance and the polarization—between the increasingly influential Communists and the reorganizing right-wing nationalists—of the political spectre.

The last months of Hungary's experiments with democratic and Communist governments provided a series of tragicomic episodes in the life of the Polanyi-Stricker family. Cecile was quick to apply to the new Minister of Culture for a fellowship abroad in order to resume the activities of the Women's Lyceum. Karl Polanyi, disenchanted by the radicals' failure and ambiguous about the rise of Communists (although many of his close friends, such as Georg Lukács, figured prominently among their leaders), left for Vienna in the early summer of 1919. Károlyi, under pressure by mounting internal opposition and amid international isolation, resigned in March 1919. He and his wife, the Countess Andrássy, invited Laura over during their last night before their escape from Hungary[110] The elections and any thoughts of a political career for Laura

Polanyi were canceled when the government of the Republic of Councils took over. During the short-lived Communist dictatorship, the Stricker villa was visited by Red Guards, ready to confiscate the animals and arrest the wealthy factory-owner. In the wife of the capitalist owner the former students recognized their lecturer at the Galileo Circle and left amid apologies.[111] It may have helped that Adolf Polanyi, as well as several cousins held high-ranking offices in the Communist government. 112

By August 1919, the Republic of Councils too collapsed under the military threat of the victorious allies and the reorganizing internal reaction. The following White terror and the reign of successive right-wing conservative governments destroyed the chances of a democratic political solution and with it the entire infrastructure of the pre-war democratic counter-culture as well. The leaders of all the left-wing parties were forced into exile, their membership decimated and silenced. To cite just two characteristic examples of the fundamental shift in the political climate, a ministerial decree in May 1920 banned all freemason organizations and in September the Parliament enacted the so-called "numerus clausus" law, limiting the ratio of Jewish students admissible to the universities.

But the shift in the political and cultural scene along nationalistic and conservative lines cannot be ascribed solely to the counter-revolutionary backlash in the aftermath of the revolutions. After all, the counter-revolutionary terror gradually subsided and in a few years the Horthy-regime put on a more respectable conservative façade, yet the democratic opposition failed to regain its pre-war influence. The decisive factors in the political make-up of the inter-war period were on one hand the Trianon Peace Treaty, in which Hungary lost two thirds of its pre-war territory and one third of its population and, on the other, the conservative-nationalistic propaganda that effectively linked the national disaster with the republican and democratic episode.[113]

The Polanyi family could claim as many losses as any as a consequence of the Trianon Treaty: the Ungvár lands and mills now belonged to the newly created Czechoslovakia, the granite mines of the Transylvanian relatives, to Romania. Yet according to the triumphant right-wing ideology, because of their association with the Radicals, Socialists, Feminists and the like, and most of all as Jews, they were the ones responsible for the territorial losses and the ensuing economic and social misery of Hungary.

I started this chapter with describing a photograph of the Pollacsek family at the height of their financial and social success; it pictured the young siblings in Cecile's salon that itself had become a symbol of the family's contribution to

Hungary's turn-of-the-century politics and culture. While one would be hard pressed to find a single photograph from the period following 1919 that would demonstrate the changed situation of the family with the same clarity, it is significant that most of the post-1919 photos show Laura Polanyi and her family in the idyllic surroundings of their garden. It underscores the involuntary withdrawal from the public to the private sphere and perhaps helps to explain why Laura's daughter, a self-confessed third-generation feminist opted for a career and the solitary life in the arts instead of following in the footsteps of her mother and grandmother in the public sphere.

Gone were the days of lively group photos as well; of the five siblings, by the end of 1919 only Michael was living in Hungary, and he too moved to Germany in 1920. Many of the younger relatives and most of the close friends had been either forced to emigrate or chose to live abroad; most of them in Austria, Germany or Italy, European countries easily accessible for Hungarians. Yet nothing illustrates the changes more than the fact that Laura Polanyi now needed a passport to visit her sister and brothers in Vienna, Berlin or Italy.[114]

Chapter 2:
The "Radical Women"

Laura Polanyi's daughter, the celebrated designer Eva Zeisel, has always been in step with the times—"Being on the Internet is cool," she commented on her website at age 89.[1] Her short biography on the site also firmly affirmed her place at the top of her family's long lineage of strong, emancipated women.

"Born as the old world empire of the Habsburgs was fraying in Hungary and Communism was on the rise, Eva Polanyi Stricker, grew up outside Budapest on a rambling estate. A solid matriarchy had begun with her salon-keeping grandmother, a journalist, and her mother, a historian and onetime parliamentary candidate."[2] Even if Eva Zeisel, the family's reigning matriarch's idenification as a "a third-generation feminist," has a whiff of journalistic excess,[3] it reflects the esteem in which the family held its feminist tradition. This tradition is also the most obvious unifying thread to connect Cecile and Laura Polanyi's forays into politics and the women's rights movement in the period beginning in the late 19th century and ending in 1919. With their contributions to psychoanalysis, education, and academia, briefly described in the previous chapter and to be further discussed later, they attest to the astonishing range and talents of mother and daughter.

In the following, I will revisit the political activities of Cecile and Laura prior to 1919. First I will describe them in the wider context of activism, both male and female, of the period. I will then assess the value of one of the central paradigms of Western women's history, the notion of separate spheres, in relation to this Central European case. Finally, I will propose an alternative definition of the private-public dichotomy and locate the source of women's activism represented by Cecile and Laura Polanyi in the progressive bourgeois counterculture of turn-of-the-century Hungary.

A much simpler alternative would be to present the public activities of Cecile and Laura as part of a larger struggle, that of the Hungarian first-wave women's rights movement. After all, it could be argued that their public roles, from the semi-private salon to participation in feminist and other political organizations, reflected an increasingly militant and public stance against the patriarchal limitations of the larger society were part and parcel of the emerging Hungarian women's rights movement. Moreover, both Cecile and Laura could be legitimately identified as bourgeois feminists, part of the Hungarian first-wave women's rights movement, whose emergence and peak coincided with the period in question, the first two decades of the twentieth century.[4]

On the other hand, Cecile's contacts with the feminists were negligible and Laura's relationship with the Hungarian bourgeois women's rights movement, although close, was far from unproblematic. One of the objectives of the following narrative is to convey the ambiguities of this relationship over time and various issues. The political loyalties and choices of Cecile and Laura Polanyi were rooted in the family's intellectual traditions, nurtured through their education, and linked to the defining social, political and intellectual influences of their era; to reduce them to the single cause of women's emancipation would not do justice to their complexity.

Yet it is a story of women fighting against the boundaries set by society that evokes similar stories of women's activism elsewhere, told through the paradigm of separate spheres. The paradigm has been successfully employed to describe the emergence of middle-class society in Britain and North America, and served as the framework in which to ground the emerging Western bourgeois women's rights movements.

In the recent assessment of a leading British historian, the opposition of the private and public spheres has been "central to much of the writing on women's history in Britain and North America from the early 1970s," and "the focus on the language of separate spheres and the dichotomies between private and public was fundamental to charting the limitations and oppression of women's lives."[5] The paradigm of separate spheres successfully established the links between the ideology of separate spheres, evangelical religion, and the cult of domesticity on the one hand and the emergence of the middle-class family as the cornerstone of middle-class society on the other.[6] Furthermore, it identified the separate spheres as the source of women's emerging public activism and placed gender relations at the heart of class formation.[7]

The notion of "separate spheres" permeated Western women's history to such a degree that it is almost impossible to sidestep it when writing about bourgeois women's movements anywhere, including the emerging scholarship on women's history in post-Communist Eastern Europe; there too, "public" and "private" became the staple of academia.[8]

Yet, despite its merits in Western women's history, one has to be sceptical about the use of the paradigm in the countries of Eastern and Central Europe. One of the more obvious challenges is the lack of evangelical Christianity outside of Britain and North America. Other, even more significant differences in political, social, and intellectual history should strongly caution against the indiscriminate use of separate spheres, as the main paradigm for the emerging woman activism and bourgeois society in the case of Austria-Hungary.[9]

The problems begin with the inherent problems of the paradigm itself. French women's historians had raised the point that the boundaries between private and public had never been clear-cut to begin with.[10] Social historians with a comparative perspective called for a widening of the notion of the public sphere. Richard Evans in particular argued for a more widely defined public sphere as a useful middle ground between old-fashioned political history and feminist historians' focus on women's experience.[11]

In the late 1980s a group of prominent women's historians proposed to widen the scope of women's history, both in a geographical sense, to include the history of women beyond Western Europe and North America, and by moving it towards an interdisciplinary approach. Their efforts contributed to the growing realization that some of the central tenets of Western women's history such as the dichotomy of separate spheres may not be relevant to the understanding of gender relations beyond these limited geographical boundaries.[12]

Barbara Einhorn's pioneering study on gender relations under the Eastern and Central European Communist regimes may seem as irrelevant to our pre-WWI case. Yet her argument, that under the vastly different experiences of Western and Eastern European women, the dichotomy of private and public spheres gained widely differing meanings, raises a singularly valid point in our context.[13]

In Western feminist interpretations, "the private sphere was pilloried for its disadvantaging of women in under-valued, unremunerated, isolated and largely invisible spheres of work. Western feminists emphasized the need to free women from the confines of the private and facilitate their entry into the public spheres of work and politics."[14] At the same time, in the oppressed civil societies of Eastern Europe, the private sphere took on opposite, positive connotations.

> At the unofficial level ... the private sphere was invested with a value in inverse proportion to state strictures. Family and friends filled the space where civil society could not exist; the private sphere was the only space for the development of individual initiative and autonomy. It was also seen as both haven from and site of resistance to the long arm of the state.[15]

Such a different perception of the private/public divide in turn effected gender politics as well, since

42 The Hungarian Pocahontas

... far from exposing gender divisions in the family, the value attributed to the private in the state socialist countries both strengthened the public/private divide, and induced solidarity within the private sphere, against the impersonal and oppressive forces to which people felt subjected in the public sphere. What this constellation did not do was highlight women's rights or gender inequalities. Rather, it pitted the collectivity of family and friendship groups against the unitary interfering state, *and* discredited any public commitment to the equality of women.[16]

This unexpected turn of gender-relations observed under the oppressive political regimes of Communist Eastern and Central Europe seems to apply in the early-twentieth-century period as well. According to this dynamics, the key to understanding Cecile's and especially Laura's political and professional motives and choices lies not in their drive to step out from the private to the public realm—although it contained this element as well—but rather in their participation in the building of a progressive, alternative public sphere.

Another, slightly longer leap, back to France in the last days of the Old Regime, will lead us to another, complementary frame of reference, defined by the German sociologist Jürgen Habermas as an "authentic public sphere," crucial in the building of an emerging bourgeois society. Cecile's salon and its role in Hungary's emerging bourgeois counterculture in the early 1900s invites the comparison to the French salons, hosted by women, in the dying days of the Ancien Régime. And the similarities turn out to be far from superficial.

In his seminal work, *The Structural Transformation of the Public Sphere*, published in German in 1962,[17] Habermas pointed to the emergence of an authentic public sphere as the main arena for the creation of modern bourgeois society in eighteenth-century Europe. This authentic public sphere, standing between the non-authentic, state and court-dictated public sphere, and the private realm of family and commodity exchange and labour, emerged from the private sphere and was further divided into three aspects: the market of cultural products, the Republic of Letters (the institutions of intellectual sociability, such as clubs, salons, cafes, the press, etc.), and the public sphere in the political realm.[18]

True to his roots in the neo-Marxist traditions of the Frankfurt School, Habermas intended his book as a critique of the degeneration of the eighteenth-century literate bourgeois public into the highly manipulated, manufactured "public opinion" of our day. It is a testament to his insight that European social historians has come to accept it as a convincing historical analysis of the emerging bourgeois political culture in the late 18th century.

The fact that Habermas's by then classic study was published in English only in 1989, made for a very different reception in the English-speaking countries.[19] In the absence of an English translation, American feminist historians went on to ignore Habermas's model as late as 1984 and define "politics and political involvement ... as activities that take place either within formal government institutions or through informal channels to power.... The activity must be conscious, organized, and leading toward some legal change or governmental response."[20] Since in their view "*salonnières* and writers did not step beyond their salons and discussions [and] they took no political action" they concluded that "they cannot be considered political women. Their study should be undertaken elsewhere."[21]

When it finally became available in English in 1989, the fashion of the Frankfurt School and the appeal of neo-Marxism had been long gone, and Habermas's seminal work was registered mainly by political scientists.[22] The reaction of historians was, at best, muted, with the notable exception of North-American and British feminist historians. They agreed that Habermas's treatment of gender, or rather, lack of it, rendered his model unacceptable.[23]

One of his rare defenders among feminist historians pointed out that Habermas's feminist critics based their negative assessment on the notion of a simple opposition between the public and private spheres; it was, however, a false opposition that failed to do justice to the complexity and fluidity of both the Old Regime and Habermas's representation of it.[24] It was exactly the ambiguity and fluidity of this authentic public sphere that "allowed women to play an important role in this public sphere so long as it remained private."[25] In her intricate argument, Goodman highlighted the connection between the fate of an authentic public sphere in general and the freedom of women to fulfill meaningful roles in it. When the men of the French Revolution drew the line between a male political sphere and a female domestic one, "it had as much to do with the collapse of the authentic public sphere as it did with misogyny," and sprang from the state's intention "to attribute all publicity to itself and to dominate a private sphere now reduced to the family."[26] "It was the authentic public sphere that was dissolved in the revolutionary process, and with it, a public role for women."[27]

Habermas's reception in Hungary was a very different story. Here, *The Structural Transformation of the Public Sphere* in 1971[28] was published not long after the bloody breakdown on the "Prague Spring," demonstrating the futility of any hope for a successful internal reform of the system. The Hungarian political opposition, eager to find historical antecedents, found one in this book: pre-revolutionary France where an authentic public sphere successfully challenged the institutions of official political culture and, ultimately, the entire political system. Such a reading of Habermas contributed to the articulation of an alternative public in Hungary; sociologists, economists and political philosophers embraced Habermas's categories when describing the emerging "second public sphere" and "second economy" of the 1970s.

The framework I propose for the purposes of this chapter is based on a broad definition of the political/public sphere, one that includes not only political institutions such as parties and associations *per se*, but also the institutions of the emerging bourgeois political culture, such as the press, the various civic and professional associations, the free-mason lodges, even the coffeehouses. Habermas's concept of an authentic public sphere as the medium of an emerging bourgeois political consciousness with its own institutions grounded in the private, allows the inclusion of the salon as one of these institutions. Despite the obvious differences between turn-of-the-century Hungary and late eighteenth-century France, the analogy is meaningful. Hungary's spectacular economic modernization took place within the context of an outdated political system. As well, the lopsided modernization of its social structure, the so-called "dual social structure," maintained much of the privileges of the traditional ruling class and raised powerful social barriers against the rise of a new, bourgeois professional and intellectual class. It is the latter's fight for political and social acceptance that lends significance to the institutions based in the private sphere, such as the salon.

In addition, Habermas's notion of the "authentic public sphere" provides a framework flexible enough in which to locate the identity of the women who participated in it. As we will see, Cecile and Laura's identification with the progressive counterculture of early twentieth-century Hungary (and, in Cecile's case, the identification early in life with the Russian revolutionary Left) won over their identification with the cause of women's emancipation. Much of the appeal of this community for women, and the explanation for their loyalty with it, was a consequence of the fluidity between private and public.

The environment in which these young women experimented (and were not only allowed but encouraged to do so) with new, public roles, was a natural extension of their private lives and identities. Cecile's salon was in every sense an extension of her family life and her family life blended flawlessly with her political activism, even with her Russian revolutionary contacts. As for Laura's generation of younger women, the leap into the realm of the public/political sphere was made smoother by the fact that it took place within the network of family and friends. When they took on new public activities, this network provided not only financial and emotional support for their education but also kept these choices in the realm of socially acceptability. It explains why young women from assimilated Jewish families were overrepresented among the newly emancipated in disproportional numbers and met fewer rather than more barriers in the process. Supported by a network of family and friends, they encountered less resistance than young women from the "traditional," Christian middle class.

The sense that they were part of a larger "alternative public sphere," the democratic counter-culture, also shaped these young women's perception of gender divisions. In their eyes, the main frontlines were drawn not between men on one side, protecting the borders of the public sphere, and women on the other, but rather, between the keepers of semi-feudal, conservative Hungary against the alliance of men and women fighting for a democratic Hungarian political system and modernist culture.

Cecile's salon, while clearly an institution of this emerging bourgeois public sphere, was also part of a long tradition although there is no indication that she or her guests were aware of this continuity. One link with the past was more coincidental than substantial: the best-known salon of 1880s Pest was the only one hosted by women, and by Cecile's namesakes, the Wohl sisters. Here, however, the similarities ended. Stefánia and Janka Wohl were dilettante writers of German extraction, and their salon gathered the cream of the political and cultural establishment, the eminent writers, academics, and politicians of the era. Conversation was deliberately kept outside of politics and in a strictly conservative spirit.[29]

Another salon of late nineteenth-century Pest was hosted by the Pulszky family, representative of the best liberal traditions of the Hungarian nobility. Ferenc Pulszky, one-time director of the Hungarian National Museum, was also the grandmaster of the largest Hungarian freemason lodge, founded in 1886. He belonged to the great liberal generation of the 1840s, fighting the anti-liberal, neo-conservative trends of the 1880s. The family was to forge important ties with the progressive movements of the new century. One of Pulszky's sons, Ágost, was a respected liberal positivist philosopher and professor of law, and as such, the mentor of the young law graduates, Oszkár Jászi and his co-founders of the Sociological Society. Ágost Pulszky was to become the first president of the Society and when he died in 1901, his library was donated to the Society and catalogued by Ervin Szabó.

His sister, Polixéna, was one of the leaders of the moderate women's association, the Hungarian Association for the Education of Women. The Association fought for women's access to higher education and founded the first girls' gymnasium, the high school Laura Polanyi was to attend from 1896. A frequent guest of the Pulszky salon, the young Henrik Marczali, later became Hungary's leading historian, Laura's future mentor at Budapest University.[30]

I had previously quoted Oszkár Jászi's eyewitness account of the early days of Cecile's salon. In his unfinished memoirs, Jászi looked back on the decisive influences of his university years in Budapest, and described, among them, the informal gatherings at the house of his future father-in-law, Geyza Moskovicz. Moskovicz was a colourful character, one of only a handful, Jewish members of the National Casino, the exclusive club of the aristocracy, and friend and advisor of Count Andrássy, the foreign minister of the Monarchy. Moskovicz married into one of the leading Jewish financier families while he himself remained a landowner, a fierce Hungarian nationalist, and a conservative anti-capitalist. He welcomed "all men of good manners from the younger generations" in his "jungle," named after the Kipling bestseller of the day. He failed in his efforts to convince his young friends of the importance of the Hungarian national struggle and, according to Jászi, only reinforced their opposition to the country's social and political elite. Yet he provided a vivid example of open discussion and tolerance of opposing views, later reincarnated in the debates of Jászi's future Sociological Society. The spirit of the Moskovicz gatherings, however, belonged to the nineteenth-century liberal tradition, represented by the Pulszkys and others whose main goal was to create the largely missing Hungarian institutions of establishment culture and middle-class audience.

It is unlikely that Cecile, who arrived from Vienna in the late 1880s with no ties to or knowledge of the Hungarian literary tradition, found her inspiration in these salons. Her role models were much more likely the French *salonnières* of the 18th century of whom she had probably learned in her high-school history lessons. Their role in the French Revolution was generously overestimated and the Goncourt brothers' book on the French *salonnières* was widely read at the time.

A recent portrait of the eighteenth-century French *salonnières* fits Cecile in many ways. Olwen Hufton defines the salon's hostess as a professional organizer of social gatherings whose "success was measured by the readiness of great minds to come and to import other luminaries from the republic of letters."[31] Her observation that "most of the *salonnières* looked upon their activities as a real career, though one without a salary"[32] is also fitting. As for Cecile's motives, she shared some of the French *salonnières*' literary ambitions, even Madame Necker's wish to find "a niche for herself in a society where she was a foreigner."[33]

We can assume with some certainty that Cecile was aware of another incarnation of the salon in early-nineteenth-century Berlin, whose bourgeois hostesses played a pivotal role in German Romanticism.

> A handful of other middle-class women managed at least for a while to step outside the narrow field of domesticity. Unusually well educated and ambitious, they secured for themselves a place in that gray area, the world that was no longer private and yet was not quite public, represented by the salon. Despite its aristocratic image, the salon was a genuinely *bürgerliche* institution to the extent that it did not select its members according to rank resulting from birth or office, but acknowledged only 'educated figures' who had individual merits. The normal social barriers between the aristocracy and bourgeoisie, Jews and Christians, men of letters and merchants, officers and civilians, were blurred in the salon; women too had the chance to be accepted as individuals and to win respect. As hostesses they gathered a public around themselves which not only paid homage to female beauty but also honoured intelligence, spontaneity and great imaginativeness.[34]

The description of early-nineteenth-century Berlin salons, located in the no man's land between the private and the public, with the normal social barriers and divisions suspended, echoes Cecile's salon a century later. The most famous of the early nineteenth-century Berlin *salonnières* was the Jewish merchant's daughter from Berlin, Rahel Levin, later Varnhagen.[35] By the turn of the century, her contributions to German Romanticism had been widely acknowledged and she became a feminist icon, popularized by the bestselling biography of Ellen Key, herself perhaps the best-known feminist of the time.[36]

As Oszkár Jászi emphasized in his memoir-fragment, Cecile's was not merely another salon, it was an "opposite jungle." Jászi's reminiscences constitute one of the very few eyewitness accounts of Cecile's salon, and the only one that attempted an assessment of the salon's significance in the coming of age of his generation. As such, they deserve to be quoted in full:

> Beside this conservative national jungle [the Moskovitz-salon] (and independently of it, although a few of its members attended both), there was another gathering, with a strongly radical, even socialist emphasis. A talented and initially very successful engineer from Northern Hungary, the builder of several railway lines, Mihaly Pollacsek and his wife, a Russian woman from Kovno (sic!), Tante Cécile, a veritable icon, even symbol, became, following their financial disaster, the guiding lights and leaders of an opposite 'jungle'. An equally mixed gathering, it increasingly fell under the spell of Nietzsche and Marx. The hostess was brilliantly witty but frequently displayed a female superficiality. At times she performed a veritable trapeze act between oft-changing ideological formulae, while kept discovering new talents and shaping them to her own taste. I remember when, during my Herbert Spencer-period, she cautioned me that the wisdom of the great English positivist should be balanced

with the resplendence of Nietzsche. The circle of "Cécile mama" was well known not only in Budapest but also enjoyed a certain international reputation and was sometimes frequented by foreign visitors who visited to immerse themselves in the air of Hungarian extreme ideas.[37]

Jászi's memoirs dated the beginnings of Cecile's salon to the Pollacseks' bankruptcy in 1899, to coincide with the founding of the journal "Twentieth Century" in the fall of 1899 and the Sociological Society in January 1901. If this is correct, the salon's influence was perhaps less significant in the making of the small circle of friends who established the two flagship institutions of the Hungarian progressive counterculture. Yet Cecile's eclectic interests continued to serve the young lawyers and social scientists well in the following years. Beside the intellectual fare, the Pollacsek house also provided a substitute home and family for the young men, many of whom arrived from the small towns of the countryside and lived in rented rooms and small flats during their university years and the early years of their professional careers. Last but not least, the salon provided these young men with a relaxed but socially acceptable environment to meet young, eligible women. Many high-profile marriages and relationships began under the not always benevolent, sharp eyes of Cecile.

To suggest that the salon was Cecile Pollacsek's most lasting legacy is something of a paradox, given the ephemeral nature of the genre. Yet, it became the achievement with which she wrote her name into the intellectual history of modern Hungary. Not only was it the perfect fit for her personality and intellectual ambitions, it also fulfilled a social need. As friendships and marriages further solidified the circle and its newlyweds settled into their own homes, Cecile had to share her "regulars" with other hosts and hostesses. By 1904, Alice Jászi, Oszkár's younger sister, also kept an open house, on Thursdays, presumably so as not to interfere with Cecile's Saturdays. Her brother-in-law, the prosperous and childless lawyer Károly Pollacsek also kept both his city and weekend house open to the young crowd.

The salon's own social microcosm kept Cecile happily isolated from the social circles of the Jewish bourgeoisie. She and her husband both detested the intellectual shallowness of the *nouveau riche*, along with their tendency to assimilate to the worst excesses of the Hungarian gentry. In any case, for women in Cecile's generation, there were not many outlets available for public activity beside the existing charitable women's associations. The only such association accessible to her, the Israelite Women's Association of Pest, although a venerable organization (it was the first of the women's organizations founded along religious lines, in 1866) was obviously too dull for her restless intellect.[38]

Cecile was also motivated by the sheer pleasure of being the centre of attention. She prided herself on the discovery of new talents and provided the link between the successes of her own generation and the promises of that of her children, as well as introduced eminent visitors from abroad to the home-grown talents. In all this, there was probably a good measure of snobbism; her letters to her children always carefully recorded the names of her most prominent visitors.[39]

She barely had any close ties to anyone from her own generation—with the notable exception of the Klatschkos—but for this she compensated with a legion of younger friends. Neither did she try to hide her age or make light of the obvious fact that most of her guests could have been her children; to the contrary, she played on her maturity and experience in a maternal fashion. She earned a notoriety for her intrusions into the private affairs of her young charges; Georg Lukács mentioned her "well-known eye and talent for gossip"[40] while trying to avoid Cecile at a summer resort where he was visiting a young, female, friend. In Lukács's case, Cecile might have felt entitled to the scrutiny as, through their mutual best friend Leó Popper, he was a friend of Karl Polanyi and because of the high-profile love affair he had with Cecile's niece, Irma Seidler a few years back.

Jászi was not the only one Cecile advised on intellectual avenues to be explored. In one of her letters that has survived in Georg Lukács's correspondence, she ominously instructed the already well-known and published young philosopher and art critic to take up the psychology of the masses, including the *Class Struggles* of Marx, in order "to understand the feelings of the masses."[41]

There is some indication that Lukács and his friends did not reciprocate Cecile's friendship or see her as their equal.[42] Their lack of respect may have originated in the justified arrogance of the young generation whose members measured everyone in terms of intellectual output, based on the considerable productivity many of them had already shown at a young age. Cecile was painfully aware of the difference between her young friends' impressive record and the lack of enduring intellectual products of her own. She described to Lukács her mental state in the somewhat affected style of the day as the depression of a "very tired woman" who is barely alive because "only those who, as yourself, can say: I work, are happy. *Lavoro ergo sum*."[43]

Such moments of depression and feeling of uselessness could not have lasted for long. Her manuscripts and the family documents provide a fascinating sample of her attempts to leave a legacy other than her salon. There is an invitation to the lecture of Cecile Pólányi-Pollacsek, using another of the many name-versions she experimented with. Since she never officially Magyarized her family name, it could be interpreted as a sign that she wanted a share of her children's growing public recognition. The invitation to the exhibition of the "Eights," the leading modernist art group, at the National Salon, indicated that she was to give a talk "about the newest direction of art."[44] No manuscript survived and we can only guess that the talk was given in German.

Cecile wrote and spoke mostly German, with only a few Hungarian words thrown in for good measure: it was highly ironic that while her salon was frequented by the best talents of the Hungarian literary avant-garde, she could not read them in the original. Characteristically , in a letter from the 1930s she correctly identified Attila József and Gyula Illyés as the two outstanding poets of the period and the prize visitors of her weekly gatherings, while at the same time badly misspelled their names.[45]

Cecile's lack of fluency in Hungarian substantially limited her journalistic ambitions. She was passionately interested in the theatre and her letters are filled of witty and summary reviews of theatre productions; but only of those that were produced in German, by visiting German and Austrian companies. In the spirit of the times, she aspired to become a sort of *kultur kritik* but her published articles were few and far between, and limited to Budapest's German-language newspapers, the *Neue Pester Journal* and, in one instance, the prestigious *Pester Lloyd*.[46] True, every educated Hungarian read and spoke German but the real action was happening in Hungarian, in the exciting modernist literature.

There are other, unpublished short pieces preserved among her manuscripts with such telling titles as "Graphology", "Fashion-chronicle," "Modern Luxury" and the more ambitious "About Beauty, Love and Others" as well as a short one-act comedy, written perhaps to be performed at a cabaret, titled: "The Miracle Doctor."[47] Occasionally insightful and witty, these pieces did not withstand the test of time; they proved to be as ephemereal as the genres themselves in which they were produced.

Cecile's frequently expressed loyalty to the Russian Left lent her the exotic aura of a Russian revolutionary, setting her further apart from the bourgeois society of turn-of-the-century Hungary. While her identification with Russian language and culture originated in her childhood and was reinforced by her father's assimilationist conviction, the revolutionary element was clearly due to the influence of the Klatschkos. Samuel Klatschko not only represented an attractive, non-sectarian socialist ethic, he also demonstrated by his lifestyle that it was possible to have it both ways: to live a morally principled life enriched by meaningful action and, at the same time, enjoy everything bourgeois culture had to offer. These were the very values Cecile successfully transplanted into her salon in Hungary. The Klatschkos may never have kept a salon but their apartment on *Belvedere Gasse* emulated all the characteristics of one: it was a meeting place in the no man's land between the private and the public, between the bourgeois and the revolutionary.

It is no accident that in the eyes of her contemporaries as well as those who met her only in her old age, Cecile was the embodiment of the legendary young Russian student girl. And it is very likely that her appearance, with her cropped hair, dark, unadorned dresses, lack of jewelry and hat, complete with cigarette, was a consciously projected image. The relations between the Klatschkos and the Pollacseks, reportedly, also included mysterious packages and visitors from and to Russia. It is difficult to tell how much of this activity was real or exaggerated by Ilona Duczynska, the future Mrs. Karl Polanyi, who later recorded her husband's reminiscences and whose own revolutionary fervour was legendary. In any case, Cecile's lecture on the 1905 Russian revolution is testimony to Cecile's deep identification with the Russian revolutionary Left.[48]

As an expert in Russian history and revolutionary movements, Cecile was invited to the *Vorwärts*, the cultural association of German-speaking socialist workers, to give a talk on the 1905-6 Russian revolutionary events. She accomplished the task in an unusually well-organized and characteristically passionate lecture. She started off with the standard socialist assessment of the time: that the events in Russia signaled the dawn of a new era in the history of class struggle, that of the proletarian phase. She then went on to outline the trends in Russian history, from Peter the Great to the Crimean War, which led to the present system of despotism and unwillingness to reform. From here, she proceeded to a detailed account of the revolutionary movements in the second half of the 19th century and the thorough Westernization of the intelligentsia. She described the period of revolutionary terrorism and *narodn'ik* movement as a dead end which was effectively superseded by a proletarian-based mass movement, with the founding of a Russian socialist party. Throughout the lecture she provided hints to her first-hand experiences. The emphasis on the Russian intelligentsia's Westernization as the direct cause for the emergence of revolutionary movements clearly shows her father's influence. She described the sacrifices of young students of the elite who, after many years of studies in Zurich, remembered their duty and returned to Russia to repay their debt to the working people; this passage of rare emotional charge clearly speaks of her own aspirations or unfulfilled dreams. She also mentioned Klatschko and, repeatedly, his utopian socialist mentor, Chaikovsky, among the most important leaders of the socialist movement, an obvious overstatement, and emphasized the role of the strong Jewish socialist parties of Lithuania and Poland.

She concluded her talk with the well-worn romantic image of a "red sunrise on the snow fields of Russia" and a passionate battle-cry: "The superhuman struggle of our Russian comrades is our fight as well, and when we see the Sun rise in the East, let us cry in unison: Hail the Russian revolution!"[49] It makes one wonder whether the workers of the *Vorwärts* Association ever registered the irony as this middle-aged wife-of-industrialist concluded her lecture with the thunderous commitment: "And we, proletarians of the world, welcome with joy and anticipation the day of freedom."[50]

Cecile who followed so keenly the new intellectual trends of the early century was bound to discover, sooner or later, psychoanalysis. Through Alfred Adler, the family's friend and physician in Vienna, she must have been informed of the Viennese psychoanalytical scene and in 1909 received treatment at the Bircher-Brenner clinic in Zurich. Dr. Bircher-Brenner, originally a dietitian and physiotherapist, the inventor of the Bircher-muesli, just opened a psychoanalytic practice.[51] Cecile, originally sceptical of the new miracle treatment, quickly turned into an enthusiastic follower of psychoanalysis. Shortly after her return from Zurich she visited Ferenczi's office in Budapest who related her visit in a letter to Freud. "This lady (the mother) is herself neurotic, you see, and was just in analysis for four months with *Bircher-Benner* in *Zurich*. At the time she was making a lot of nasty remarks about my 'obscene' lectures; now she has been completely converted, is full of enthusiasm for the cause, and wants to go back to *Bircher* in order to dedicate herself there to ¥A., as a *nurse*."[52] Cecile's newly-found passion for psychoanalysis was part of a larger phenomenon; in the same letter, Ferenczi sarcastically commented on the cult-like atmosphere at the Bircher-clinic, describing the patients-turned-followers of the movement, "many Dutch women among them, who want to make a theosophical science out of ¥A."[53] The remark was actually based on Cecile's own experiences at the clinic, related by her to Ferenczi. Naturally, she was reluctant to include herself in this crowd. And Ferenczi agreed, adding that, unlike these women, "Frau Pollatschek is, incidentally, a very intellectual, very well educated lady, who has an excellent grasp of the sense of psychoanalysis."[54]

Cecile never followed up on her plans to take up psychoanalysis in a more professional manner, despite the fact that the psychoanalytical movement was relatively open to women, physicians as well as interested amateurs. In Hungary, some of the first analysts were women and, although younger than Cecile, belonged to the same social circle.[55] She would occasionally subject her friends and acquaintances to short analytical sessions; György Pólya, the famous mathematician remembered that she effectively cured him of his habit of repeating every sentence.[56] (According to the family, tongue-and-cheek version of the anecdote, Pólya himself reports: "Mama Cecile cured my habit, cured my habit.") Cecile realized that of all her intellectual passions, psychoanalysis was her "great, unrequited love affair."[57] But to focus on any one of her intellectual passions for long would have ran counter to her restless intellect, always in search of the next new thing. In the process, she may have missed her best opportunity to find a creative and useful outlet the lack of which she lamented so often.

Laura's first lessons in women's emancipation were undoubtedly taken from her mother; brilliant, creative, widely traveled and read, living an utterly nonconformist lifestyle, Cecile provided an example of rare creative and intellectual freedom. Yet despite the claim that Cecile was the decisive inspiration for her children's intellectual development,[58] she may have had an opposite influence on Laura. Perhaps it was a question of different personalities; Laura's systematic and analytic mind as well as her guardedness and self-deprecating irony were more reminiscent of her father. From early on, Laura's interests (the bibliography, her library work) and her choice of academic subjects (such as the early modern economic history she chose for her doctorate) required steady work and promised no instant return, in sharp contrast to the oft-changing, sometimes superficial interests and intellectual fireworks of Cecile.

Their differences were also due to a generational shift. Whereas Cecile was unique in her generation with her mix of intellectual ambitions, Laura was a member of the first generation that benefited from the opening up of opportunities for young women to pursue higher education and professional careers. Last but not least, while Cecile was never attached to any single political party or organization, Laura was committed, from an early age, to both of the two main streams of the Hungarian women's movement and, later on, worked for various political and cultural organizations.

Laura's connection to the older, moderate stream of the Hungarian women's movements came about as a matter of chance rather than choice. The opening of the first girls' gymmnasium in 1896, where Laura was a member of the first graduating class, was the result of a long fight by the Hungarian Association for the Education of Women ["Magyar Nöképzö Egyesület"], founded in 1868 by a Hungarian aristocrat, the Countess Pál Veress. Until the end of the nineteenth century, it was the largest women's association in Hungary, and its main goal was to secure women's access to secondary and higher education. For lack of an educated middle class, its leaders were, almost without exception, aristocrats.[59]

If the aristocratic leaders of the Association had hopes that the school would raise a loyal young generation, committed to the moderate liberal ideals of their organization, they came to be disappointed. Instead of becoming followers of the moderate women's movement or at least expressing gratitude for the work of the pioneers, the young women of the first graduating class went on to claim full credit for their accomplishments. To their chagrin, leaders of the Association had to witness some of the graduates ending up in the ranks of the emerging bourgeois feminist movement, and suffer the final blow as the feminists too claimed credit for this turning point in women's emancipation.

These upcoming infights between the various strands of the Hungarian women's movements indicate that leaders of both the moderate and the radical women's movement realized very early the significance of opening up the faculties to women and establishing a girls' gymnasium. In hindsight, these acts symbolized the changing of the guard in the history of the Hungarian women's movement. The class of Laura Polanyi, and her own path more than anyone else's, at once effectively provided the connection between the two main streams of the Hungarian women's movement and created a watershed between them.

These changes, of course, reflected more than the graduation of a single high-school class. From the 1880s, women's employment underwent a fundamental change. Girls' trade schools and teacher colleges, coupled with the growing demand for cheap female labour in the white-collar occupations, created a marked rise in the number of women working in the civil service and industry. The elementary school teacher, the post office clerk, the typist, and the stenographer became female occupations par excellence, underpaid, abused, and discriminated against. It was this fast-growing urban white-collar female labour force that produced the first grass-roots women's organization, the Hungarian Association of Women Clerks [Magyar Nőtisztviselők Egyesülete]. Founded in 1897, it became the first and largest women's organization that represented the economic interests and welfare of a large occupational group, and, eventually, provided political education for a whole generation of feminist leaders. From the late 1890s, the new leaders of the bourgeois first-wave feminist movement came exclusively from the ranks of the middle class and mostly from the ranks of the Association of Women Clerks. Individual aristocrats, however, such as the Countess Teleki (under the pen name "Spark", she was also a journalist), continued to play a role on the moderate wing of the women's rights movement. Simultaneously, a number of philanthropic women's organizations were founded by women with ties to the traditional elite and the churches and influenced by the emerging social Catholicism.

The parallels between the paths of the Hungarian women's movements and Laura's own continued when, in the summer of 1904, her graduation from university coincided with the raising of the flag of the first feminist organization in Hungary. In the summer of 1904, the Hungarian Association of Women Clerks sent its two leaders, Róza Schwimmer and Vilma Glücklich, to the Berlin conference of the International Council of Women. On their return, they founded the Coalition of Hungarian Women's Associations, an umbrella organization encompassing practically all existing women's organizations, which continued to exist throughout the entire period without much real influence and, in December 1904, the Association of Feminists.[60]

Under the guidance of the international first-wave feminist movement, the Hungarian Association of Feminists launched an ambitious program to raise public awareness of the problems of child welfare, the protection of mothers and newborns, illegitimacy, the exploitation of and discrimination against women in the work place, prostitution, alcoholism and sexual education in schools, and suggested solutions.[61] Above all, they became engaged in a concentrated effort for women's suffrage, supported by the leaders of the International Alliance of Women, the more radical of the two largest international women's organizations. The Hungarian Association of Feminists had become a member of the Alliance in 1906.[62]

It is entirely possible that Laura seriously considered a career within the feminist association. After all, not only was this the first political organization representing women's political and educational rights and fighting for their equal rights in employment, but it was also led by women whose education and background were very similar to her own. A composite picture of the feminist leadership would show a highly educated woman with a high school diploma (Vilma Glücklich, second-in-command to the uncontested leader, Rózsa Bédy-Schwimmer, was actually the first woman to enroll at the Faculty of Arts of the Budapest University in 1896). She would be fluent in German, French, perhaps even in English, and born around the late 1870s.

A member of the feminist leadership would be then, typically, somewhat older than Laura but would come, more likely than not, from the assimilated Jewish upper-middle and middle class.[63]

In addition, Laura's language and social skills, not to mention her financially secure background by marriage would have made her an ideal candidate. And her continuing commitment to women's rights issues was demonstrated by her first appearance on the feminist "lecture-circuit" in 1905. Following a short period of withdrawal and the birth of her first child, she delivered a talk that cut to the heart of the issue of women's emancipation. And if she had indeed aspired to take up a permanent engagement in the feminist leadership, there are other signs that the demands of her growing family and her intensifying interest in pedagogy made her reconsider.

The talk in question, titled "A few words about the woman and women's education" was given at the end of 1905 and published in 1906.[64] In it, the young university graduate and mother presented an unorthodox approach to the "woman's question." It was one that could not have pleased the feminist camp very much, for she argued that there was no such thing as woman's question only woman's question*s*. She proved her point by sidestepping the whole problematic of bourgeois feminism and, in true Marxist fashion, turning it on its feet. Approaching the question as a social, rather than a psychological, physiological, ethical, or esthetic problem, she went on to demolish most of the accepted bourgeois feminist wisdom. The feminist leadership repeatedly argued that the struggle for women's rights superseded the struggle between classes and was, in fact, the only legitimate class struggle, a position developed, in part, as a reaction to the attacks of the Social Democrats.[65]

Laura argued that if there were no such thing as a single women's question and "the woman is always more closely associated with the men of her own socio-economic class than with any other woman,"[66] there was no single solution for the multiple problems facing working women or bourgeois women. From here, Laura went on to discuss the second part of what may have been the initial question of the debate and prescribe the potential solutions in women's education.

The public appearance of the 23-year-old Laura in full Marxist armour was no accident: it largely corresponded to a phase undertaken by the circle of the *Twentieth Century*. If it did not quite manifest itself in a conversion to the teachings of historical materialism, it certainly meant that Jászi and his friends were taking account of the most important works of Marx and contemporary Marxism and trying to draw their own conclusions as to the application of Marxist and socialist prescriptions to their reform programme. Their Marxist phase, lasting from 1903 to the first half of 1906, was signaled by the publication of such important works as Jászi's *The State Theory of Historical Materialism* in 1905 and, above all, the first volume of Ervin Szabó's monumental *Selected*

Works of Marx and Engels in the same year.

Yet, despite their ideological differences, Laura kept up her collaboration with the bourgeois feminists. She maintained a correct if not necessarily warm relationship with one of their two leaders, Vilma Glücklich.[67] There are sporadic signs over the course of the next few years, testifying to her continuing commitment, including a talk at the Feminist Section of Lugos (a small town in Transylvania) on "Feminism and Marriage" and her article on "The woman of the middle-class intelligentsia."[68]

The article was published as part of a series addressing the perceived problems of the intellectual element within the middle class. These problems, detected by the watchful eyes of the radical sociologists, consisted of the falling marriage and birthrates as well as a rising age at marriage. The author of the leading article of the series, the young sociologist Ede Harkányi, was the designated expert of the Jászi-circle of the gender question and a friend of the Polanyis.[69] Following a cursory analysis of the dismal statistics, he concluded that the liberation of women, i.e. their access to education and employment would instantly solve the problems. To which Laura Polanyi added, in her by now customary "Marxist" manner, that the right of middle-class women to employment was to be handled as a practical question of economics rather than one of ethics. Middle-class women's employment was not, she argued, a question of liberating women from the oppression of men, but a question of liberating middle-class men from the responsibility of being the sole breadwinners in the family.

Finally, there is one more sign, in the form of a letter in Laura Polanyi's correspondence, that shows her continuing ambiguity toward both the feminist organization and any commitment to take up an official position in it. Written by Ede Harkanyi in the fall of 1909, at the end of her summer holiday, it sheds light on Laura's ambitions and professional plans. "Your girlfriends live their life, flirt, etc., etc. The Freemason daily, reportedly, is about to be published; there you will have space, sphere of authority; at least I hope so. Perhaps there will be some positive changes in the feminist camp as well. About all this we will chat after your return. Now just keep gathering the arms for the struggle: strength, calmness, beauty."[70]

Could the reference to the hoped-for changes be interpreted as her generation's attempt to take over the feminist leadership or, perhaps, as a matter of personal dislike for the present leaders? The answer is much more complex and goes back to the 1905-6 political crisis in Hungary when, for a short period, universal male suffrage suddenly seemed an immediate possibility. Seeing their hopes evaporate soon after the consolidation of the dualist system and of limited parliamentary democracy in Hungary, the extra-parliamentary democratic opposition doubled its efforts for the suffrage. In the process, the formerly allied forces of the democratic Left, such as the Social Democrats, the Radicals as well as the Feminists, turned against each other with unprecedented venom. In the elaborate choreography of post-1906 political life, all sides, equally guilty of giving up principles for immediate, temporary gains, of negotiating with former enemies, accused everyone else of the same sins. The Social Democrats kept the demand of universal suffrage (male and female) in their programme but only in principle. In practice, as in Austria in 1906 when the Party dropped the demand for women's vote in exchange for the guarantee of universal male suffrage, it ceased to be a priority.[71] The Hungarian Radicals too ceased to openly demand the vote for women, since "it would have meant the strengthening of the forces of reaction"[72] and weakening their own chances. At least the Radicals were mildly understanding when the feminists decided "to follow very reasonable tactics: if I don't get help from my friends, I take advantage of the desperate situation of my enemy and squeeze him as much as possible."[73]

According to the Radicals, the fact that they and the Social Democrats temporarily dropped women's vote off their agenda was a minor fallacy because their struggle for universal male suffrage brought the antidemocratic political system closer to its end. In their eyes, the feminists' pacts with the Conservatives (such as their acceptance, in 1912, of educational and property criteria in the granting of the vote), were much more harmful because they helped to strengthen the system.[74] These differences in tactics and in the principles and practice of the struggle for the vote led to considerable rifts within the democratic opposition and go a long way to explain both Laura Polanyi's mixed feelings toward the feminist leadership and her final decision to not join it.

While the democratic opposition became increasingly tangled up in party politics and the struggle for the vote, Laura proceeded in the opposite direction and turned her attention first back to academia then to pedagogy. From 1913 when Laura and her family moved to Vienna, she seems to have completely withdrawn from politics; though this is more an assumption than a documented fact, supported by the almost total lack of documents in the family archives from this period that would show any political or intellectual commitment on her part. The only exception is an invitation to a talk by Dr. Laura Stricker on "The Women's Rights Movement in Austria and Hungary" at the section of the 18th and 19th section of the Austrian Women's Rights Committee.[75] Unfortunately, the date—22 January—on the invitation does not include the year; we can only assume that it took place in 1914 for the coming war effectively took the issue of women's rights off the agenda.

World War I proved to be the ultimate watershed for the generation of intellectuals that had come of age in the previous decade, and for the left-wing Hungarian intellectuals of Laura Polanyi's generation it was doubly so. If the war demolished their faith in scientific and social progress, the following revolutions finished off any remaining hope for a democratic political and social reorganization. Finally, the peace settlement tore apart the country itself and helped to power a right-wing regime which in turn detroyed the lifelines of their intellectual and political community. The war completed the process started by the crisis less than a decade earlier, by provoking a wide range of reactions, and dividing former friends and allies.

Initially, most of the intellectuals, even on the progressive side, took a pro-war stand, or at best were of two minds.[76] The Hungarian Social Democrats were not included in the parliamentary process, but had they been put to the test, they would have voted in favour of the war just like their Austrian and German counterparts. By mid-1915, however, influenced by the rising death toll and the Zimmerwald Conference, the Social Democrats came around. The leading writers of the *Nyugat*, as well as the Lukács-circle, the Radicals, and leaders of the liberal nationalists, all committed themselves to an antiwar position. Thus the future coalition of the 1918 democratic revolution started to fall into place.

To their credit, of all the parties of the democratic opposition in Hungary, the feminists were the only political force immediately and consistently taking a pacifist stand.[77] Rózsa Schwimmer, the leader of the Hungarian bourgeois feminists was in London in the weeks leading up to the war; she immediately sprung into action and from then on, was instrumental in the organization of all the pacifist activities by the suffragists, including the founding of the Women's International League for Peace and Freedom, and its Congresses at The Hague (1915) and Zurich (1918).[78]

Laura Polanyi, like everyone else, was closely affected by the events. Her husband, a reserve officer, was not called up, because of his age and family responsibilities. But Karl Polanyi completed his officer's training in 1914, was called up early in 1915 and served on the Galician front as a lieutenant.[79] He wrote to Laura on a field-postcard in September 1915:

My Dear Mauzi!

Here, there is nothing, nothing. If Dante had written from the 7 circles of Hell with an English aluminum pen, on a *feldpostkarte*, it would have looked just like this, just as grotesque, displaced. Here one should not be able to write, only bark. Not to think, just to feel your way in the scenes of a nightmare. The raid of the Mongolian hordes is a [illeg.] in the genre of Th[omas] Cook and Co., in an idyllic mood and of educational value, compared to today's war.[80]

His wartime experiences marked Karl Polanyi for life. He must have provided more details of the horrible carnage (for the fall and winter of 1915 in the trenches of the Galician front became notorious for its high casualty rates) to his sister. On his leaves, he found refuge in Laura's Vienna apartment: photographs from the war years show the uniformed "uncle Karli," visibly exhausted and melancholic, cuddled by Laura's three children.

It is not entirely surprising then that Laura Polanyi's curriculum vitae, written in the 1950s, includes the following line: "Delegate of the International Women's League for Peace and Freedom, Date: 1917, Stockholm, Copenhagen, Oslo."[81] Apparently, during the war she mended her ties with the Hungarian feminist leaders, in particular with Rózsa Schwimmer, who was the organizing genius behind the WILPF. Laura, after all, was in an ideal position to represent both Hungarian and Austrian women, members of the international pacifist organization from 1915. She also had the means to travel in a time of great economic distress. Curiously enough, studies covering the history of the feminist pacifist movement mention no pacifist women's conference in 1917 in any of these cities, and agree that the WILPF had only one conference during the war, in The Hague in 1915, and another immediately after, in May 1919 in Zurich.[82] If we accept Laura Polanyi's version, there are several possible explanations: she may have been one of the five representatives the WILPF designated in 1915 from each of its then member countries—Hungary and Austria were both among the first twelve countries that joined. These women were supposed to stand by to travel to the first conference, to be called immediately as the war ended.[83] Another explanation is that she was mistaken by one year: it was in fact in the early weeks of 1916, not 1917 that Rosika Schwimmer's ill-fated Peace Ship expedition reached Sweden. Funded by Henry Ford, the ship traveled from America to neutral Scandinavia, with American pacifist women on board, to promote a peace-initiative. Once in Sweden, delegates from European countries joined the Americans, and together, proceeded to the other countries of Scandinavia.[84] Taken together, these two versions probably provide the outlines of Laura's involvement in Schwimmer's pacifist activities.

Two years later, Laura and Rózsa Schwimmer had the opportunity to meet again. Laura's family returned to Budapest in the summer of 1918, in the final months of the war. We do not know the exact reasons: but the fact that they immediately bought a house on the hills of Buda, seems to suggest that in the fourth year of the war, and with food shortages on the horizon, Budapest was a more pleasant environment in which to raise a young family than Vienna. The house on the hills may have been short of grand but its surroundings were magical; Laura's daughter, Eva, later credited the garden with inspiring her to become an artist.[85]

At the end of October, the army of the Monarchy collapsed, the nationalities rebelled and proclaimed their independence and the returning soldiers carried Count Károlyi, leader of the liberal nationalists, to power. His government consisted of the left wing of his own National Independence Party, Jászi's Bourgeois Radical Party, and the Social Democrats. The Association of Feminists became a member of the National Council, the interim legislative body. In one of several of its desperate measures, the Károlyi-government appointed Rózsika Schwimmer to the post of Ambassador to Switzerland.[86] She would be able to use her war-time pacifist activities and connections with Entente politicians, so they hoped, to favourably influence the post-war settlement.

The first decree of the revolutionary government in November 1918 called for the election of a legislative assembly by universal suffrage, including women. There were limitations on women's eligibility (over 24 years of age as opposed to 21 for men and the requirement of literacy), but these seemed relatively minor in a country where previously less than 6% of the male population had the vote. The question of how women would use their vote under a democratic government remained hypothetical. The decree was never put into practice as the elections, called for April 1919, were automatically canceled by the next revolutionary wave, the Bolshevik-led Republic of Councils.

Family lore held that in 1918 Laura Polanyi was a candidate for Parliament.[87] Was she a candidate for the Feminists or the Radicals? Her daughter could not be sure but leaned toward the Radical version.[88] This seemed to corroborate the passing remark of the family's Hungarian historian that "in 1918 she [Laura] organized the women's section of the Radical Party."[89] In the Hungarian historiography of the revolutions, there is no hint of women candidates in the elections; not surprising, since there is not a single word about women getting the vote or the Feminists participating in the National Council either. Unfortunately, official archival sources to confirm this family information were impossible to come by; periods of revolutionary upheavals are usually not known for their meticulous record-keeping.

Without any documentary evidence to support it, Laura Polanyi's candidacy seemed to belong to the realm of family legend. That is, until I came across a short document in Hungarian in the Polanyi Collection at the Széchenyi National Library. It consisted of two yellowed sheets in small print with the title: "What do the Radical Women Want?"[90] A cross between a political manifesto and an electoral flyer, it appears to have been written in the winter of 1918-1919, as the programme of the female auxiliary of the Hungarian Bourgeois Radical Party.

The manifesto of the "radical women" was clearly aimed at first-time women voters. The list of their demands: equal rights within marriage, equal wages for equal work, the de-stigmatization of unwed mothers and their children, the condemnation of prostitution, the introduction of "communal households," were all familiar demands, included in the pre-war programme of the Hungarian Association of Feminists.

As for the authorship of the manifesto, both its style and its location among the family's documents pointed to Laura Polanyi and it seemed logical to conclude that the manifesto was evidence that Laura Polanyi organized or was involved in a women's section for the Party and that she inserted the feminist agenda into the party's platform as a way of attracting first-time women voters. Another copy of the same document among the family's private documents[91] signed by "the women executive of the Radical Party," offered unmistakable proof that Laura Polanyi was indeed involved in the composition of the document and was actively engaged in the electoral campaign of 1918.

Shortly after finding these documents, two manuscripts turned up in the handwriting of Laura Polanyi in a pile of unorganized papers in the family's possession. One was the draft of the "Radical Women Manifesto," confirming that she was indeed its author; the other, the manuscript of what seemed to be an electoral speech, actually listed the names of women candidates for the Radical Party.

If I ended my account here, the result would be the addition of a small but significant detail to Hungarian political history. As it stands, the official date for the introduction of women's suffrage in Hungary is 1920 (first put into effect, as stipulated by the Trianon Peace Treaty, at the elections of January 1920). Even recent contributions to the emerging field of women's history ignore the earlier date and focus on the fact that women's suffrage in Hungary was introduced after the revolutions, under a counter-revolutionary, right-wing regime.[92] The above evidence of women politicians actively participating in the electoral politics of

1918, to the degree of drawing up the Radicals' platform aimed at women, and running as the party's candidates, deserves more than a footnote in the Hungarian history textbooks.

In addition, the two manuscripts documented the final rift between the women who called themselves "radical" and were led by Laura Polanyi, and the Feminists. On many issues, the "Radical Women" manifesto went further than the accepted bourgeois feminist position. Among its demands were the complete separation of secular and religious education and the legalization of abortion, unheard of in the bourgeois feminist agenda. The emphasis on the need for state intervention in child and family welfare was also much stronger than it had ever been in the feminist programme of the pre-war period. Finally, its call for radical women and mothers to raise their children in the spirit of a new society, based on work instead of capital, underlined the difference from the emphatically class-neutral Hungarian bourgeois feminism, a point familiar from Laura Polanyi's pre-war pamphlet.[93]

In the second manuscript, Polanyi went even further, not only identifying the "radical women" as an entirely separate entity from the bourgeois feminists, but also retroactively severing all ties, past and present, between the two groups. First of all, she argued, the feminists had no right to take credit for the advancement of Hungarian women in the professions for it had been achieved without resistance on the part of the faculties and the male intellectual elite. If and when a fight was needed, she argued, it was put up by the young daughters of the middle class such as herself, driven by the love of learning, not by the women's rights agenda.

What followed was a devastating look at equal-rights feminism, as represented by Hungarian bourgeois feminists. The theory of women's alleged universal servitude and common interests, Polanyi pointed out, masked deeply conflicting class interests. It was a familiar point, raised time and time again by socialist critics of bourgeois feminism before the war as well as by herself. The new element in her argument was her denying the feminists' right to represent middle-class women. Their objectives, she argued, had no relevance beyond the small circle of "privileged" women, those of aristocratic or upper-middle-class background.

Finally, she qualified the bourgeois feminists' political record in the last 15 years as an unmitigated disaster. Their fixation on the vote and the long series of compromises they committed in its pursuit deprived them of any moral capital they may have accumulated. Their class-neutral, apolitical stance had been narrow-minded in the pre-war period, and turned downright amoral and irresponsible during the revolution—because it jeopardized the chances of the progressive political parties. Here, we find traces of the old Radical argument about the differences between useful compromises in the service of progress on the one hand and amoral, degrading alliances, helping the reaction on the other.

When the Károlyi-government came to power, the bourgeois feminists, perhaps trying to avoid the mistakes of 1905-6, agreed to keep their organization out of and above party politics. On this point, Laura Polanyi charges that this step not only accelerated the feminists' own demise but betrayed their responsibility toward the women voters and their partnership with the progressive political forces as well. As a result, she concluded, the last months saw the complete disintegration of the formerly 30,000 strong feminist organization, with its members joining parties from the counter-revolutionary, nationalistic Right to the Communists.[94]

Harsh words from someone who, before the war, had been a frequent lecturer on the feminist circuit and a delegate of the Hungarian feminist pacifists, under the guidance of their leader, Rózsa Schwimmer. Why was it necessary to make a clean break, why then and why with such vehemence?[95]

Above all, Laura felt the need to make absolutely clear where her loyalty lay. There was an election campaign going on, and the Radical Party needed the first-time women voters. She used everything in her power to prove that the Radicals' programme provided the best guarantees for women's rights and advancement. Her own generation of emancipated professional women, she argued, should not feel indebted to the women's rights movement. Their sense of accomplishment, their self-perception as emancipated women was based on their individual efforts. If there was a community they felt they belonged to, it wasn't the feminist party but the progressive counter-culture.

This picture was unfair and distorted on at least three counts. First, her description of women's emancipation in turn-of-the-century Hungary as entirely unproblematic was exaggerated at best. If the opening of some of the university faculties itself was not strictly the achievement of the women's rights movement, the acceptance of women in the professions would not have been possible without the relentless campaigns of the Feminists. Another point on which Polanyi suffered from a politically induced amnesia is the relationship between the Feminist leadership and the "radical women." Looking back in 1918, she categorically denied any co-operation between the two groups. This interpretation not only denied the Feminists' initial success in co-opting the younger, professional women but also blurred the stages of the gradual alienation between the two groups. Polanyi also remained silent on the less than stellar pre-war record of the Social Democrats and Radicals on the issue of women's vote.

Polanyi's final, negative assessment of the bourgeois feminists was justified: with the vote achieved, the Feminists were unable to renew their platform and watched helplessly as their membership evaporated. Despite the many points on which she was on target, her critique was also very much the product of the times. She could not escape the trappings of narrow-minded party politics that she so keenly observed in others. The intensity of her attack was clearly out of proportion, if understandable in light of the emerging right and left-wing extremism, and justified by future developments; the counter-revolutionary regime was welcomed by a number of former Feminists, now representatives of the emerging right-wing conservative women's group.[96]

In the final analysis, all this had very little bearing on the turn of events. International power politics, rather than political principles, brought about the triumph of a counter-revolutionary regime in August 1919. The cause of women's emancipation, once again and this time for good, was out of the hands of women.

The progressive counterculture, turn-of-the-century Hungary's version of "authentic public sphere" was among the first casualties. The short lesson in democratic governance ended in complete failure and the tremendous bloodletting of emigration included the whole Radical and most of the Feminist leadership. The neo-conservative reordering of the political system effectively demolished the entire network of this counterculture and, in the process, the gains in women's emancipation. Cecile's salon, cut off from this web of institutions, lost its previous significance as a mediator between the private and the public, and as the training ground for politically committed intellectuals. She kept hosting her weekly gatherings, frequented by a crowd of leftist intellectuals and artists, probably without ever realizing the magnitude of the change.[97]

Laura, on the other hand, was painfully aware of the defeat that rendered her a full-time housewife. Less than a year later, in February 1920, her neighbour presented the 38-year-old Laura with a greeting written in bittersweet rhymes. Looking back on the tumultuous years of war and revolutions, one of the verses summarized the effect of the events on her life: "Politics have failed, Let's be just housewives, We can only hope though, That it won't disappoint us!"[98]

If the liberal educational measures and the progressive community of the pre-war years provided Laura Polanyi with the opportunity to experiment with a range of public roles, the democratic revolutionary regime allowed her and fellow members of the "woman section of the Radical Party" an unprecedented level of political activism. The short months of the Károlyi government were to remain the only period for the pre-war leftist political coalition—and to most of its members, the only one—that gave them a chance to validate their principles and theories in practice.[99] For the women of the circle, the same period had gained a particular significance when they not only acquired the vote but also the authority to directly influence a meaningful political process.

The final political service provided by Laura to the Károlyi government symbolized the backward turn to the private, as it were. Count Károlyi, realizing the futility of resisting the Communist tide, resigned. Before leaving the country, he summoned Laura's neigbourly help—the Strickers' villa was within walking distance of the Count's summer residence—by asking her to hide some of the Károlyis' valuables: a few paintings and their family silverware.[100]

To the members of this circle, this period of failed aspirations and defeated hopes but also of unprecedented opportunities, remained frozen in time and became the yardstick against which they measured all their future political and ethical decisions and actions. Almost 25 years later, at the end of the Second World War, Oszkár Jászi and Laura Polanyi, by then both exiles in the United States, exchanged letters on the feasibility of a democratic settlement in post-war Hungary. Laura reasoned that it did indeed have a chance and advised Jászi, the conscience of the democratic Left, to consider supporting it and, eventually, even returning to Hungary.[101] Jászi, as usual, was more realistic in his pessimism.[102] While disagreeing with her final assessment, he took her advice and her reports on the Hungarian émigré organizations seriously. At that point, as Laura mentioned,[103] they had been friends for more than forty years, and Jászi trusted and respected her as a friend, scholar and political ally. The self-assured authority, however, radiating from Laura's letters to Jászi—who was, after all, the undisputed moral leader of the Hungarian democratic Left in exile—was grounded in more than the memories of a shared past. It was rooted in the legacy of an intellectual community where women were treated as equals and in the short months in the fall and winter of 1918 when they acted as equals.

Chapter 3:
"The Hungarian Jug was Shattered, Scattered into a Hundred Pieces"[1]

"Of course for now the wildly progressing events have thrown all our affairs into disarray. But the White madness will not last any longer than the Red did," wrote Oszkár Jászi on 30 August 1919, a few months into his Viennese exile.[2] His prognosis exemplified the exile state of mind that tended to regard the condition as strictly temporary.

"This is the second time I am going through this experience but, unbroken, always have the strength to start anew," wrote Karl Mannheim to Jászi in April 1933.[3] By then, both men had lived in exile for fourteen years. Jászi exchanged "the brutality of Central-European climate"[4] for a professorship at Oberlin College, Ohio, in 1925. Mannheim, Jászi's junior by 18 years, had successfully remade himself as a German academic, and only recently was appointed to the chair of sociology at Frankfurt University. It was not, however, the loss of a brilliant career or his livelihood he regretted the most; he lamented the defeat, for the second time in his lifetime, of "a progressive generation."[5]

Mannheim and Jászi demonstrated two of the possible trajectories of members of their generation, ranging from internal to temporary or permanent exile, from return to Hungary to a second emigration in the 1930s. Two dates represented defining moments for all of them. The first, 1919, signified defeat as well as the beginning of a long exile for many, while the second, 1933, marked the merging of the Hungarian émigrés into the flow of the Central-European intellectual migration; for by the mid-1930s they had all become refugees from Hitler's Europe.

This chapter takes up the story of Laura Polányi and her family at the defeat of the revolutions in Hungary in 1919 and follows their itineraries during the 1920s and 30s, from their leaving Hungary to passing through, or temporarily settling in Austria, Germany, the Soviet Union, and England. The last leg of this gradual process, their emigration to the United States, is the subject of a separate chapter. While Laura and her immediate family remain at the centre of the narrative, her extended family—her siblings and their families—are included to illustrate the degree of displacement that affected the Polanyis and, by extension, the entire Hungarian and Central-European intellectual community.[6]

When Laura and her husband had decided to remain in Hungary after 1919, they were motivated, among other things, by the desire to spare their young family yet another move; after all, they had moved back from Vienna to Hungary only a year earlier. At the time, it seemed the safer of the two alternatives: the children stayed in their familiar environment, surrounded by a large circle of relatives. In the long run, however, the parents' desire to provide the children with stability as well as an education and prospects in keeping with the family's tradition, proved to be incompatible. Their choice in 1919 not to emigrate did not prevent, only postponed the painful decision to uproot the family. Paradoxically, instead of reinforcing the children's ties to Hungary, it resulted in a cosmopolitan upbringing that provided them with the skills to live and succeed outside Hungary.

Laura's decision to stay—although it was not something she could foresee at the time—put an abrupt end to her political and professional activities. For two developments, the annihilation of her intellectual community and Hungary's sharp turn to the Right, both closely related to the triumph of the counter-revolutionary regime, resulted in a hostile climate for women's political and professional advancement. Knowing Laura's history of battling unfavourable conditions, it is not surprising that by the late 1920s and early 1930s, she seemed to renew her search for intellectual outlets. From 1932, however, there were growing indications that the future of her family lay away from Nazism-infested Central Europe. At this point, with her two older children independent and professionally secure and the youngest on his way to an engineering diploma, Laura, at fifty certifiably middle-aged, could have settled for a life as the wife of a successful businessman with intellectual ambitions. Instead, she became increasingly involved in her children's lives. Out of a sense of adventure as much as duty, she followed them not only to familiar places such as Vienna and Berlin but also ventured as far as Kharkov and Moscow in the Soviet Union.

As a result of her involvement and the relationships she forged with her children and their spouses, by 1938, the time of the family's escape to the U.S., she had become the moral and emotional anchor of her family, and as such, was greatly responsible for their success in emigration and beyond.

Chapter 1 ended with the Fall of 1919 when the White Terror was raging in Hungary and Laura was soon the only Polányi sibling still living there. The first one to leave was Sophie, who, for reasons unrelated to politics, had moved to Vienna before the war. Her husband, Egon Szécsi (whose sister, Frida, married Adolf Polányi) had been a member of Ervin Szabó's Circle of Socialist Students during his years at Budapest University, at the beginning of the century. He served in World War I for four years then returned to Vienna to practice law. Two daughters, Marika and Edith, were born in 1912 and 1914, respectively, and in 1919, a mentally disabled son, Karl.[7]

Adolf Polányi, the family's notorious political hothead, served in the Comissariat for Commerce under the Republic of Councils and, as a result, was forced into exile. For a while, he was active in the Hungarian immigrant circles in Vienna,[8] then moved to Italy to start over. A paternal aunt, Teréz Pollacsek, and her children, Adolf's one-time fellow socialist student Ernö Pór and Médi (Matild) with her husband, the sculptor Márk Vedres, had already been living in Italy since around 1915. Struggling themselves, they were unable to help financially but at least provided some sense of family.

Having failed to find success in politics, where he had been the most ambitious of all the Polányi brothers, or to emulate their scholarly achievements, Adolf reluctantly turned into a businessman. He experimented with various enterprises, among them a translator's agency and a dry-cleaning business (his wife's family, after all, had owned one of the first steam-laundries in pre-war Budapest), none very successful. In the mid-1920s, he divorced Frida and married the much younger Lily, a photographer.[9] His siblings vacillated between hope and skepticism as Adolf struggled with the high order of supporting two families.[10]

Adolf may have lost the ambitions of his youth, but not his notorious restlessness and, as we will see, never seemed to reconcile himself to his responsibilities as a family man. His two daughters, Vera and Eszter, often came back to Budapest to visit, experiencing, with mixed feelings, the lifestyle of their wealthier cousins.[11] Vera later returned to Italy to attend medical school, while Eszter moved back to Budapest and married there. Adolf's two sons, Michael and Thomas, had been born in Hungary in 1913 and 1918, respectively. They both became scientists, studying in Rome under Enrico Fermi in the early 1930s.

Karl Polanyi left Hungary in June 1919, physically and mentally a broken man. In Vienna, he first worked as Oszkár Jászi's secretary, and editor of the Hungarian émigré paper *Bécsi Magyar Ujság*. In the early 1920s, his interests increasingly turned to economics, and he became editor of the *Österreichischer Volkswirt*, the influential left-liberal economic weekly. In 1920 he met and two years later married Ilona Duczynska whom he credited with re-awakening his creative energies.

Duczynska was a most worthy addition to the line-up of extraordinary women in the Polányi family,[12] invariably described by everyone who met her as a "sovereign revolutionary,"[13] "a revolutionary flame"[14] and "a tireless wanderer through revolutions."[15] Her background, Hungarian gentry on her mother's side and Polish nobility on her father's, could not have been more different from Polanyi's. They rarely agreed on politics and were worlds apart in their temperament, Polanyi favouring the quiet life of the scholar, Duczynska, until the end of her days, drawn to revolutionary action. Despite their differences, their marriage turned out to be a lifelong partnership, described by her biographer as "the fidelity of equals."[16]

At the time of their meeting in 1920, Ilona was 23 years old, 11 years Polanyi's junior, and already a seasoned revolutionary. As one of the leaders of an anti-militarist student movement in Hungary, she had been arrested in January 1918 and tried in September of the same year. Liberated by the Károlyi-revolution, she subsequently worked for the Commissariat for Foreign Affairs of the Republic of Councils which sent the then 22-year-old Ilona to Switzerland on a propaganda mission. When the Republic of Councils fell, she went on to Moscow where she worked in the Comintern as Karl Radek's secretary and took part in the Second Congress of the Comintern in the summer of 1920. She was sent to Vienna as a courier for the Hungarian Communist Party in exile. (In her sparse luggage, she hid a tube of toothpaste with thirty diamonds, to be delivered to Georg Lukács, one of the leaders of the Hungarian Communist Party in Vienna.[17])

Following her article on the fractional infights within the Party, Duczynska was expelled for "Luxembourgist deviation."[18] Reluctantly, she went on to join the Austrian Social Democratic Party. In 1923 Ilona and Karl Polanyi had a daughter, Karoline (Kari).

The youngest brother, Michael Polanyi, left Hungary for Germany in 1920. He quickly rose to the pinnacle of his field and by 1930 he became the chair of the department of physico-chemistry of the Kaiser Wilhelm Insitute in Dalheim, near Berlin. He married the chemist Magda Kemény who had attended university in Germany in the 1920s and they had two sons.

The early 1920s in the Polanyi brothers' life were not only a time to make the political and ideological decisions normally involved in emigration, but also those about life-style and family. Born between 1883 and 1891, they reached the age when men of the educated middle class were supposed to settle down, start families, and establish their professional careers and standing in society. This process may have been postponed by their emigration but did not fundamentally alter the choices they made. In their personal lives, the Polányi siblings never challenged the accepted bourgeois norms of family life, despite their association with progressive political causes, or Laura's feminist ideas about child-rearing and communal households. True, they were part of the social and intellectual circle in Hungary that introduced substantial changes into the social mores; by supporting the rights of women to education, treating them as their equals, accepting their right to a professional career within marriage, and making divorce socially acceptable. These changes, however, had taken place gradually and, apart from a few notable exceptions, were never accompanied with the radical lifestyle experiments so prevalent, for instance, in the Russian revolutionary movements of the late 19th century.[19] Close to home, the marriage of their parents, Mihály and Cecile Pollacsek provided the siblings with an example attesting to the flexibility and feasibility of the bourgeois marriage.

The Polányis' choices of life-partners and life-styles reflected this ambivalence: the acceptance of women's changing role within and outside marriage but also an unshaken faith in the institution itself. Their marriages represented a range of solutions all well within the monogamous marriage. Sophie's marriage stood at one end of the spectrum; there is no sign she ever worked outside the home after her marriage. Karl and Michael both married university graduates, thus by contemporary standards exceptionally well educated women, although Michael Polanyi's wife, a chemist, does not seem to have worked in her profession following their marriage, nor did she seem to have any ambitions for a career on her own. Adolf's first wife was not educated beyond high school but as a young woman she worked in the family business in Budapest. As family legend has it, she also singlehandedly unionized the employees there.[20] Adolf's second wife, a photographer, most probably had to work in her profession to support the family.

While still within the traditional framework of bourgeois marriage, the family life of Karl Polanyi and Ilona Duczynska was the most unconventional of all the siblings. The Viennese exile was a return of sorts for both of them; Karl was born in Vienna, while Ilona, a native of Austria, spent her childhood there. Vienna in the 1920s, governed by the socialist municipal government as a utopian city-state, was an exciting place to live and they were proudly sharing the experiment by, among other things, hanging out the red flag and marching in the workers' parade every May Day. Duczynska ended her reluctant association with the Austrian Social Democrats in 1928 and, after a decade-long hiatus (she had studied mathematics in Zurich in 1916-17), returned to her studies in physics. Her temporary withdrawal from political action, however, did not lend any more orderliness to the family's everyday life. The Polanyi-tradition lived on as their apartment served as a subsidiary of the *Volkswirt*, as well as a meeting place for Karl's impromptu seminars. Increasingly, it also became Ilona's "political and intellectual salon, with the political aspect obviously in the forefront."[21]

In a family where everything was directed toward the future, two people represented the past: Erzsi, the maid, imported from the estate of Ilona's landowner relatives and Ilona's mother. Mrs. Duczynska, née Helén Békássy lived in a room off the Polanyis' living room, surrounded by the ancestors' portraits and other remnants of her family's feudal glory, and took care of her young grand-daughter. Meals were notoriously poor, household rules, clothing and other niceties of middle-class existence neglected to the extreme. As a friend of Ilona commented: "She was one for essentials, she never wasted time on unnecessary things."[22]

It is highly ironic that, despite their obvious similarities, Cecile, of all people, was deeply unhappy with Karl's choice of spouse. According to Duczynska's memoirs, their relationship was determined from the start by Cecile's icy rejection. "Cecile, in her own person," Duczynska explained, "was a *bohème*, a '*Barfüssler*'; she looked down on worldly goods, status, and standing; but for all that, she wished for her sons brilliant careers and wealthy wives."[23] Equally ironically, Duczynska never missed an opportunity to comment on Cecile's inability to cope "with the complexities of the large middle-class household," in wealth or poverty.[24] To wit, Ilona's description of the Pollacsek household in the days of Karl's childhood, "where the necessities of life such as food and clothing were of such extraordinary simplicity that no discernible change was brought about when financial catastrophe struck the family" should be taken with a grain of salt.[25] It seems to reflect more Duczynska's own priorities than the actual state of the Pollacsek household at the turn of the century—photos from the family's prosperous period show all the attributes of an upper-middle-class lifestyle—and underscores the ambiguity of the two women's relationship.

In comparison, Laura's family lived a life of undisturbed domestic idyll. Their house in Budapest with its large garden was perched on a hill and its remoteness provided a degree of safety even in the worst months of the city's Romanian occupation and White Terror.[26] There was the occasional Romanian dispatch riding up the alley leading to the house and Laura's daughter, Eva remembers the Whites rounding up the rich Jewish merchants of the neighbourhood.[27]

Eva was thirteen years old at the time. In her memories it was all part of a "high comedy," played out by the soldiers of various regimes and their domestic animals, going wild in their improvised farm.[28] To the adults, the overall tone of the rapidly progressing events must have been far from comic. In August 1919, in the face of growing internal opposition and the Romanian military offensive, the Communist government resigned. Its leaders fled to Vienna and a government of trade union leaders took office. After only six days, they too were forced to resign under a counter-revolutionary coup, aided by the Romanian occupying army. The Friedrich-government effectively dismantled not only the measures of the Republic of Councils but also the achievements of the previous, democratic revolution. Meanwhile, Vice-Admiral Horthy's National Army (it was organized during the months of the Bolshevik dictatorship in the Eastern half of the country) and its paramilitary detachments unleashed an anti-Bolshevik and anti-Semitic terror on the countryside. Over two thousand people were executed, and about seventy thousand imprisoned or sent to internment camps.[29] The Allies' mission, sent to Budapest to bring the situation under control, achieved the withdrawal of the Romanian troops and allowed Horthy's National Army, the only military force capable of maintaining order, to take over. Horthy entered the city in November 1919 on a white horse and, setting the tone for the coming decades, pronounced Budapest the "sinful city," ready to be cleansed of its Judeo-Bolshevik vices by his Christian-national forces.

Within a month, a new coalition government was formed, recognized by both the Allies and Horthy, consisting mainly of representatives of the conservative-agrarian parties. Prescribed by the Paris Peace Conference, national elections were held in January 1920, by universal and secret ballot, including women. It is highly unlikely, however, that Laura, champion of women's political rights and one-time candidate of the Bourgeois Radical Party, exercised her finally achieved right to vote. Her party was dismembered, the other liberal parties were intimidated by the unchecked terror of the paramilitaries, and the only remaining left-wing party, the Social Democrats, boycotted the elections in protest.

Judging from the pace of the events of the last year and a half, it was not unreasonable to think that political conditions might soon stabilize.[30] In the meantime, Laura, true to her optimistic and practical nature, occupied herself with the tasks at hand. Her husband had gradually rebuilt his textile business; a certificate of incorporation from January 1921 listed his business address and its nature as "trading in wool, worsted, and woolen fabric."[31] Despite the catastrophic consequences of the war and the Peace Treaty for the Hungarian economy, textile industry was among the few areas quickly recuperating;[32] and

Sándor Stricker's recovered business interests, now located in the newly formed Czechoslovakia, soon proved to be useful in unexpected ways.

As accounted earlier, back in the summer of 1919, Count Károlyi had left some of his valuables with the Strickers the night before he left Hungary. After the fall of the revolutions, Károlyi, with his wife, the Countess Andrássy, and their three young children, found temporary refuge in Czechoslovakia. Hunted by the Hungarian counter-revolutionary regime and vilified by his own family, he was cut off from his properties and transformed from one of Hungary's wealthiest landlords to a penniless refugee. Laura was among the very few that offered assistance. In the course of 1920, using her husband's business activities in Czechoslovakia as a cover, she helped to smuggle out of Hungary the Károlyis' silverware and paintings—to be sold and used to support the family and the émigré cause.[33]

The task involved considerable dangers. Mail was heavily censored, and in January 1920 the White regime stepped up surveillance of the Károlyi correspondence. Károlyi's loyal sister was interrogated and threatened with internment, his butler driven to suicide, one of his couriers arrested and tortured.[34] The actual deed of smuggling letters and money was most likely done by Laura; for the correspondence of the Károlyis repeatedly names her as one of only a handful of confidants who could be trusted to carry letters and money.[35]

This episode highlights the suddenly narrowed space for women's political activity and also hints at another consequence of the change of regimes for women. As a woman, Laura was less likely to arouse the suspicion of the authorities for, ironically, the conservative turn favoured women, at least bourgeois women, in one respect over men. While the latter, regardless of their social standing, were hunted down and persecuted for their role in the revolutionary regimes, of the many women who had held public office during the revolutions, only those with the highest profiles, such as Rózsa Schwimmer or Ilona Duczynska, were forced to flee. Many others chose to stay, under the tacit understanding that they would retreat into their private life; but many found ways to overstep these invisible boundaries.[36]

Following the elections in January 1920 and the signing of the Trianon Peace Treaty, Hungary's political life slowly normalized although the resulting framework was markedly different from the pre-war one.[37] The Peace Treaty deprived Hungary of two-thirds of its former territory and almost sixty percent of its population. Thirty percent—almost 3.2 million—of ethnic Hungarians found themselves in minority status, living across the new borders in the newly created Czechoslovakia, Romania and Yugoslavia. Hungary also lost most of its natural resources and industry, and became extremely dependent on exports and imports as well as vulnerable to the changes of world economy. Yet gradual economic recovery followed hand in hand with political stabilization and, by the early 1920s, both were achieved by the governments of Counts Teleki and Bethlen, representatives of the old landed-agrarian elite.

The political framework consisted of a mixture of old and new: under Teleki, Hungary was proclaimed a kingdom without a king, with Horthy appointed as Regent. Parliament was elected by an electoral law more democratic than any prior to the war, although a 1922 decree reduced the proportion of voters from 40% to 28% of the population. The political landscape of the coming decade was determined by the anti-liberal measures of the 1921 Bethlen-government.[38]

A half-hearted land reform in 1921 failed to solve the country's most pressing social problem, that of the landless agricultural labourers.[39] The Catholic Church maintained possession of its lands, roughly equal to the amount of land distributed in 1921, along with its influence in public life and education. In striking contrast to the liberal principles and practices of the pre-war era, education and official culture now emphasized Christian and nationalist values. With the Social Democratic Party and trade unions largely restricted, the activities of leftist, even liberal parties and public life in general, were limited by strict anti-liberal measures such as censorship and other limitations on civil rights. To legitimize these measures, government propaganda blamed the Left for the Trianon Treaty, and made the revision of the Treaty its *raison d'être* and the cure for the country's economic and social ills.

The pre-war period's fundamental cleavage between the nationalist-conservatives and the left-democratic reformers widened considerably, with the latter effectively "quarantined."[40] The strength of the pre-war democratic reform movement had never been in its numbers, but after 1919 these numbers fell below the critical mass. Of its two flagship institutions, the Sociological Society was banned. The modest heir of the *Twentieth Century*, the review *Századunk* (Our Century) was edited and written by a handful of Jászi's followers, from a single table at their coffeehouse.

The fate of the freemason lodges exemplifies how liberal bourgeois institutions fared under the successive Bolshevik and counter-revolutionary regimes. The lodges were among the bourgeois-liberal organizations banned under the Bolshevik dictatorship, as possible hotbeds of counter-revolutionary activities. Then, under the White regime, they were declared part of the Jewish conspiracy for Hungary's betrayal and as such, disbanded by decree.

Under these conditions, the modernist and progressive literary trends that had emerged so strikingly in *fin-de-siècle* culture in close partnership with the political reformers, were unable to exert a comparable influence in the interwar period.[41] Finally, the most important new intellectual movement emerging in the 1930s, that of the "populist" (literally: "of the people") writers, with its emphasis on a peasantry-based social and cultural renewal and its inevitable racial undertones[42] refused any association with the pre-war democratic Left.[43]

The stifling intellectual climate, Hungary's increasing lag behind the European leaders in science and the arts, along with the bleak economic prospects, drove many young intellectuals out of the country, even if they were not directly threatened for their political views. The most important factor in driving young Jewish intellectuals abroad was the notorious *numerus clausus* law that had the dubious merit of being the first example of anti-Semitic legislation in post-war Europe.

Introduced by the Teleki-government in 1920 as a measure to placate the anti-Semitic Christian middle class and solve the problem of white-collar surplus, the law fixed the number of admissible university students at the ratio of their "nation-race and nationality" in the general population. In its initial version, the law intended to stop the admission of women, and during the early 1920s effectively fulfilled that aim as well. The final version and its application, however, were openly directed against Jews, and successfully reduced their proportion among university students to between 6 and 15% from the pre-war 28-34%.[44] And if the law did not pronounce clearly enough on the prospects of young Jewish professionals in Hungary, the practice of officially tolerated intimidation, including regular beatings of the legally enrolled Jewish students by anti-Semitic student organizations, did.

These were the conditions that defined the options of Laura Polányi's children when, by the early-mid 1920s, they reached the age to enter university. The decision of her two sons to study abroad, in Vienna, was far from unique; as a reaction to the anti-Semitic university policies, large numbers of Hungarian-Jewish students took the same road.[45] Vienna, with its university's superior academic standards and prestige, had been the first choice of Hungarian students studying abroad even before the war. Now that for many the only chance of a university education lay outside of Hungary, it was a choice no more limited, as it had been before, to children of the privileged and those with strong family ties and financial support in the imperial capital.[46] Prior to the war, when the Monarchy's university credits and degrees were mutually recognized, Hungarian students opted for universities outside of their home country to further their administrative and professional careers. Now they were more likely to use them as a springboard to careers abroad; it is estimated that less than one quarter of them had their degrees naturalized,[47] possibly even fewer chose to return to Hungary.

Laura's eldest son Mihály (Michael), born in 1905, enrolled in Engineering at the Vienna Technical University in the mid-1920s. His younger brother, György (George) Ottó (he was born in November 1913 in Vienna) was to follow him as a student of applied physics in the early 1930s, after his initial studies in Berlin.

The Stricker boys' life in Vienna was quite different from that of the average Hungarian student who, typically, lived in unheated rooms and relied on soup kitchens; Laura's sons were surrounded by close relatives, and they had neither immediate financial needs nor language problems. In the mid to late 1920s, the family kept an apartment in Vienna, "always as open to the friends of their sons and only daughter as a Viennese café."[48] There old family friends, such as the Klatschkos, the Schwarzwalds (among her many projects, the socialist educator Eugenia Schwarzwald ran a soup kitchen for Hungarian émigrés in the early twenties), and the Rundts (Arthur Rundt was a director of the famous Reinhardt Theatre, his wife, Recha later married Oszkár Jászi) but also friends from the younger generation. Arthur Koestler, who was also studying in Vienna, young members of the Adler circle, including the Adler favourite Manès Sperber, as well as young sociologists, Paul Lazarsfeld and Hans Zeisel and physicists, Alex Weissberg, Victor Weisskopf, met and developed lifelong friendships in Vienna. But unlike the guests of Cecile's salon in the early days of the century, the young émigrés and natives of Vienna were less passionate about the literary avant-garde than the great political movements of the time, Communism, Socialism, and Zionism.

Laura's daughter, Eva possibly met both her future husbands there. Alexander Weissberg, who was to become her first husband, was born into an orthodox Polish-Jewish family in Krakow in 1901. He studied physics at the Vienna Technical University and became a Communist. Under the guise of thoroughly bourgeois appearance and habits, he had a lucid and trenchant mind, and his fondness for sweets was only matched by his passion for dialectical materialism. His absolute loyalty to friends and family was to be tested under the most difficult circumstances.[49]

Hans Zeisel, Eva's future second husband, was the son of an assimilated Czech-Jewish family. He was born in 1905, studied law and economics in Berlin and Vienna, and became a socialist and a participant in Karl Polanyi's seminars. In the early 1930s, he worked with Paul Lazarsfeld in the pioneering field of market research and, with Lazarsfeld and Marie Jahoda, co-authored an important study on unemployment.[50]

Laura's only daughter, Eva, was to become the most important person in her life in the coming decade. She was born in 1906 and showed early signs of artistic talent. She remembers converting a greenhouse into her studio and painting outdoors in the garden of their house.[51] Following her graduation from high school, she enrolled at the Academy of Fine Arts of Budapest to study painting. She quit after a year and a half to join a potter's workshop as an apprentice. She was not the first woman in the family to become an artist; Laura's cousin, Irma Seidler as well as a paternal aunt of Eva were both accomplished artists. Pottery, however, was an unusual career choice for a young woman from a good family; more a trade than an art form, it was associated with a life of physical work in working-class conditions. Eva became the first Hungarian woman to be admitted as a journeyman into the Guild of Chimney Sweeps, Oven Makers, Roof Tilers, Well Diggers and Potters, an accomplishment she never fails to mention to this day.[52] Her choice represented at once a rebellion against the family tradition that prized intellectual achievement above everything else, and loyalty to another family tradition, that of women's pioneering accomplishments.

Her ensuing career and personal choices reflected the same independent and rebellious spirit. They took her on a trajectory that was not only fundamentally different from that of her mother's and grandmother's but distinguished her even in her own generation. From 1926, Eva worked in Germany, first for the *Hansa Kunstkeramik* in Hamburg then the *Schramberger Majolika Fabrik* (Schramberg was a small town in the Black Forest), training as an industrial designer of tableware. In her memoirs and interviews, she described the rented rooms in the slums of Hamburg and the working-class neighbourhood of Schramberg as well as her life in the shops and factories. Once again, it was a rebellion on several levels: not only did she live by her hands' work, but did so in a man's world. She recalled an incident in the Hamburg factory when "they wanted to surprise me as a young lady to be shocked. When I came in, there was a life-size male organ of clay. With great objectivity and no fuss, I disposed of it— that was my hazing."[53]

Even more unusually for an unmarried young woman from a good family, she lived independently. It was a sign of the changing times that, unlike her grandmother and mother, she could postpone marriage while pursuing a career.

The rules, however, were still fluid, and what may have been acceptable in decadent Berlin, was just barely tolerated in the countryside; in an interview, Eva talked about getting a reputation in the small town of Schramberg when seen visited by young men.[54]

She may have broken every rule in her lifestyle, yet remained, in many respects, the dutiful little girl of her family. As a self-confessed innocent in the overcharged political atmosphere of the Weimar Republic—"at this time in Germany you had to belong to a politically identifiable unit"[55]—she joined the Social Democrats, the party of the working class. In this, she was equally guided by her instinct ("the white-collar workers were the most disgusting kind of German middle class"[56] and a sense of duty to her family and friends, knowing that it was what her friends in Vienna expected of her. In her memoirs, written almost 50 years later, she explained: "Although I was not a participant in any political activity, I was of course a member of the union because of my work at the factory. I was also a member of the Socialist Democratic Party, which didn't mean much to me, but it was what most of my friends in Vienna expected me to do."[57]

In 1929, Eva moved to Berlin to work for the prestigious Carstens company. The time she spent in Berlin between 1929 and 1932 coincided with the high point of Weimar culture. In her memoirs and interviews she described the experience in all its cultural splendour and political decadence. Laura rented a large, light-filled two-story studio for Eva and her brother, Michael. It was only a few doors away from the *Romanische Café*, "considered by progressive intellectuals as the centre of the world."[58]

The statement from a historian of Weimar, "it is only a slight exaggeration to say that exiled Hungarians *created* Weimar culture"[59] may be somewhat partial, yet he is right to note that in Weimar culture "at almost every turn one meets with a Hungarian émigré."[60] Among them, the Polányi-Stricker family had a substantial contingent, well represented at the gatherings in the studio that "became an annex of the *Romanische Café*, the Forum Romanum for the exchange of ideas on how best to save the world."[61] Emil Lederer, married to Laura's cousin, Emmi Seidler, was a professor of economics in Heidelberg and came to visit often. Michael Polanyi who by this time headed the Department of Physico-Chemistry at the Kaiser Wilhelm Institute at Berlin-Dahlem, often brought his physicist friends, including the young Leo Szilard and Eugen Wigner. Through Wigner, Eva met another talented young physicist, the Viennese Victor Weisskopf who became a lifelong friend. Weisskopf remembered Eva's apartment as "the kind of perpetual open houise that was common in those days—you could simply come and go as you pleased."[62] Eva's cousin on her father's side, László Radványi, a brilliant sociologist and a student of Karl Mannheim, came with his wife, the Communist writer Anna Seghers.[63] Cecile, "my legendary grandmother, who was living a bachelor's life in Berlin... brought all sorts of sparkling wits."[64] Germany was at the time the unquestionable centre of the universe in terms of modernist art and design, and the years spent there proved invaluable for Eva's artistic development. During the same period, she rose as the next female star of the family, who moved with ease between the various "nuclei" of their social circle, be they writers, sociologists, economists, or scientists.

Eva shared the studio with her brother, Michael, who began working as a patent attorney. He met his wife, Hilde in Berlin. The young German woman was pretty, hardworking, very useful at the office then and later. They made a stunning couple. But she was not an intellectual, not even particularly educated and was terribly intimidated by the intellectualism of the Polányis. According to Hilde, Cecile was the only one in the family who understood and took her under her wing.[65] Cecile's kindness—a quality she very seldom displayed—was not forgotten. Photos of Hilde and her baby daughter with Cecile, taken in Budapest in 1938, record Cecile's last meeting with her first great-grandchild before the young family was to leave for America and suggest a special bond between the two women.

Michael was the first "finished product" of Laura's three children. His rise as a patent attorney was proof that the educational strategy and the hard work of son and mother paid off; he was becoming a professional success. At the same time, his choice of business and wife demonstrated that he completely detached himself from the family's Hungarian roots and intellectual and political passions. The weakening of Hungarian identity among the Hungarian-Jewish students studying abroad was a common phenomenon, resulting in a high rate of emigration in this group.[66] In a family so deeply steeped in Hungarian culture and politics, it signaled a strikingly new trend.

The relatively worry-free years between 1928 and 1932 gave Laura a chance to focus on her own projects. Eva and Michael were safely ensconced in the Berlin studio and her youngest, Ottó was beginning his university studies there. At around the same time, Laura and Sándor sold the garden in Budapest[67] and moved their smaller and simpler household into an apartment, closer to the city centre. In 1929 Laura was only a youthful forty seven while Sándor Stricker turned sixty. He never shared his wife's cosmopolitanism and eagerness to travel; traveling for him, after all, was business, rather than pleasure. Always the devoted family man, he was not happy to see the children leave Hungary but resigned himself to the fact for their sake. As far as he was concerned, he was happy to settle for a quiet life in Budapest. In the course of the next decade, as his wife and children were experiencing new adventures all over Europe, the physical and intellectual distance between him and the rest of the family widened. While the tenderness in their relationships remained, his involvement in the children's lives became marginal.

In 1931 Laura contributed to a round-table discussion on the problem of marriage, organized by the youth organization of the small oppositional Liberal Party and published by its daily.[68] The topic and the format was a throwback to the debates of the Sociological Society of the pre-war period and generated a reportedly sizable audience at the party's headquarters. Laura's short commentary repeated her familiar argument about the incompatibility of modern marriage with feudal morality, the patriarchal ideal of woman, and the bourgeois notion of the husband as the primary wage-earner. The invitation confirmed her status as an expert but did not change the fact that, in light of the negligible influence of the tiny Liberal Party, the event was played out in a social and political vacuum.

Between 1928 and 1932 she also collected material and wrote a study on the economic policy of Maria Theresa, killing two birds with one stone. It was submitted for her son, Michael's doctoral degree in economics at the University of Budapest and provided further proof, if needed, that he was not interested in the family's scholarly pursuits.[69] The real author's identity was an open secret, at least within the family. As for the ghostwriting of doctoral theses, it was established, widespread practice at the University of Budapest, especially among law students, providing poor but brilliant students with much-needed extra income.[70]

Always on the practical side, Laura was apparently also considering publishing the study under her own name, with her own doctoral thesis; the topic, after all, was a natural extension of her previous study on the economic policies of Maria Theresa' father, Charles VI.[71]

Yet the plans to return to her original field remained suspended and the Maria Theresa study unpublished; instead, in 1932 Laura Polanyi followed her daughter to the Soviet Union. Between 1932 and 1937, the main geographical axis of Laura's immediate family switched from the Budapest-Vienna-Berlin triangle to Kharkov and Moscow in the Soviet Union, with her youngest son, studying there from 1933, holding up the Vienna end. In terms of family dynamics, from this point on, the third generation, Laura's children, took over in making the decisions and determining the family's future direction. Laura was increasingly forsaking her own plans in exchange for participating in her children's lives and—in her unobtrusive way—preserving the right to partake in these decisions. Cecile, who had still been an active participant of the family scene in Vienna and Berlin, was by now permanently left behind, settled in an apartment hotel in Budapest.

The chronology of the Central-European intellectual refugees began with 1933, the year Hitler came to power. This was also the case for the Hungarian immigrants who had made Weimar Germany their home and in 1933 became refugees twice over. Their fate was shared by some members of the extended Polányi family, including Laura's youngest brother Michael Polanyi. In the life of Laura's immediate family, however, the central event of the 1930s was their Soviet adventure. It took up half of the decade and determined, to a great degree, the family's future. The main outline of these years can be summarized in a paragraph.

Eva Stricker visited the Soviet Union in 1932. Mainly in order to get a visa, she became engaged to Alexander Weissberg who had been working there as a foreign expert. Soon after arriving, she began to work in the Soviet china industry and in 1935, at age 29, was promoted to Chief Designer of the China and Glass Industry of the Russian Republic.[72] Some time after 1933, her older brother, Michael also came to work in Moscow as a foreign expert. Laura visited with both of her children for periods of time. Eva was shortly married to Weissberg, and after an amicable separation, moved to Moscow. It was there that she was arrested in May 1936. Accused of conspiring to murder Stalin, she was kept in prison for 16 months then released and expelled to Austria in September 1937.

The story did not end with Eva's miraculous escape. While she was in prison, Alex Weissberg was also arrested; through a string of incredibly close escapes, he also survived. Eva—and at some point, her brother—returned to Vienna, where Hans Zeisel had been waiting for her. On the night of the *Anschluss*, in March 1938, Eva escaped to Switzerland and then on to England. In London, she met up with her childhood friend, Arthur Koestler and the account she had given him of her interrogations in Stalin's prison served as background material for Koestler's *Darkness at Noon*.

The Soviet episode has come to occupy a central place in the Polányi mythology. In its above, concise version it figures in the many popular articles written on the family, with its main points repeated almost verbatim. American journalists find especially irresistible the story's Hollywood-like plot and its triumph-over-adversity ending.[73] In recent years, as Eva's body of work has undergone a revival and she was recognized as one of the outstanding designers of the 20th century, the numerous articles written on her work and legacy have used the story of her imprisonment as a counterpoint to the timeless beauty she created in her designs. It has been cited over and over again to epitomize the striking contrast between her "indomitable love of life," "visible in every piece she has ever made"[74] and the potentially devastating, extraordinary trials she had endured.

The journalists who wrote these articles, of course, had no choice but to rely on information Eva herself provided and there is no reason to doubt that her version is a truthful record of her experiences. At the same time, we have to take into consideration that it is also the product of a long process, of her coming to terms with a series of traumatic experiences, her 16 months-long imprisonment, followed by the dramatic escape from Austria and emigration to the United States. It is also the result of a conscious—and understandable—effort on her part to control the public exposure of a deeply personal part of her past.

In addition to the personal aspects, there were political reasons that stopped Eva Zeisel from making her experiences public for decades. Following the end of WWII, during the worst years of the Cold War, she had a fallout with Koestler over the latter's rabidly anti-Communist politics. Rather than becoming an accessory to what she regarded as anti-Soviet warmongering, she insisted that Koestler keep her identity secret in his memoirs where he explained the origins of *Darkness at Noon.* Betraying the deep ambiguity she felt over her own contribution to the novel, in light of its role in the Cold War and, she refused to read *Darkness at Noon* until after Koestler's death in 1983.

In the late 1970s, however, Eva began to revisit the painful memories and by 1977 she had a hundred pages of her "prison memoirs" completed. The memoirs provided a detailed description of her imprisonment, interjected with episodes from the years spent in Germany and her travels in the Soviet Union. Originally, she intended the memoirs for her children but also sent a copy to Koestler, asking for his opinion. At the time, despite Koestler's encouraging words, she stopped short of considering its publication.[75] After Koestler's death in 1983, she reconsidered, then, because of discouraging reaction from, among others, Koestler's agent, dropped the plans to publish it. Ever since, she has treated the memoirs ambiguously: as semi-classified information, to be given as background material to the journalists and art historians writing about her on the one hand, and as deeply personal confessions, to be kept secret on the other, or even both at the same time.[76]

If I attempt to retell the adventures of Eva and her family in the Soviet Union, it is because I believe that this five-year-long episode is of key importance to our understanding of the dynamics in Laura Polányi's family as well as of the decisions she and her children were to make in the following years. A critical analysis of the dramatic events of this episode, as is always the case with this family, highlights more than the experiences of a single family; it will also illustrate a wide range of motives for the fascination of European left-wing intellectuals with the Soviet Union in the 1930s.

Such a retelling will, inevitably, involve confronting Eva's memories with alternative sources and, on occasion, finding inconsistencies or missing bits in her version. It is a delicate task that should be undertaken with the understanding that, historically accurate or not, this is her own, and a very personal, story.[77]

It all started on a whim. Eva Stricker "left Carstens in the lurch, and at the last minute, in order to get a visa, she became engaged to her friend Alex Weissberg, who was working in Kharkov as a physicist."[78] In 1932, to leftist intellectuals everywhere, but especially in Central Europe, the Soviet Union represented the last great hope. Yet in her memoirs, Eva insisted that her motives were different from the many left-leaning intellectuals who were longing to go and see with their own eyes the great experiment in the East; that she was a political innocent. Her way of participation in the world, she claimed, never manifested itself in embracing political causes or joining parties but by following her instincts.[79] In Berlin, she recalled with a mixture of irony and nostalgia, "I listened to a great amount of theoretical discussion concerning politics and the labour movement. Everybody around me was very much involved in the rights and wrongs of daily politics."[80] Her views were unaffected by the Communists in the family. She related an episode when one of them, her cousin's wife, Anna Seghers, tore Eva's Social Democratic party card into pieces, as an illustration of the overcharged political atmosphere of Weimar, not as a value judgment. Her likes and dislikes of people were independent of their political convictions.

Alex Weissberg became a Communist during his university years in Vienna. More importantly, when Eva decided to visit the Soviet Union, he had already worked at the Ukrainian Physico-Technical Institute since 1931.[81] The Soviet government, in the midst of its monumental industrialization campaign, the First Five-Year Plan, was desperate for well-trained professionals and agressively recruited so-called "foreign experts." Weissberg was put in charge of the building of an important department of the new complex, shaping up to be "one of the largest experimental laboratories in Europe."[82]

Berlin at the time was full of Russian émigrés, and their music and dance, the sense of different colours and rhythms aroused Eva's curiosity. To her, these impressions conveyed the hope that there existed a younger, healthier culture in Soviet Russia and that it was a potential antidote to the political and moral decadence of the West.[83] And perhaps, although Eva did not consider it at the time or later, it is possible that she wanted to find out more about the Russian roots of her own family.[84]

She left Germany on January 1st, 1932 and moved in with Weissberg who lived in the new residence built for the staff of the Kharkov Institute. In the fall of 1932, Arthur Koestler came to the Soviet Union to write a book commissioned by the Comintern, and visited his old friends for a fortnight. He described the "small but, by Russian standards, luxurious flat," consisting of three rooms and a kitchen, shared by Alex, Eva and Eva's mother where "frequently they also had visiting physicists from abroad billeted on them."[85] Eva planned to stay for only a short vacation in the Soviet Union but soon after arriving, in January of 1932, she visited the offices of the Ukrainian China and Glass Industry, was offered work, and accepted it.[86] Over the next couple of years, she was given the assignment to visit china factories in remote areas of the Ukraine. Her arrival in the Soviet Union coincided with the peak of the great Ukrainian famine, the result of Stalin's forced collectivization campaign. Everywhere she went, there were signs of starvation and the pictures of the famine, which officially did not exist, were etched in her memory.[87]

Eva also remembered her first encounter with the world of the *shtetls*. She described one small town as "a sad little place; there were more hunchbacks and cripples than in other places"[88] but was impressed by the skills and spirit of the young Jews who ran the local china factory. It was a world removed by only two generations from her own family's (her maternal grandmother's) past; and yet in her own admission, this young assimilated Jewish woman had never even heard of the *shtetls* or realized that the Yiddish-speaking workers would understand her lecture delivered in German. Only much later, reading Sholem Aleichem's books in America, would she recognize the little towns she had seen in retrospect.[89]

Eva quickly realized that the Soviet Union was not a country to be judged by Western standards, with most of the population just one step removed from their primitive, almost medieval peasant lifestyle. She found an Oriental acceptance of suffering and deprivation, that "time was timeless here, and that the patience of the Russian peasant was as alarming as his poverty."[90] Two weeks out of Berlin, she was stunned by the degree of poverty but also the grace with which it was accepted. Most of all, she remembered the episodes of kindness and acceptance she had seen.[91]

For Koestler, who toured the Soviet Union at the same time and encountered the same famine and poverty, the experience proved deeply traumatic. The striking gap between reality and official propaganda ultimately made him realize the incompatibility of his ideals with its realization and kickstarted the process of his disenchantment in Communism. (All this, however, did not stop him from dutifully completing his book contract with the Comintern.)

Never a Communist, Eva was immune to the disturbing clash between ideals and reality, experienced by most of the visiting Western Communists. If she had any preconceived notions about the Russian people at all, it was rooted in the classic Russian literature of Tolstoi and Dostoevski, reminiscent of the romanticized notion of Russia held by turn-of-the-century intellectuals. The "sentimental love ... with all its tints of pity and respect"[92] was not based on political ideals and is something she had come to hold and continues to hold to this day for the Russian people.

In January 1933, Hitler was elected chancellor of Germany. In Eva's memoirs, there is not a word of reaction to the events in Germany, a significant omission because it shows the degree to which she distanced herself from the turmoil in Central Europe by moving to the Soviet Union. Despite her silence, the events in Germany must have played a significant role in turning her intended short visit in the Soviet Union into a prolonged stay. We do not know if she had ever planned to return to her German employer and her professional life in Germany, in any case, the way back was now effectively cut and her professional life tied exclusively to the Soviet Union.

Contemporaries, including those living there, almost uniformly regarded the turn of events in Germany with guarded optimism. Leo Szilard, the Hungarian physicist working in Berlin, was the exception, living with "literally packed" suitcases since January 1933.[93] Szilard's anecdote is highly characteristic of the climate of German academia at the beginning of 1933.

> After the Reichstag fire [February 27, 1933], I went to see my friend Michael Polanyi and told him what happened, and he looked at me and said, "Do you really think that the secretary of the interior had anything to do with this?" and I said, "Yes, that is precisely what I mean," and he just looked at me with incredulous eyes. At the time he had an offer to go to England and to accept a professorship in Manchester. I very strongly urged him to accept this, but he said that if he now went to Manchester, he could not be productive for at least another year, because it takes that much time to install a laboratory, and I said to him, "Well, how long do you think you will remain

productive if you *stay* in Berlin?"[94]

Szilard's portrayal of Polanyi as the naive academic living in his ivory tower was not entirely fair. Polanyi was in the majority with the likes of Karl Mannheim, all convinced that the rise of Hitler and the Nazis was a short-term phenomenon. Mannheim and Oszkár Jászi, both among the sharpest observers of European social and political trends, were still discussing the possibility of sending Jászi's son to a German university as late as March 1933.[95] In April 1933, these plans were abruptly canceled and replaced by Mannheim's desperate pleas to secure an appointment in the United States.[96]

By April, a decree of the German Ministry of the Interior ordered all university professors of Jewish origin to be fired immediately; Szilard, always "a day earlier" than most people, was already busy organizing the Academic Assistance Council in London, to help the German academic refugees. Eva's uncle, Michael Polanyi, accepted the Manchester position in the summer of 1933. Others affected in the family included Eva's younger brother, who left Berlin to continue his university studies in Vienna. Eva's cousin, László Radványi and his wife Anna Seghers, found refuge in France, along with the majority of émigré German writers.

Following his extensive travels in the Soviet Union, Arthur Koestler returned to the Weissbergs' hospitable flat in Kharkov to fulfill his obligation and complete the manuscript of his Soviet travel book. He recalled the night they learned about the turning point in Germany with an anecdote that highlights the tremendous isolation of the Soviet Union from the rest of Europe.

> We were playing a peaceful poker game for kopecks—Alex, myself, and Professor Shubnikov, head of the Institute's laboratory for low-temperature research. Shubnikov was an endearing elderly Professor, very absent-minded and something of an eccentric. While one of us was dealing, he remarked dreamily, apropos of nothing:
> '...And so they have burnt down the Reichstag. I wonder now what Hitler did that for?'
> '*What*?' we shouted.
> 'Don't you know? The Nazis have burnt down your Parliament. It was on the wireless.'[97]

Alex and he, continued Koestler, understood the significance of the event; the terror had started, Germany became a totalitarian state.[98] The news abruptly changed Koestler's life; it turned him from traveler into a refugee overnight. After obtaining his exit permit—which proved to be, he writes, as difficult as it had been to get his entry visa, Koestler left for France in the summer of 1933.[99]

Around the same time, the frequency of guests billeted in the Weissbergs' Kharkov flat suddenly increased. They brought news of the developments in Germany, unmentioned by the Soviet press and confirming the gut reaction of Koestler and Weissberg that Germany's Nazification was well under way.

After their long engagement, Eva and Weissberg got married in July 1933, a decision prompted at least partly by the developments in Germany.[100] In her memoirs, Eva underplays the importance of the relationship. Their engagement, she says, was primarily a ruse to get her a visa to the Soviet Union, and they only got married at her mother's insistence.[101] This, however, does not add up with other facts, pointing to inconsistencies in her story. In this case, it concerns only a minor, probably even insignificant detail but exemplifies the larger problem of verifying her narrative, in the absence of alternative sources. According to Koestler's account, Laura had lived with the Weissbergs since the summer of 1932. If a legal marriage was Laura's wish—and it is not difficult to picture her insisting on some sort of propriety—why would they wait for more than a year and a half after Eva's arrival? Also, once entering the Soviet Union, foreign citizens, including those invited as experts, had to reapply for residency permit every six months. It was a tedious, bureaucratic process, with several references required, including some from party officials. Eva's work for the Ukrainian china industry may have been considered important enough to allow her to stay but hardly important enough to secure a visa for her mother. (It required months, even years before Communist activists from abroad, such as Koestler, received clearance for an entry visa.[102]) And if it was Weissberg's work that was considered so valuable to the Soviet authorities that it had already guaranteed the permits for his fiancee and her mother, why the sudden need for them to get married? Furthermore, according to Eva, it became clear quite soon after her arrival that the arrangement was not working. Obviously, there were some details Eva failed to mention in her memoirs. It is possible, for instance, that Laura and Eva had connections, perhaps through Ilona Duczynska, in the higher Comintern and Party echelons that helped with these bureaucratic procedures.

This hypothesis seems to be borne out by the fact that, around the same time, Michael Stricker, Eva's older brother, also came to the Soviet Union. He was invited to Moscow as a foreign expert of patent law. According to a family member's recollection, the invitation came courtesy of an old family friend, Gyula Hevesi. A Communist and one of the people's commissars during the Hungarian Republic of Councils, Hevesi emigrated to the Soviet Union and occupied a high position in the Soviet film industry.[103] Michael, by all accounts, was not interested in politics nor engaged in the cause of Socialist construction in the Soviet Union. His motives for accepting the offer must have been more practical. It came along at the right time, when he had to leave Germany, and offered a relatively good salary as well as the usual privileges enjoyed by foreign experts in the Soviet Union.

Moscow in the mid-1930s had a sizeable Hungarian émigré population, including the Communist Party brass, Béla Kun and Georg Lukács among them, and the commissars of the 1919 Hungarian Republic of Councils. (Members of the last cabinet of Hungary's Bolshevik dictatorship, Communists and Left Socialists, were tried by the Horthy regime in 1920 and subsequently expelled to Soviet Russia, in exchange for Hungarian officer prisoners of war.) During the 1920s, leaders and prominent members of the underground Hungarian Communist Party were also stationed, temporarily or permanently, in the Soviet Union. They were usually employed at the Comintern and the Hungarian broadcast of the Soviet State Radio, or taught at the Marx-Engels-Lenin Institute and the Academy of Foreign Languages. In exceptional cases, some of the Hungarian Communists were allowed to work in their original fields, as physicians, scientists or academics.

But even then, they were kept in almost complete isolation from ordinary people, confined to their own, comparatively privileged circles. If that was the case for foreign Communists seeking refuge in the Soviet Union, foreign experts whose loyalty could not be taken for granted, were even more carefully sheltered from the reality of Soviet life. They had their own, relatively well supplied shops and thus were exempt from the food shortages and the lack of most elementary consumer goods affecting the general population. They were provided with chauffeured cars and, perhaps most importantly, their own apartments, instead of the infamous communal apartments, so prevalent in the large Soviet cities.

Among the Hungarians living in Moscow at the time, there was a number of Polányi relatives, including Ernö Seidler, a cousin of Laura. Seidler, the son of Laura's paternal aunt, had served as an officer in the Monarchy's army, became a Communist in the Russian prisoner-of-war camp and was sent back to Hungary at the end of 1918 to found the Hungarian Communist Party. An engineer by profession and a kind and gentle man, he was a commissar during the Republic of Councils, in charge of the defense of Budapest. ("That's why we lost it," went the family saying.[104]) Seidler's wife, the German-born Stella Münch, taught German at the Lenin Academy; a family picture shows her with Eva and Laura on an outing near Moscow. Other acquaintances of the Polanyis in Moscow included József Madzsar, Oszkár Jászi's brother-in-law. A sometime Bourgeois Radical, he became a member of the underground Communist Party around 1924-25.[105] With much difficulty, he made his way to Moscow in March 1936, hoping to work in his profession; he was a dentist and an internationally known expert of social medicine. László Dienes, a friend and colleague of Ervin Szabó, was teaching at the Marx-Lenin Institute and the Pedagogical College of Foreign Languages from 1933, and two of Adolf Polányi's old friends from the days of the Socialist Students' Circle, Ernö Czóbel and Béla Vágó, also lived in Moscow at the time.

Following an amicable separation from Weissberg in 1934, Eva moved to Leningrad (the former and today's St. Petersburg), where she stayed at a luxurious hotel and worked for the Lomonosov (formerly the Imperial Porcelain) Factory. Her designs ranged from plates for mass consumption to perfume bottles for Molotov's wife. Her shapely but ornament-free designs were judged too decadent and the geometric motives she used to decorate them, too "Western;" so the factory had local artists paint the dishes she had designed.[106] Nevertheless, she rose quickly in the ranks. Soon she moved to Moscow where she worked at the Dulevo Porcelain Factory outside the city and in the following year was named Artistic Director of the China and Glass Industry of the Russian Republic. In a picture taken with leaders of the industry, she was yet again the sole woman.[107]

In the spring of 1936 Eva shared a room with Laura in her older brother's Moscow apartment. Michael Stricker and his wife had just had a baby girl. When her daughter's marriage ended in 1934, Laura also left Kharkov and returned to Hungary where she underwent a series of illnesses and operations. A year later she returned to the Soviet Union, this time to Moscow, in her new role as a grandmother. She stayed at her son's apartment to help care for the baby but also to work on a new project; she collected material for a study on Soviet family policies.[108]

In 1935, Stalin's propaganda machine started a campaign for the restoration of the family and marriage, followed by legal measures, such as the reversal of the previously liberal abortion law and the tightening of marriage and divorce laws.[109] Laura regarded these changes in Soviet family and social policies as indication that the Soviet leadership was moving towards a normalization along Western liberal principles. In her view, 1934-35 represented a period when the Soviet leadership became genuinely concerned with the wellbeing of its citizens, especially the welfare of families and children.[110]

Another Hungarian visitor in the Soviet Union recorded his reaction to the same developments in his diary entries. The Hungarian writer Ervin Sinkó moved in the same intellectual circles in Moscow and even had mutual acquaintances with Laura. A Communist since the 1919 Hungarian Bolshevik revolution, Sinkó came to Moscow in 1935 as a true believer. During his two-year stay he tried earnestly to keep the faith, explaining away his disappointing experiences with the usual excuses: the backwardness of the population, the imperialist and fascist threat, the economic priorities.

It was exactly the campaign for the restoration of family and marriage that prompted his final disenchantment with the Stalinist system. Sinkó, with his refined esthetic sensitivities, could not help noticing the artistic untruthfulness of the writerly contributions to the obviously orchestrated campaign. If the lack of artistic quality of the articles, often by excellent writers, made Sinkó instantly suspicious, he found the ideas they expressed morally repulsive. The praise of the sacred institutions of marriage and motherhood as woman's main calling reminded him of both the clerical propaganda of his childhood in the pre-war Monarchy and Mussolini's fascist campaign that regarded women as breeding stock.[111] He also found the artificial, tourist-like lifestyle of foreign Communists an indignity that prevented them from witnessing the reality of Soviet life.[112]

We can only speculate on the reasons that made Laura less conscious of the deceptiveness of Stalin's campaign that carefully timed the expression of the government's concern with its citizens' wellbeing for the period leading up to the Great Terror. First of all, Laura was not a Communist, thus she may have been less critical of Soviet reality because her expectations had not been very high to begin with. Secondly, because she had not moved in Communist circles before, she was less familiar with the practice of falsifications and lies, the common currency of the Soviet propaganda machine by the mid-thirties.[113]

Finally, because of her background, Laura may have been oblivious of her relatively privileged surroundings in Moscow—after all, it was merely adequate, and far from luxurious, compared to her previous lifestyle in Budapest and Vienna. In any case, the fact that Laura continued collecting material for her study, even while Eva was in prison, and was entertaining plans to complete the study until the mid-1940s, calls for further explanation. Perhaps she needed the project to keep a sense of usefulness during the months of her daughter's imprisonment. Or, as Eva would explain later, Laura wanted to prove to herself that she was an impartial observer, able to keep her scholarly objectivity even with her daughter's life in danger.[114]

Eva was about to move into her own apartment, an indication of her considerable standing; in a city with a housing shortage so severe that even professionals and party members shared kitchens and bathrooms with half a dozen families, to have one's own apartment was the highest privilege. But on the night of the 28th of May, 1936, she was arrested by the NKVD.

In her prison memoirs she described the months of interrogation. She was accused of counter-revolutionary activities and organizing a plot to assassinate Stalin. Although she was not subjected to physical torture, the long periods of solitary confinement and the relentless mental pressure of the interrogations broke her spirit and she finally signed a confession admitting to counter-revolutionary activities. Realizing that her interrogators succeeded in destroying her dignity, Eva tried to commit suicide. She was saved and kept in an isolation cell for almost another year, until, in September 1937, she was called out, put on a train under guard, and released in Poland.

Eva's memoirs provide a vivid and moving description of her 16 months in prison. Memorable details of her account, including the mental exercises in the solitary cell, the portraits of her two interrogators (the first: decent and idealistic, the second: brutal and cynical), the prisoners' "knocking" communication, found their way into Koestler's *Darkness at Noon*. If her aim was to leave a testimony of her extraordinary experiences for her children, she succeeded. The underlying motive of her memoirs, however, seems to go beyond the wish to leave a record; it is to find a rational explanation for both her arrest and eventual release.

Eva's arrest, in May 1936, somewhat preceded the beginning of the Great Terror in its earnest that was to sweep away most of the foreigners in the Soviet Union, Communists and non-Communist experts alike. Yet to be just one of Stalin's countless victims was not for Eva; and she found a more personal, alluringly tailor-made explanation for her arrest many years after the fact. One day, she accidentally took a book off the shelf at the New York Public Library, titled *The Secret History of Stalin's Crimes*.[115]

The author, Alexander Orlov, was one of the NKVD's leading operatives in Western Europe. He defected to the United States during the Spanish Civil War and waited until after Stalin's death to publish his memoirs. His testimony, at the time of its publication regarded as suspect and based on second-hand information, has been proven mainly accurate by more recent accounts.[116] In Orlov's book, Eva found a reference to a meeting that took place in the Kremlin in the middle of May 1936. At this meeting, Stalin, who supervised the preparation of the first show trial (the Zinoviev-Kamenev trial that was to take place in September 1936), reminded the leaders of the NKVD that their script for the trial lacked "a prisoner who would testify that he had been sent to the Soviet Union by Trotsky for the purpose of committing a terroristic act."[117] From here, Eva made the contention that because the NKVD knew about her vacation in

Paris in the summer of 1935, she was arrested at Stalin's direct order, as it were, to fulfill the role of Trotsky's courier. What she did not mention in the memoirs was that Orlov continued his account with describing at length how, as a result of Stalin's request, the NKVD sacrificed two of its valuable agents who went on to perform the roles of Trotsky's agents at the trial.[118]

The real reason for her arrest may have been much more banal: as one of the recent articles written on her remarked, "her success brought her enemies."[119] In a climate of increasing xenophobia and fear, the meteor-like rise of the 29-year old, talented and pretty young woman, with the German-sounding name, must have attracted jealousy and suspicion. Once arrested, it is possible that the NKVD tried to use her, with a suitable confession, as one of many potential witnesses for the coming trials; and that, eventually, they dropped the plan because she proved to be too difficult to handle.[120]

Eva must have been aware that her eventual release was nothing short of a miracle and needed explanation. Yet her suggestions on this point are neither clear nor entirely convincing. Of the several, somewhat overlapping explanations provided in her memoirs, the first is based on her assumption that during the preparation for the show trials, the NKVD was instructed to observe due process, or, as she put it, "everything had to be very clean and legal on paper"[121] and "an appearance of legality was extremely important to the high command."[122] When her interrogator tricked her with threats and promises into signing a confession and, consequently, she tried to kill herself, she finally had a chance, she writes, to make a complaint to the state prosecutor about the illegal methods employed against her.[123] As a result, she writes, her interrogator was arrested and she eventually released.

To keep up the appearance of legality on paper was of course one thing and obtaining confessions from innocent people was another. And everyone involved, from Stalin to the NKVD interrogators knew perfectly well that threats and false promises, as well as physical and mental torture were an integral part of the job of obtaining confessions. Eva wants us to believe that the NKVD was so concerned with legality that her knowledge of the illegal methods employed in itself was sufficient to successfully stand up to the entire Stalinist system.

In order to make this argument more convincing, Eva again points at Orlov's book for evidence: "Orlov's account also states that Stalin was concerned at this point that the record not show any misconduct, and directed that all interrogations be performed legally, without devices such as threats and false promises."[124] In fact, there is nothing in Orlov's book to suggest this. Another problematic point concerns the issue of legality; the definition of legality in the Soviet Union in 1935 was quite different from what an American reader in 1987 would take for granted.[125]

Another, complementary explanation for Eva's release, one she repeatedly referred to in her memoirs and interviews was the role played by her mother. "Eva never learned exactly why she was released from prison," goes the already quoted *New Yorker* interview, whose author heavily relied on Eva's memoirs.[126] "A contributing factor may have been the efforts of her mother, who collected statements from eminent Russian physicists attesting to Eva's good character. ... That they signed is evidence of the persuasive force and charm of Laura Polanyi Striker," adds the journalist.[127]

Alexander Weissberg's autobiography offers a somewhat different version and reveals that it was Eva's then husband who went around soliciting these references from his physicist colleagues. "When my wife was arrested in the spring of 1936, I approached various highly placed persons on her behalf. My wife was very well liked and most of them gave me written declarations in her favour. Six months later, after the trial of Zinoviev, that would have been out of the question; even the highest placed and most powerful had begun to fear for their own safety."[128] Koestler also mentioned his friend's efforts on Eva's behalf: instead of saving himself, he went to Moscow and Leningrad to obtain testimonies from influential people, an act that would have been lunacy in 1937. "In 1936 it was merely reckless."[129]

One can easily picture the partnership of Weissberg and Laura, both well suited to tackle the formidable task, trying to figure out the best way to proceed and the best people to contact to save Eva. Weissberg's truly selfless efforts (after all, at the time of Eva's arrest, they had been separated for years) cemented the friendship that had begun between mother-in-law and son-in-law in the Kharkov days. Weissberg's affection was clearly expressed in his letters— *"meine alte Flamme*, Laura Mikhailovna", he wrote many years later,[130] even in the formal Russian way he addressed her, half-jokingly, by her first and paternal names, to the end of her days.[131] Looking back with fondness on their relationship after Laura's death, Weissberg described it as one forged in their joint fight to free Eva.[132]

Eva always emphasized Laura's role in her release, especially Laura's persistence in working her way into the Soviet legal system and finding the State Attorney (or procurator, in the Russian terminology) responsible for her case. In a letter to Eva, Weissberg described the occasion when Laura and himself walked up to the building of the Office of the Military Procurator of the Leningrad

District, with Laura entering it to officially launch an appeal on her daughter's behalf.[133] It must have been an exceptional event in the city that, since the Kirov murder two years earlier, was subjected to an unprecedented series of mass arrests and deportations, and beaten into submission. The explanation Eva suggested—repeated in numerous articles and told me during our first interview—was that Laura, armed with references, made such an impression that the military procurator, now convinced of Eva's innocence, went on to acquire her release.[134] Such a move by a procurator seems most unlikely in light of our present knowledge of the Soviet judicial system of the period. Instead of guardians of legality—as Eva presented them—procurators were just as obedient and hapless tools of the Stalinist system of repression as anyone else. After the first show trial in September 1936, intervention in a political case by a procurator would have been nothing short of suicidal.[135] From the summer of 1937, former executors of the Purge, procurators and judges themselves became its victims in growing numbers.[136] Moreover, even if the procurator became convinced of Eva's innocence and decided to intervene, he could not have been successful in a time when, as we are told, procurators making complaints about the illegal methods of the NKVD were routinely arrested.[137]

Eva's insistence on crediting her mother with the deed can be explained by sentimental reasons. The account of her release may not be fully accurate, but there is no doubt about the sincerity of the emotional attachment to her mother that she developed after her prison experience. As there is no doubt that, regardless of the effectiveness of her efforts, Laura left no stone unturned to save her daughter; and that in a foreign country, far from her familiar surroundings, in the intensifying climate of xenophobia, this was an act of considerable courage.

As for additional explanations for Eva's release, Koestler forwarded a suggestion, according to which she was freed due to the Austrian consul's "heroic efforts."[138] Eva was not an Austrian citizen but Laura was born in Austria; it seems highly likely that she would try to use her connections in Austria to that end. Yet to be an Austrian citizen was no help in many other cases; and Eva herself referred repeatedly to an Austrian friend, one of Alfred Adler's daughters, who perished in the Gulag. Finally, Eva casually mentioned in her memoirs that just before her release, the NKVD officers specifically asked her to spy on her uncle, Michael Polanyi, as well as Viennese Social Democrats.[139] With the disclaimer that, most likely, we will never know the exact circumstances of her release, the most educated guess one can make is that the NKVD decided she was, potentially, more useful for them alive and free than in jail.

Eva was put on a train heading to Poland in September 1937.[140] By that time, Weissberg, along with most of the physicists at the Kharkov Physico-Technical Institute, had already been arrested, and accused of the usual crimes of counter-revolutionary activities and Trotskyist plots against Stalin and the Soviet leadership. As Weissberg almost instantly realized, his case was part of a larger plan, directed against all foreigners, especially Communists; non-Communist foreign experts, in most cases, were only expelled. He also recognized that this was only the tip of the iceberg and, his analytical mind always ready for a challenge, set out to translate the enormity of the Terror into numbers.[141]

The Terror swallowed up the Hungarian Communists in Moscow as well. Ervin Sinkó, the disenchanted writer, luckily kept his French passport and was able to secure an exit visa in 1937. By 1938, József Madzsar, Béla Kun, Eva's uncle Ernö Seidler, along with the majority of Hungarian Communists and their German, Polish, and Romanian comrades, were in camps or shot. Hevesi, Eva's brother's employer was lucky: arrested not long after Eva, he survived 9 years in the camps and returned to Hungary after 1945.

As for Eva's brother and his young family, they safely arrived in Vienna in August 1937.[142] In October 1937, a month after her daughter's release, Laura returned to the Soviet Union. This episode also remains a bit mystifying. With her daughter just released and her son-in-law still in prison, how did Laura ever get a visa to re-enter the Soviet Union? And yet, she appeared in Kharkov, sending to Weissberg in the Kharkov prison a divorce petition to sign, along with a package of much-needed food supplies.[143] On her return to Vienna, Eva met up with Hans Zeisel, a friend of the family since the late 1920s who had waited for her all these years—that is all we can learn from her. In order to marry him, she had to finalize the divorce from Weissberg.[144] In the next chapter, I will return to Weissberg's fate and the future efforts of Eva and Laura, as well as Koestler, to save him.

Vienna in the fall of 1937 was very different from the city Laura and her children called second home before the war and in the 1920s. Red Vienna, governed by the Socialist Democrats and proud of its exemplary housing and social services, lived in a state of a virtual civil war since the late 1920s. Eva's younger brother, George, moved there from Berlin after 1933 to finish his studies in applied physics at the Technical University of Vienna.[145] In sharp contrast to the majority of Hungarian students in Vienna, he was well provided for: he rented a large room near the University as a study, in addition to a small apartment that he soon shared with his new wife, the chemistry student Barbara.[146]

In the family, George was called by his middle name, Ottó, reportedly a memento of Laura's youthful admiration for the Habsburgs; the last Habsburg heir, Otto, was born a year before him. But his political persuasions were far removed from his monarchist middle name. He became involved in the political struggles that divided not only Vienna but soon emerged in the midst of the Polányi family. Karl Polanyi had left Austria in November 1933 when, due to increasing pressure from the Right, the *Volkswirt* could not afford to keep him on board anymore. He went to England, where he taught adult working-class students, "under the auspices of the Workers" Educational Association and the Extramural Delegacies of the Universities of Oxford and London."[147] Soon his daughter followed him. Ilona stayed on in Vienna, swept up once again in political activism. As a member of the left (independent Communist) wing of the Austrian Social Democratic Party, she participated in the February 1934 rise of the *Schutzbund*. She was in charge of the radio broadcast of the Schutzbund, enlisting the help of her young nephew, George Stricker.[148] Ilona spent the following two years underground, editing the *Schutzbund*'s bulletin, by now as a member of the Austrian Communist Party. In 1936, because of ill health, she finally joined her husband in England.[149]

The two Polányi brothers, Michael and Karl, living yet again in the same country, went through a difficult period in their relationship. Family reunions were out of the question, since the two wives, one, the consummate faculty wife, the other, the eternal revolutionary, could not be brought into the same room. More importantly, the brothers' fundamentally different views on the Soviet Union almost led to a breaking point in their relations. Eva's imprisonment and the show trials reinforced Michael Polanyi's already well-developed doubts about the moral, political, and economic virtues of the Soviet system. Karl, on the other hand, reached a virtually uncritical position toward the Soviet Union. By 1939, he called those who had doubts about the trials, "sentimental intellectuals;" and those who did not equate Russia with socialism, the traitors of socialism.[150]

In the fall of 1937, Laura and her three children were reunited in Vienna. It was a time to take stock: they all had been through a series of potentially life-threatening adventures. All three had chosen life-long partners. They had their differences in political outlook and affiliations. Michael was never political and his Soviet experiences only reinforced his position. Eva remained her impulsive and defiantly outsider self, her future husband, the liberal Social Democrat Hans Zeisel providing a moderating influence. Finally, young Ottó and his new wife were and remained Communists. Unlike their uncles, however, they were able to set aside these differences, in the interest of their next, collective undertaking.

Among the family's monumental collections of correspondence and documents, there is not one piece of evidence that records the actual decision. Yet, in light of the events that were to follow, there can be no doubt that with all three of her children and their spouses as well as Laura gathered in Vienna, a family council took place, a decision was made and, almost certainly, a detailed plan was laid out. The most important part of this plan concerned the decision to go, collectively, to the United States. A multitude of practical tasks had to be performed: affidavits and visas to be requested, travel plans specified, and most importantly, a certain division of labour decided upon. It was agreed that Michael and Hilde, on the strength of their ability to quickly establish a business and generate an income, would go first, leaving their 2-year old daughter behind in Laura's care. Laura would go next with the child, followed by Ottó and Eva, and their respective spouses. Once safely settled in New York and Chicago (the direction of Ottó and his wife), they would make arrangements for Sándor Stricker to follow.[151] Meanwhile, Cecile would remain in her comfortable hotel suite in Budapest, provided for by Michael Polanyi. Sophie and Egon Szécsi in Vienna, expecting their American visas any moment from their daughter living there, were soon to follow.

There were last-minute visits to Budapest, to introduce Eva's new husband-to-be to the family there and to say good-byes.[152] Some of the relatives questioned the wisdom of the drastic step of leaving the continent, at a time when war in Europe did not seem imminent. If Vienna was not the old, familiar place anymore and Germany was out of the question, could the young couples perhaps move back to Hungary? Yet, in the many letters and notes between Laura and her children, meticulously outlining the travel and shipping arrangements stretching over half of Europe, Hungary is mentioned only as the place where one goes to say good-bye to old relatives or take care of unfinished business, never even as a place for nostalgia.

The children had started the process of detaching themselves from Hungary a long time ago; it is significant that two of them chose non-Hungarian spouses. Their recent experiences in Germany, Austria, and the Soviet Union only reinforced the conviction that their future lay away from Hungary and the continent. For Laura however, whose ties to Hungary were much stronger, the decision must have been agonizing and involved changes few people of her age would undertake voluntarily. It was not the first time the Polanyis had lived through historical cataclisms and they took a certain pride in always being among those who actively influenced the events. Now Laura had to make the final decision and pull up the stakes her family had invested in Hungary's fate for generations. Yet what must have been even more difficult was the admission that events, at least for now, were beyond their control.

Given her less than robust health, it would have seemed more sensible to return home to Hungary until, eventually, she and her husband could rejoin their children. Her decision, instead, of embarking on the trip with them was a true measure of her youthful energy and the place she came to occupy in their lives. For participating in their children's adventures rather than opting for a more comfortable plan, she was to pay a heavy price, subjecting herself to a series of physical and mental trials. But that is another story.

Chapter 4:
The Odyssey of the Polanyis

In August 1939, waiting in England to embark on her trip to the U.S., Laura wrote her farewell letters to relatives and friends in Hungary. A nephew on her husband's side replied, gently scolding Laura for her pessimistic outlook. There was no reason to be overly dramatic, he wrote, a mere two weeks before the outbreak of WWII. "Here, so far everything has been really quiet and peaceful and if we did not have the newspapers and the radio, we could not feel any effect of the historical times."[1] As far as "Adolf was concerned," the nephew added in a transparently coded aside, he was speculating "for *baisse*"[2] and suggested that in a year or two, the whole thing would blow over. Then Laura and her children would be able to return to Hungary or he to visit them in New York.

Six years later, at war's end, Laura received a letter from an old friend of the family, György Polgár.[3] He headed a small agency, the *Bureau de Recherches Hongrois* in Geneva, and Laura had written to him seeking his help in finding the husband of her niece, Eszter Polanyi, deported to Dachau.

> I cannot tell you how glad I was to receive your kind letter dated on the 28th of October. It was my long-time sincere wish to hear detailed news about the Polanyi family and you were kind enough to fulfill it without even knowing about it. *The report is extraordinary and displays, within one family, our entire life, at once marvellous and tragic.*[4]

Polgár went on to do what most letters crossing the former frontlines did at the time: counting the losses. His account of the terrible human toll on their families and friends put in perspective the blind optimism of the first letter, that of Laura's nephew, shared so many in the assimilated Hungarian-Jewish middle class.

This chapter continues to focus on Laura and her children. It will retrace the itinerary of their flight from Hitler's Europe and highlight the significance of this period in Laura's life. As Polgár rightly pointed out, the extended Polanyi-Stricker family represented, on a small scale, almost the full range of the Hungarian Jewish experience. The resounding success of Laura's immediate family's emigration, however, cannot be fully appreciated without at least providing a glimpse of the fate of relatives and friends who could not escape and perished or barely survived in Europe.

Even when safely settled in England and the United States, Laura and her children were haunted by the terrible fate hanging over their friends and relatives trapped in Nazi-occupied Europe. They continued to help them escape throughout the rest of the war, at times turning the rescue efforts into a family entreprise as it were. Laura's talent at pooling and organizing the family's resources—be they practical, intellectual or financial—to this end was soon realized. Following her own escape in August 1939, she devoted most of her time and energy to this task.

The Polanyis, fleeing from Central Europe in 1938-39, were part of the great wave of intellectual refugees reaching the United States. Of the 23 family members of the second and third generations of the Polanyis, 19 changed their country of residence between 1919 and 1942. In addition, the Stricker relatives, on the side of Laura's husband, were also generously represented in the ranks of the intellectual refugees. These numbers in themselves would make the Polanyis an ideal subject for a case study in the history of the intellectual emigration. Their example should be expected to illustrate the main patterns described by the sizeable literature on the intellectual emigration to the U.S. as, conversely, this literature should help explain their remarkable success in emigration and after.

Upon closer inspection, the Polanyis' case turned out to offer more than merely an illustration. In the literature on the intellectual refugees, one comes across itineraries and narratives very similar to those of the Polanyis or even references to illustrious members of the family and praise for their remarkable accomplishments in emigration.[5] Yet, the picture emerging from the documents of the family's flight, instead of fitting into its main narrative, pointed to significant gaps in the American scholarship on the refugee intellectuals.

It was not for lack of interest, be that academic or popular; on the contrary, the refugee intellectual wave sparked an instant and still lasting fascination in the American popular imagination and was recognized as a worthy academic subject. The first studies appeared during the war and have continued at a steady flow ever since. Unlike any other emerging academic field, it was one whose scholars happened to be often its subjects as well and in which the studies often displayed an unorthodox mix of genres, combining the tools of the memoir and literary essay with those of the historical and sociological study.[6]

From the first statistical surveys, pointing to the potential effect of the massive influx of intellectuals,[7] to the affirmation that "the exiles Hitler made were the greatest collection of transplanted intellect, talent, and scholarship the world has ever seen,"[8] there emerged the consensus that the intellectual migration from Europe signaled a turning point in American intellectual and academic life.

Almost simultaneously followed the realization that the study of intellectual immigrants required a different set of tools from those applied to immigrants in general. As early as 1953, the introduction of a small collection of essays by such eminent émigré scholars as Franz Neumann, Erwin Panowsky and Paul Tillich expressed frustration over the inability of American social science, "inclined to think in terms of millions rather than individuals," to grasp the magnitude of this change.[9] The contributions of this volume demonstrated the potential gains of an interdisciplinary approach, one that weaves the threads of personal, as well as intellectual and institutional histories together, and makes full use of the émigré scholars' position, at once insider and outsider. The essays of Tillich and Neumann also introduced the perception of the exile experience as a paradigm for the intellectual in general, especially in modern Western history.[10]

A new interest in intellectual history from the late 1960s spearheaded a few outstanding collections of essays. They successfully combined the insights of former émigré but by then fully established American scholars with the fresh energy and broad outlook of a new generation of young scholars in the by now full-fledged academic field for the study of intellectual émigrés.[11]

As the period of the 1930s and 1940s became sufficiently removed in time, the intellectual migration took its place as a chapter in American immigration history. The study of American immigration policy of the period and the attitude of the Roosevelt-administration toward the refugees, in particular, was an overdue and necessary task. It was, however, accomplished at a price, by shifting the emphasis from the refugees and their interaction with American society to the role and responsibility of various government bodies, political factors and public opinion. Although these studies never claimed to focus on the intellectual emigration, their approach still resulted in the intellectual refugees being lumped together with refugees in general or, if the focus was on Jewish immigrants, limited to Jews.[12] While government policy and its shortcomings were intensely scrutinized, the vital role of non-government organizations and individuals in the rescue effort was often overlooked. It is telling that the heroic efforts of Varian Fry, instrumental in rescuing more than 2,000 mostly prominent intellectual refugees from Vichy France, remained largely unheralded. Following a conference contribution more than two decades ago,[13] a first, popular, biography was published only in recent years.[14]

It is a testament to the intellectual émigrés' lasting influence that there is now a new generation of scholars studying their influence in American academia and intellectual and artistic life. There is renewed interest in institutions such as the New School and the Bauhaus in America, and the most famed among the refugees, like Hannah Arendt, Thomas Mann or Arnold Schönberg, on the one hand, and signs of the prevailing interdisciplinary approach on the other.[15] Finally, in recent years we have witnessed what is probably one last surge of memoirs, written by the younger members of the refugee wave.[16]

What are the implications of all this for an account of the Polanyis' Odyssey? First of all, the Polanyis do not fit readily into a scholarship that has shown increasing compartmentalization and often limits the scope of its query according to the refugees' country of origin and academic or creative field.[17] By virtue of their accomplishments, often within the career of one person, in fields ranging from physics to the arts, education, literature, economics, and philosophy, not to mention politics, the Polanyis always resisted easy classification. Because of the multiple stages of their emigration, and their temporary settlement in Austria, Weimar Germany, and England, not even their country of origin could be clearly determined.[18] The same applies to their ethnic background; their complex identities, developed through multiple affiliations with Austrian, Hungarian, German, and an increasingly secular Jewish culture are not easily fitted into a clear-cut ethnic or religious framework. Meanwhile, even relatively recent examples of the refugee scholarship display a tendency to ethnic or religious stereotyping that harks back to the popular perception of the refugees at the time of their arrival.[19]

Another lacuna in the history of the exodus of European scholars to America concerns the stage between departure and arrival, the flight itself. With so much attention focused on the organizations and individuals, instrumental in their rescue (and, conversely, the hostility of government officials to be overcome), only marginal interest has been paid to the refugees' own efforts to save themselves. By overlooking this aspect, scholarship not only failed to do justice to the efforts of the refugees, it also created an artificial discontinuity, turning the leading lights of Central European intelligentsia into helpless victims, unexplainably reinvigorated once in America. Yet, if the Polanyis' example is any indication, the intellectual refugees did not passively wait to be rescued. One of the underlying patterns in the family's immigration was the reliance on their own resources and the use of organized outside help only as a last resort. A new focus on agency would not only bring the study of intellectual refugees in line with that of ordinary immigrants to the U.S. but could also point to additional, unexplored aspects of the emigration process itself.[20] I already mentioned the "headstart" enjoyed by Hungarian intellectual émigrés of the 1918-19 revolutions.[21] Disruptive as it had been, the emigration from Hungary offered invaluable lessons, a dress rehearsal for the next flight, this time from Hitler's Europe. In addition, Laura and her children's experiences in the Soviet Union taught them the skills necessary to cut through the bureaucratic and legal hurdles of a dictatorship and the importance of co-operation with family members, friends, and fellow intellectuals.

For, if there was one crucial factor in the flight of the intellectuals escaping from Hitler, it was the role played by their academic and intellectual networks. And that is exactly why the Polanyis, with their family and intellectual connections spread all over Europe, provide such a paradigmatic case. Through their involvement in the progressive movements in Hungary and Austria as well as their achievements in academic fields, they were firmly grounded in the Central European intellectual, political and academic networks from the late 19th century. The post-1919 wave of emigration from Hungary did not disrupt, only expanded these ties into every corner of Europe, carrying relatives and friends everywhere from Paris to Vienna, Berlin, Moscow, and Manchester. In addition to the significance of these networks in transplanting the intellectual, scientific and artistic talent into America, they also forecasted a trend, the internationalization of modern academia, science and the arts.

The experience of Laura and the younger women in her family highlights another, relatively underdeveloped area in the study of intellectual refugees: the study of intellectual refugee women.[22] In addition to Laura and Eva, most women in the Polanyi family were intellectuals in their own right, armed with university degrees—some in science and engineering, almost unheard of for American women at the time—and a long list of professional and political accomplishments. They no doubt shared these characteristics with a much larger group of refugee intellectual women.

In their everyday lives these women encountered countless examples of American progress and the blessings of modern technology. Ironically, when it came to social norms and expectations concerning women, especially those in academia and the professions, they found conditions much less hospitable than in the countries they had come from. Even a cursory look at their collective experience suggests that the success of Laura and Eva was the exception rather than the rule: the majority of intellectual immigrant women had to settle for the role of the faculty wife and hostess or find socially acceptable creative outlets.[23] Their undeniable impact on the North American notions of women in the professions and academia is still waiting its historian.

Despite the support of old- and new-world networks, the Polanyis were not exempt of the difficulties normally associated with emigration as they rebuilt their lives. That included the confrontation with the oft-simplistic American perceptions concerning the refugees' identity. The reason for their flight, as in the case of many of the refugees, was a combination of their political opposition to Nazism and the anti-Semitic measures of Hitler and his allies. Like many of the refugee intellectuals, they too refused to adjust their identity to Hitler's racial laws.[24]

It is because of the combination of these factors: the international renown of some of the family members as well as the family's ties to the European academic and intellectual elite, the prominence of women professionals in their ranks, the fact that they represented a wide cross-section of the intellectual migration, and last but not least the extensive documentation of their flight that the Polanyis' case offers such a rich material for the study of the intellectual migration from Hitler's Europe to North America.

By March 1938, Laura and her children had completed the preparations to leave for America. The *Anschluss*, declared on the 13th of March, served as a timely justification of their decision to leave the Continent behind. It also complicated matters. When the news of Hitler's troops marching into Austria reached Vienna, Eva, still suffering from the trauma of her recent imprisonment, was not going to take any chances; with her British visitor's visa in hand, she boarded the train and reached England a few days later.[25] She was supported by her uncle Michael, stayed with her other uncle, Karl, for a while, then with an exceptionally kind English woman, Mrs. Bruce who regularly helped refugees and became almost a surrogate mother to Eva during these difficult months.[26] The sudden flight left her affairs in disarray; the divorce from Weissberg was still uncompleted, forcing her to postpone her marriage with Hans Zeisel and her American visa application pending; it was Laura who was to take care of finalizing the divorce a month after Eva had fled Vienna.

More alarmingly, Egon Szécsi, Sophie's husband, was arrested during a coffeehouse raid, a random victim of the terror of the first days of Nazi takeover in Vienna. But even Egon's arrest and the news that he was taken to Dachau concentration camp could not shake the family's optimism. The Szécsis' eldest daughter who had been living in the States for some years, was making arrangements to bring her parents over.[27]

The Polanyis proceeded with their plan; Michael and Hilde Stricker sailed to the U. S. on the 13th of April 1938, leaving their 2-year old daughter, Michelle, in Laura's care.[28] Michael who had business connections in the States (their affidavits were provided by a Mr. Benjamin Liebowitz of the Trubenizing

Company, stating a yearly income of 80,000 dollars[29]) did not waste his time. By the end of April, he and Hilde had already opened their office on Broadway—Dr. Michael S. Striker, Patents and Trade Marks—promptly Americanizing the spelling of the family name to Striker. They rented an apartment nearby[30] and, most importantly, went about the business of securing affidavits for the rest of the family, sending almost daily dispatches of the developments.[31] It seemed that American visas were granted largely on the strength of affidavits; and while immediate family members made the best sponsors, in their absence, the length of American residency and the amount of income and assets were considered crucial. By May 1938, Michael secured multiple affidavits for his mother as well as for Eva and Hans, and made sure that the relatives of Otto's wife submitted the necessary documents. The names circulating as possible guarantors give a good indication of the breadth of the family's connections already transplanted to the States from Central Europe, from Emil Lederer to the Jászis, Paul Lazarsfeld, and Leó Szilard's brother, Béla.[32]

American immigration policy further complicated matters, requiring that potential immigrants apply on the quota assigned to each country based on their birthplace. Thus Ottó and Laura had to apply on the German quota (by force of their Austrian birth and because now it was part of Nazi Germany), while Eva and Barbara were to be considered within the Hungarian quota.[33] Meanwhile, Sándor Stricker in Budapest worried whether his youngest, Ottó, would be able to complete his studies before his departure and his daughter, Eva, finally get married.[34]

June and July 1938 brought more positive developments; Hans and Eva traveled to Prague (as a Czech citizen, he had to apply for his American visa there), received his American visa and returned to England to marry in July. At the end of June, a family friend optimistically reported to Michael Polanyi in Manchester that Ottó, his wife, and Laura all expected to receive their American visas in a few weeks.[35] As far as Sophie's husband, Egon was concerned, continued the letter, they were hopeful that he would be released in a couple of weeks. The optimism was not entirely unfounded; it corresponded to a period that lasted only a few months before the November 1938 *Kristallnacht* during which Nazi policy granted passports to bearers of valid visas, even to those arrested and in prison or concentration camp. The Polanyi "brain trust," always on top of new developments, sprung into action accordingly: on June 28, Michael Polanyi rushed to cable the Szécsis' daughter in Chicago with the news. If they could provide strong affidavits, have them approved in Washington at the State

Department, and cable the approval to the American consul in Vienna, there was a chance that her father could be released.[36] As a result, Sophie applied for an American visa (both for herself and her husband) in July.[37] As Laura assured Michael Polanyi in late August, Sophie, nearing her fiftieth birthday, was healthy and full of energy.[38]

Laura herself was wrapping up her affairs in Vienna. Always the thoughtful mother, she ordered a new easel for Eva and packed her photography equipment.[39] She was also planning a last visit to Budapest. The short side trip necessitated queuing for a number of extra transit visas (French, Italian and Yugoslavian visas on top of the Czech and British she already had), yet she was determined to go home one last time, to say good-bye, to see her mother.[40] Her brother Michael, anxious to see her leave Austria, urged her to cut the trip short.[41]

In August the family got one more step closer to the completion of the plan: Ottó and Barbara left for the U.S. When they reached England on their way, Eva awaited them with ashen face and the news: Laura had been arrested in Vienna.[42] Laura's arrest, as it turned out, had nothing to do with political or "racial" reasons; she invited the unwanted attention of the Austrian police by holding numerous business meetings and making too many phone calls on her son's behalf in the lobby of her hotel. Her position, in the custody of the Austrian police, waiting for the review of her case, was precarious and prompted frantic action from her family and friends in Budapest and London.

In the absence of her children, already on their way to or in the U.S., the remaining family members and friends organized the battle lines with admirable speed. Sophie took over the care of Laura's grandchild, visited her sister in prison, and sent detailed reports to family members. The Stricker relatives in Budapest held an "emergency council meeting" and decided to dispatch the best lawyers to Vienna, to explore official and semi-official avenues. They relayed the news and developments to Eva and her uncles in England.[43]

The disastrous event sounded painful echos in Eva, herself only recently liberated from prison. The thought of her mother languishing in a Viennese jail cell in Nazi-annexed Austria was unbearable.[44] While the Budapest relatives debated the chances of various courses of action and Laura was waiting for her case to go to a hearing,[45] Eva made desperate attempts to acquire the help of the Quakers. The origins of the family's Quaker connection are not entirely clear.[46] It may have been Karl Polanyi's suggestion[47] who possibly met Quakers through his connections with the English Christian Left. It is also likely that Eva's host in England, Mrs. Bruce, also a Quaker[48] and herself involved in helping the refugees, had first-hand knowledge about the Friends' activities in the rescue work.[49]

A few days later, a Mrs. Richards, a representative of the Friends Service Committee reported to Eva that despite her best efforts in Vienna, she was not able to bring her mother home with her, "but as long as there was the smallest suspicion of any money transactions it was quite impossible to get her out before the hearing of the case. I wish I could have stayed there longer," she continued "but I *had* to get home to get my children ready and off to school, and to look after some of my other cases, which are all urgent."[50] Due to the combined efforts of Mrs. Richards, the Hungarian lawyers, the medical certificates, gathered by the Budapest relatives, attesting to Laura's poor health, and the leniency or, possibly, corruption of the Austrian police official handling the case, Laura was released on the day of her scheduled hearing.[51] On the 22nd of September, she announced in a telegram: "Coming Friday 7 pm flight Mummy."[52]

The traumatic experience had left little effect on Laura's fighting spirit. On her arrival in London, she immediately picked up where she had left off in Vienna: organizing her own and her granddaughter's passage to America. She was in almost daily correspondence with her brothers, Karl and Michael, only worrying about the slow progress of the Szécsis' affairs. Once Eva and Hans sailed too—they left for the U. S. in October 1938, taking with them their niece, little Michelle—Laura was left with no one to take care of and nothing else to do but wait. She spent almost an entire year waiting for her American visa, possibly the darkest period for her in the entire endeavour. She longed to see her family in Hungary but with her Austrian passport and the recent, close encounter in Vienna, could not risk a visit.[53] In December 1938 she was taken to hospital for tests and treatment of her feverish bouts. She was frequently visited by her brothers, yet the physical weakness, the inactivity, the anticipation of war, the worries about her family still trapped on the Continent drove her, perhaps the first time in her life, to complaints. In a letter to Andor Németh, a Hungarian writer living in Paris, whom she contacted to find out Koestler's address, she burst out: "I'm not healthy and stayed behind all alone, with my children already having left for America. My visa is still delayed but because of a grotesque accident I have an Austrian passport, I cannot go home either. It is a bad situation, being paralyzed and with many other troubles."[54] Christmas, a time of family gatherings, still spent in the French Hospital in London, was the lowest point, although the telegram she received on Christmas Eve must have brought some relief: "Don't feel lonely children united as never before are with you good health many kisses aurevoir. Hans Eva."[55]

By spring, things were looking up. Following a long stay in the hospital, in February she was feeling better, staying with Mrs. Bruce, admiring her garden and trying to push developments along. Her correspondence testifies to her hopes for a spring or summer sailing date, pending receipt of the American visa, postponed over and over.[56] In March 1939, Adolf Polanyi arrived in England; according to anti-Semitic legislation introduced in the fall of 1938, that was the deadline for foreign-born Jews to leave Italy.[57] There was a long-overdue reunion of four of the Polanyi siblings. It was agreed upon that, with no prospects in England, Adolf should pursue emigration to the Americas, preferably to a South American country where he could use his business and language skills. He should, however, take advantage of his stay in England to speed up the exit of his four children from Italy, all about to finish their university studies.[58]

The surge of new anti-Semitic measures introduced in Hungary and Germany seriously limited the chances of helping the relatives there. Michael Polanyi who carried the responsibility of financially supporting his mother in Budapest and his sister, Sophie, in Vienna, grew increasingly concerned as his property in Germany was, to all intents and purposes, confiscated and his regular income in Hungary (as scientific advisor for the reputable electric company Egyesült Izzó) used to support Cecile blocked.[59] The window of opportunity for the release of Egon Szécsi and, with it, Sophie's emigration seemed to close up. The Szécsis had had their English visa since July 1938 and could expect their American visa reasonably soon. Egon, however, was still in the hands of the Gestapo and an American visa for their mentally disabled son was out of the question. Michael Polanyi, the mastermind behind the efforts to save them, reported in February that matters had reached an impasse; following a denunciation, the Gestapo called in Sophie, took away her passport, and made it clear that her husband would not be released and their passports given back, unless they procured a visa for the boy or left him behind in the care of an institution.[60]

In the end, Laura slipped out of England in late August, 1939, mere days before war broke out.[61] A few weeks after arriving in New York, Laura received news from Budapest: on September 5 Cecile had died. Condolences poured in. Aunt Irma described Cecile's last day—a beautiful, sunny day, spent in the park and reading in her bed—and the funeral that she had organized in the absence of Cecile's children.[62] The widow of Károly Pollacsek, Laura's aunt had always been a reliable presence, frequently reporting on Cecile's physical and mental well-being and only a few months earlier reminding the "children" to mail their birthday greetings to her.[63] A friend sent the obituary of the Social Democratic daily *Népszava*.[64] Its author wrote of Cecile's Russian roots and international Socialist connections, a gesture of remarkable courage at the time, before turning to praise her beautiful eyes, pathbreaking reform-dresses, and short hairdo. An old friend, Sandor (Alexander) Vince now living in Chicago, commented bitterly on "the shackled writer of the *Népszava*" who was afraid to write of Cecile's real significance. "To us and to the entire progressive Hungary she was the mother of the Gracchi," inspiring the intelligentsia of a generation.[65]

Recha Jászi summed up perhaps best the mixed feelings over Cecile's passing: "The time is so sad and tragic that I do know very well that it is best so. She was old and sick and she had lived her life. But a landmark is gone..."[66] As if marking the end of an era and the passing of the torch between generations, Aunt Irma died not long after, in June 1940.

Laura's welcome in New York quickly erased the memory of her lonely and miserable months in London. Michael and Hilde, who as Aunt Irma had predicted, were "people made for America" were thriving.[67] Eva began to work in design and teach at the Pratt Institute within months of her arrival, and Otto soon procured a job as an engineer at the Zenith Company in Chicago. The inevitable hurdles of social adjustment were eased by the wide circle of old friends already settled in America. Laura's Riverside apartment as well as Michael's on 115th Street were right in the middle of the Upper West Side neighbourhood preferred by the Central European refugees, creating a social environment not very different from that of Budapest or Berlin.[68] Even Julius (Gyula) Holló, the Polanyis' physician in Budapest made it out and set up practice in Manhattan. In addition to the friends and relatives already mentioned above, Alfred Adler's widow and the artist Anna Lesznai, Jászi's first wife, also lived nearby. Jászi and his second wife, Laura's Viennese friend from her youth, Recha had made their home in Oberlin, Ohio since the late 1920s.[69]

The Jászis were among the first ones to greet Laura in America on her arrival. "Dearest Mausi, welcome, welcome! How good to know that you are here, safe and happy with your children. And all of them working! I have read your 'Odysee' with great emotion and joy—knowing the happy end![70] I cannot tell you how I admire your courage! You have done a good job, Mausi!"[71] To which Oszkár Jászi added in Hungarian: "Dear Mauzi, Heartfelt greetings in the new homeland, wishing you all the best, Oszkár."[72]

Recha, delighted to know that her oldest friend was near and safe, was also the first to remind Laura of the immediate reversal of roles; that as soon as they arrived, the rescued became rescuers.

There is an "aching" point in every family, Mausi. I have more than one. Shall I begin
to tell you my "Odysee," a ghastly year in which I suffered not by being an actor, but
only a spectator, in a distance. Arthur[73] arrived and was soon not *bien venue* with them.
Poor, sick, helpless. I helped him as much as I could. He died in a N. Y. Sanatorium—
alone.

   My sister's husband, whom I know only slightly (and herself I know almost as
little,) is a very decent but indolent type. Only by late November [1938] he woke up to
the idea to leave Germany. We have sent affidavits, ours and of a well to do friend, but
their turn might come—when? For Mother I have sent a preference visa. She was
sailing August 23d with the "Hansa." August 25th the boat was recalled from
Southampton. Nobody allowed to land. Poor thing! Now I have paid a passage for her
on an Italian boat but being without competition the Italians are sitting on a high horse.
I cannot get any information on which boat Mother will get accommodation, when she
will sail, etc. No news from her, though I have cabled three times, reply prepaid. It is a
nerve wrecking experience.[74]

   Recha's letters described the Jászis' efforts to help friends and relatives
flee Hitler as an all-consuming, full-time undertaking that not only exacted a
heavy mental, physical toll on the Jászis, but ate up their savings as well. "Ghosts
sit on my bedside" she wrote, capturing the anxiety that was only heightened by
their own safety. Laura's letters must have revealed her own worries to Recha[75]
with whom she shared not only their former Viennese social circle, now dispersed
all over the world, but also the agony of having a sister stranded in Hilter's
Germany. The outbreak of the war in Europe made communication with family
members in Budapest and Vienna even more fragile and increased the sense of
urgency to act on their behalf.

   Despite his relative safety, the most urgent task was to bring Sándor over.
His children did not waste any time and submitted the applications for him in
August 1938.[76] Even if his was a relatively simple case, Laura and the children
did not take any chances. By this time, they were almost certainly aware that the
Hungarian quota for 1940 was taken up entirely, even if parents over the age of
65 of American residents were exempt from quota regulations.[77] Laura asked an
old family friend, the former Hungarian Social Democrat activist, now Chicago
businessman Alexander (Sándor) Vince for help, who in turn approached the
local Representatives.[78] The latter promised to immediately intervene with the
American consul in Budapest and by February 1940, the Republican congressman
assured his constituent of his "very best efforts" in the matter, in exchange for his
"unqualified support."[79] Still, it took another year and half to complete the
preparations. Sándor's trip began on the 20th of July, 1941, and, with stopovers
in Vienna, Switzerland, Spain and Lisbon, he arrived almost a month later in New

York.[80] His meticulously organized journey, with relatives and friends to contact in case of emergency at every step of the way, was a monument to the organizational skills, "sustained efforts and considerable sacrifices" of Michael Striker.[81] It completed the transplanting of Laura's immediate family.

Although Sándor's arrival to America was the result of a truly collective effort by his children, Laura's role in reassembling the family was crucial. On her 60th birthday in February 1942, her brother Adolf summed it up in the following: "You have saved all or nearly all of what had and has meaning to, things born and formed by you and forces revolving around you in a closed and self-supporting circle. I feel that life has given you a birthday present for the 60th recurrence as few people have received in this uprooted world."[82]

The success of reuniting, in a remarkably short time, Laura's closest family, only highlighted the tragedy concerning her sister and her family. The efforts to save them, directed by Michael Polanyi, did not let up and in 1939 accomplished bringing the Szécsis' younger daughter, Edith, to England. She died there, in February 1944, probably a suicide.[83] The urgency of the Szécsis' situation became more evident by the day, even if no one could possibly foresee the full extent of the coming disaster. By September 1939, Sophie and Egon would have got their American visa. His release from the concentration camp and their freedom hinged on finding a solution for their mentally disabled son, Karl. Earlier, in 1938, relatives had offered to place him at an institution in Hungary yet back then, still hopeful to keep the family together, Sophie was reluctant to leave the boy behind.[84] Last-minute attempts to acquire a visa for him to Mexico or the Dominican Republic fell through.[85] And by the time Sophie decided to leave without her husband, it was too late. In March 1941 she and the boy were taken to the Kielce ghetto in Poland.[86] As for Egon, he was killed in the concentration camp in April of 1941.[87]

For another two years, the family miraculously managed to keep in touch with Sophie, even send her money via Hungary. In March 1942, news was relayed that the boy was taken away from her, prompting one last push to save her. By then, the family must have had some understanding of the fate of Jews taken to the East.[88] But Sophie was already beyond reach, despite the American visa waiting for her in Vienna.[89] After the spring of 1943, she was not heard from any more. "My last postcard came back with the note: 'Addressee moved to address unknown.' The rest is silence," wrote a friend to Laura.[90]

As the Nazis' hold was tightening on the Continent, there came news of other tragedies. The widow of Samuel Klatschko, Anna, starved to death, abandoned in occupied Paris. Her daughter, Lina, Laura's childhood friend made it to New York, but died shortly after.[91] The fate of Anna Klatschko, Cecile's friend from the Vilna and Vienna of their youth confirmed that Cecile's peaceful end was for the better. Laura's nephew, an "enemy alien" in a French internment camp, cut off from his wife and children who were trapped in the occupied zone, sent desperate messages to New York.[92] Recha's sister and brother-in-law in Germany perished in a concentration camp. By February 1943, she lost touch with them entirely.[93] What made Sophie's fate perhaps more difficult to accept than that of the other victims was that she had the chance to escape and, guided by moral obligation or indecision, she chose not to take it. Adolf expressed what must have been on everyone's mind, writing on receiving the news of Egon's death and Sophie's deportation. "What you write about Sophy is terrible. We cannot help but feel that Egon could have probably been saved and Sophy living with a new lease of life in America if it had not been for the unfortunate idiot boy, whose fate has in no way been changed or altered by all this. She is certainly the most tragic victim of her loyalty, to a lost cause."[94]

At the time he wrote this letter, Adolf had his own worries. Of his four children, Eszter had earlier moved back to Hungary. (She was mentioned at the beginning of this chapter and we will hear more of her fate later.) When Adolf and Lily, his second wife, had to leave Italy in the early spring of 1939, his other daughter, Vera and two sons, Thomas and Michael, stayed on in Rome to finish their studies. Vera was training to be a psychiatrist and the two sons were completing their Ph.D.'s in Enrico Fermi's institute. After unsuccessful attempts to stay closer to them, in France or England, Adolf found employment with a company in Brazil. In May 1941, the Polanyi boys, with their freshly earned degrees earned but their prospects cut off in Italy, were ready to leave. They enlisted as deck hands on a neutral merchant ship, heading for New York, with valid Italian passports but without any visas.[95] Forewarned by Adolf, Laura watched the arrival times of merchant ships in the newspapers and when six weeks later the ship docked "in a godforsaken dock on Bayonne, N.J.,"[96] she waited for them, in time to convince the authorities to take them to Ellis Island.[97] Meanwhile Adolf mobilized his connections and his company's lawyer in Washington who acquired Cuban visas for the boys.

In the course of the following months and years, Laura remained in almost daily contact with her nephews, who were cooling their heels in Cuba for over two years. She provided them with moral and financial support, while orchestrating a widespread campaign to bring them into the States. It is an extensively documented story whose value goes beyond the sheer human interest it represents; it casts a light on the *modus operandi* of Laura, her incredible grasp of the bureaucratic obstacles raised by the authorities, and the way the family pulled ranks around two of its members. Moreover, it provides an insight into the issue of the Polanyis' Jewish identity, a topic only seldom mentioned in the family's correspondence.

Within days after the boys' arrival, Laura contacted prestigious members of the Italian refugee community, including professors Giuseppe Borgese at Columbia and Lionello Venturi at the University of Chicago, Enrico Fermi, and various other potential sponsors. Everyone in the family, including all earners in both generations, was instructed to fill out affidavits for them and, at the same time, Adolf also took steps to engage his company's support (he was employed by the South American affiliate of an American company in Rio de Janeiro).[98] By an unfortunate coincidence, the State Department's visa policy had been considerably tightened to correspond exactly with the arrival of the boys. Purportedly introduced to protect the country from subversive aliens, the new visa regulations took effect on June 5th, 1941. On that day, instructions went to diplomatic and consular officers to withhold visas from "all applicants who had parents, children, husband, wife, brothers, or sisters resident in territory under the control of Germany, Italy, or Russia."[99] These instructions, meant to be secret, barred the Polanyi boys' entry on multiple counts; they had sisters, their mother, and countless relatives in Italy, Hungary, even Germany and Austria. However, following a leak, the State Department was forced to make the new policy regulations public; and the instant reaction of Laura is obvious from the photocopy of the related *New York Times* article, found in her file containing the boys' documents as well as her request for the new sets of visa application forms.[100]

More importantly, she instructed her nephews to avoid a serious mistake in the visa application.

> When you fill out the emigration application, try to make sure AT ALL COSTS that under "race" they write Hungarian. I don't know if you have taken care of the religious matters, I heard from Brazil that it was the case, it would be useful in any case. ... If they write in your application, as they do with pleasure that the race is: Hebrew, that will remain in all your documents that you will have to show at every job application, and that is not to your advantage but in your field almost prohibitive. Neither Otto nor the others claim their ancestors' race and religion![101]

It was an only slightly coded warning to the boys, intended not only to guide them through the bureaucratic procedures but to make them aware that anti-Semitism was not limited to the Fascist and Nazi countries they escaped from; that it was alive and well in the U.S. too.[102] And if they needed further proof, the fact that their application was promptly refused provided one. In July, Michael Polanyi reacted to the new visa policy and his nephews' failure to enter the States in an uncharacteristically passionate outburst:

> The Polanyi boys have been refused entry to the U.S. because they have relatives living in a Fascist country. I think they are now in Cuba awaiting the results of Mausi's further strenuous efforts to get them access to some place on the Western Hemisphere. This new law of the U.S. which prevents their entry is one of the worst piece of cruel and hypocritical legislation, pursuing a policy of antisemitism under the pretext of protecting the country against Hitler's influence.[103]

In December 1941, their application was rejected again, the refusal signed by A. M. Warren, one of the authors of the new policy.[104] Adolf, in faraway Brazil, was desperately searching for a way to bring the boys to South America but concluded that "the United States are the only reasonable hope left."[105] Despite the unfair and unjust position of the American Government, evident in the visa regulations, he had "too strong a belief in American Ideas of fairness as to accept the situation as final."[106]

As for the role of Laura in bringing the Polanyi boys to America, she displayed a commitment that went even beyond her usual determination. Always the responsible eldest sibling, she was motivated primarily by the sympathy she felt for the boys who (although not exactly children; they were 27 and 23 years of age, respectively, in 1941) had not had their own parents around to help them. Adolf, himself too far away to act, and never the model father, also delegated her as his proxy. He repeatedly asked her to look after matters, as he doubted whether "Karli has the push and ... Misi the time,"[107] and to go to Washington where her "energy and tenacity would do a lot more than all the rest put together."[108] The December 1941 rejection of the boys' application prompted Karl Polanyi to blame it all on Laura, illustrating the tensions running high and his impulsive nature. A few weeks earlier he too had recommended that she "try to push matters personnally in Washington."[109] Now he expressed disappointment: "I greatly admired you for your cautious and tactful reserve these last few months, and it came as a very bad shock to me that you, without any warning, plunged headlong again into criminal maternal activism..."[110]

An additional motive for Laura to pour all her energies into the boys' cause may have been that she felt she was handed another chance; she could help them while there was nothing left she could do for her sister. It would take an additional two years and several rounds of reviews before the two could enter the U.S. Even then, one of the brothers, eager to offer his Ph.D. in physics for defense projects, was denied clearance.[111]

But what to make of the advice Laura had given the boys: to hide the fact that they were Jews? Was this not pure opportunism? Or the chameleon-like behaviour of the parvenu German Jew Hannah Arendt satirized so memorably?[112] I think not. First of all, the existence of strong anti-Semitism in the U.S. had come as a shock to the Central-European intellectual refugees for whom Roosevelt's America was associated with the best liberal values. Laura felt she had to warn her nephews about it. After all, the Polanyi boys' future depended on their chances to work in their field; their university degrees came at a price of substantial sacrifices from Adolf's entire family. And in the Polanyis' value system, the boys' academic brilliance, their Hungarian birth, even their Italian upbringing and culture defined them more than the Jewish religion of their ancestors. They could not risk their entire future life because of one question on an application form that served, in their eyes, an anti-Semitic immigration policy.

Their Jewish ancestry was an indelible part of the Polanyis and one they had never hidden or denied. Yet they felt nothing in common with the Yiddish-speaking Eastern-European Jewish world of New York.[113] Laura's advice for her nephews about hiding their religion in the application was only one angle of a wider strategy. The future choices of Laura's children and grandchildren in their education and professional life demonstrated that the family continued in its long-standing tradition to strive for intellectual and academic excellence. They kept on producing academic high achievers who attended the best schools and rose to the highest echelons of American academic and cultural life. If, under the circustances they found in America, that meant to underplay their Jewish identity, it was a small price to pay.

The Polanyis also had the luxury to make choices free from immediate financial pressures. The majority of intellectual refugees, made up of German Jews, had to leave everything behind because of the Nazi regulations and reached America penniless. They had no choice but to rely on the refugee aid organizations, organized along ethnic and religious lines. One refugee, an assimilated German Jew, summed up the circumstances that forced him to reluctantly shift his identity in the following: "in New York, you were either Jewish or nothing; otherwise nobody would help you."[114]

While maintaining their numerous ties with fellow émigrés, Laura and her children quickly developed connections with the local non-immigrant community. The family attended the Unitarian church in Brooklyn where Laura was a highly regarded member of the congregation.[115] Her granddaughter remembered that they had to take Sunday school lessons at Laura's insistence. She also explained to her grandchildren that they chose the Unitarian church because of its ties to 16th-century Transylvania.[116] Again, a seemingly opportunistic move had originated in long-standing cultural tradition. Their membership in the Unitarian congregation was also an indication that they recognized the community-building role of the local churches in their new homeland. The family's encounter with the Quakers and Laura and Eva's temporary stay in England when they had occasion to witness their help to the refugees could have played a role as well.[117]

One last case among Laura's files demonstrates that the solidarity displayed in the rescue efforts went beyond family responsibilities and blood ties. It concerns the fate of Alex Weissberg, Eva's first husband. When we last met him, he was in a Kharkov jail, waiting for his trial. Perhaps because Weissberg was one of only a very few who never confessed to any of the crimes he was accused of, he never went to trial or received a sentence. As soon as Eva reached England, she began a relentless campaign to free him. Weissberg's valiant efforts in the Soviet Union to save Eva created a solidarity between them that survived the break-up of their marriage.

In 1936, at the time of Eva's arrest, Weissberg had solicited reference letters for Eva, regardless of the risks involved. Now the roles were reversed yet the method and the network they used remained the same. The details of this fight and his own part in it are described in Arthur Koestler's *The Invisible Writing*.[118] Koestler's efforts, motivated by his friendship with Weissberg and Eva and his growing disenchantment with Communism were reinforced by his own recent imprisonment and near-execution by Franco's forces in Spain. Eva's uncle, Michael Polanyi, played at least an equal part by contacting his colleagues, members of the community of physicists. Koestler's idea of soliciting letters from three French Nobel-Prize laureates, all Communists, masterfully combined the professional and political aspects while Michael Polanyi arranged for a separate letter from Einstein.[119] Einstein's letter and Joliot Curie's telegram were duly sent to Stalin in 1938 and although they did not achieve the freedom of Alex, they were credited with saving Alex'life.[120]

No news of his fate reached the Polanyis until April 1940 when Eva received a telegram from Aunt Irma in Budapest. Weissberg was alive and free in German-occupied Krakow, begging for help to get out of Poland.[121] Weissberg, according to the stipulations of the Molotov-Ribbentrop pact, had been among the German nationals handed over by the NKVD to the Gestapo a month earlier. He escaped from the Lublin prison and ended up in the newly established Krakow ghetto.[122]

Weissberg's letters and postcards, mailed under the Gestapo's nose in the Krakow ghetto and miraculously delivered to New York, chronicle the indomitable spirit of this "human Jack-in-the-box," in Koestler's words, and Eva and Laura's efforts to save him from the seemingly inevitable end. Hoping to reach a neutral country (since the Allies no longer had consulates granting visas in German-occupied Poland), Weissberg tried to contact Niels Bohr who could bring him to Denmark. He also urged Eva to turn, one more time, to the physicists' network.[123] A last chance to save Alex would be, she wrote to his old collegues (her own friends from the Berlin days), by now settled in the States, to get him out through Lisbon on a non-quota visa. Eva managed to collect the $600 deposit needed.[124] Then she called on Einstein, reminding him of his intervention two years earlier. In order to acquire a non-quota visa, she asked him to write to a Mr. Charles Liebmann, president of the Refugee Economic Corporation, one of the organizations assisting refugees.[125]

Einstein produced the letter in a mere five days. Interestingly, he avoided any reference to Weissberg's long stay in the Soviet Union. Instead, he emphasized his three years of imprisonment by the Germans (in fact it lasted only a few months) and made a strong case for Weissberg as a candidate for a non-quota emergency visa, not only as a potential university professor but also as a valuable expert who could contribute to the war effort.[126] Normally, a university professor applying for a non-quota visa had to have a position secured at an American institution and a two-year minimum teaching experience in Europe[127] and Weissberg did not meet these criteria.[128] But the times called for desperate measures and Einstein's name may have carried enough weight to secure Weissberg a non-quota visa. In any case, it was too late. In September 1940, a HIAS (Hebrew Sheltering and Immigrant Aid Society) official Laura had previously contacted to make travel arrangements for Weissberg informed her: "We are in receipt of a letter from Warsaw advising us that at the present time the emigration of the above named [Weissberg] is impossible for the reason that the Italian border has been closed."[129] It was the contemporary equivalent of a death sentence and the last the Polanyis heard from Weissberg for the rest of the war.

Despite the failure of the rescue mission, the efforts to save Weissberg highlighted the strength of old-world networks. First among them was the community of physicists, the forerunner of the internationalization of academia, a trend that came to be predominant by the second half of the 20th century. The reasons physics emerged as the model of international academic networks were complex and included the pioneering practice of international exchanges and collaboration from the 1920s.[130] Another Hungarian physicist, already mentioned as Michael Polanyi's friend and collegue in Berlin, the great Leó Szilárd, described how his own professional and social connections in the world of physics laid the ground for the first organized rescue efforts in 1933.[131] To these ties of solidarity, grounded in professional interests and ties, the Polanyis' social circle during their Viennese and Berlin years added layers of friendship and a shared cultural and social experience.

Attesting to his amazing resilience, Weissberg survived the war in Poland, and resurfaced in Stockholm in 1946, eventually ending his life in France.[132] His escape added a fitting postscript to the already outstanding success of the Polanyis in emigration.

In an almost equally surprising development, Laura's younger son, Ottó, decided to return to Hungary after the war. The decision prompted a carefully worded remark from the Stricker relatives, picking up the pieces of their former life among the ruins of Budapest. "I'm surprised to hear that Ottó wants to come back. Needless to say we are very glad to have him back, only wondering as for the reasons when everyone else is trying to go the other way."[133]

Ottó had been and remained a Communist since his youthful commitment in 1934 Vienna. He participated in the war-time émigré activities in Chicago, and was elected as acting secretary of the Chicago section of the "Hungarian American Relief" in April 1945. He was the representative of the "Hungarian American Democratic Council" whose president was László Moholy-Nagy, the eminent Bauhaus artist and professor at the University of Chicago.[134] As soon as the war drew to a close, the temporary unity of émigré Hungarian organizations, brought on by the relief work of the war years, were quickly dissolving into an infight between the various political agendas. While conservatives as well as members of the pre-war democratic opposition turned pro-Communist in increasing numbers and many of the émigré politicians decided to return, Jászi remained entirely sceptical.[135] In an exchange with her old friend, Laura urged him to take a stand in Hungary one last time.[136] The democratic Left in Hungary, she argued, needed his moral leadership. And the Soviet Union which, as she believed, continued to support a limited parliamentary democracy in Hungary, needed political leaders representing the ideals of the old progressive camp. Jászi, the creator of the idea of the "Switzerland of the East," a peaceful, democratic, multi-ethnic East-Central Europe, was the only one left to stop the Communist tide.[137] Jászi was not convinced. Laura's hopes for a democratic development in Hungary and the Soviets' need for his moral leadership were "pure fantasy," he replied.[138] "You cannot seriously think that the Soviet needs me. I am afraid they don't even need Károlyi who is much closer to them."[139] Jászi was soon proven right in his assessment. Soviet foreign policy and the Communist Party in Hungary insisted for another three years on their sincere desire to keep the framework of a parliamentary democracy in place. Yet the beginning of the Cold War was followed by unmistakable signs of an imminent Communist takeover.[140]

It was another indication that when it came to politics, Laura, in sharp contrast to her unerring instinct in practical matters, was driven more by wishful thinking than reality. She may have been also influenced by Ottó's plans to move back to Hungary and her maternal instinct to justify his decision. Ottó, anxious to participate in the rebuilding of a new, Communist Hungary, and prompted by the signs of increasing anti-Communism in the States, returned in 1948. By the 1950s, he rose to become a high-level functionary in the Hungarian scientific hierarchy, enjoying such limited—but by contemporary Hungarian standards, substantial—advantages as frequent trips to the West and a relatively comfortable lifestyle.

His decision to move back to Hungary also helped to maintain Laura's ties to the family's Hungarian contingent. She kept up correspondence with the relatives and sent a steady supply of much-needed and appreciated food packages.[141] As soon as the the worst years of the Cold War were over, she visited her son and her three grandchildren on an almost yearly basis.

Laura's continuing ties to Hungary resulted in her last feat of rescuing a relative, six years after the war had ended. Eszter Polanyi, Adolf's daughter survived the Holocaust and was living in Hungary when in 1951 the Communist regime introduced the internment of "former bourgeois elements" in makeshift camps in the countryside. In one last concentrated effort that had all the trademark elements of her old skills, Laura saved Eszter Polanyi from "a second deportation within seven years!"[142]

It was a case that showcased the multiple layers of the Polanyis' old loyalties and connections; it also highlighted the universality of methods, used by Laura and the family when it came to successfully fighting dictatorships, whether it was Stalin's, Hitler's or Rákosi's. Rákosi, the Communist dictator of Hungary, had been a former deputy commissar and as such, Adolf's boss, in the heady days of the Hungarian Republic of Councils in 1919. Adolf who was desperate to bring his daughter, lonely and ill, to Brazil, had already tried to contact Rákosi, "being fully convinced that my name would carry weight with him!"[143] When his efforts failed—no one was brave enough to deliver the letter—Laura wrote to Rákosi herself, reminding him of the old connections and achieving, in a matter of days, Eszter's release.[144]

Laura's regular visits to Europe highlighted the fact that her family, the Polanyis and Stickers, were now represented by a large contingent living in the United States and South America as well as spread over Europe from Hungary to Italy, Switzerland, France and England. Her visits and correspondence helped maintain the ties between them and keep up the family traditions. The collection of family documents that she preserved was only one of the signs that it was a role she consciously cultivated. Among her last notes, there were detailed lists of lesser-known Stricker ancestors and their academic and intellectual contributions.[145] After a 1957 visit to Italy where she met up with the daughter of her cousin, she reflected on the continuity of old connections with the "beautiful new ones that you represent."[146] She also sent them the family tree, for the sake of the grandchildren.[147] It was a role that she earned and cherished: to be the link between generations and the custodian of the family's history.[148]

Chapter 5:
"The Hungarian Pocahontas"

In 1957 Laura Polanyi looked back on more than half a century of her academic career. In reply to the query of an American historian, she submitted the following account:

> When in 1900 the Hungarian universities admitted women students, I was with the first group of girls which invaded the holy halls. I received there my Ph.D. in History and English Literature as subsidiary subject.
>
> I had to register my main occupations since for the Virginia Historical Society publicity and am sending you a copy. You will find that the 'occupations' seem very erratic. This is due to the fact that they were influenced by the possibilities, trends, and impossibilities of this semicentury. For example when my habilitation thesis would have been recognized as valid for an assistant professorship (*Dozentur*), my university decided never to admit women to the faculty. I turned my main interest from history to pedagogics. This was also motivated by my son and my daughter reaching the age when I would have had to send them to schools I trusted less if I did not organize a school of our own. We started it trying out most of the ideas and methods the first decennium of this century brought forth.
>
> War and Peace, defeat and occupation, revolutions and inflation supplied us with problems 1914-1924.
>
> With the approach of Fascism and Communism my historical interest revived. The planned economy of 18th century mercantilism and the trends in economics and politics of the time tempted to [sic!] historical research and comparative studies. Maria Theresia.
>
> Since October 1951 when Bradford Smith was led to me as to a Hungarian historian who could look into the question of the truthfulness of Captain John Smith's report on his alleged Hungarian adventures and thus help him with his biography of Captain John Smith, I am exclusively interested in this problem. I regard it as a great gift and privilege that I was given this opportunity to serve as a Hungarian historian to vindicate the honor and valor of America's most enthusiastic champion.[1]

This remarkable document shows Laura as the consummate historian, able to turn her own, admittedly unconventional track record into a cohesive narrative.

This chapter, an overview of Laura's intellectual and academic contributions, takes its cue from this, her own assessment. On the one hand, it treats her contributions as a continuum, regardless of the academic or intellectual field in which she made her mark. For Laura's auspicious beginnings in academia, her pedagogical experiments, her attempts to convert her Soviet

123

experiences into a scholarly form, and, finally, her contribution to American historiography, all reflected her lifelong struggle to find a middle ground between her scholarly ambitions and the enormous challenges of her life and times. The result was, at best, mixed; hence her need to explain the obstacles she had faced.

Laura's work on Captain John Smith in the 1950s was so well-received that it earned her the epithet of a "latter-day Pocahontas."[2] Yet it was not only Laura Polanyi who "saved" John Smith by restoring his reputation; the American hero amply returned the favour. He made, figuratively speaking, the last few years of Laura's life by far her most rewarding in terms of academic success. These last years brought her a string of accolades, from numerous publications and glowing reviews, to membership in the American Academy of Political and Social Science.

At first glance, the life of the early seventeenth-century English soldier, explorer, and adventurer John Smith could not have been further removed from the experiences of Laura Polanyi, by then in her seventies and, to all appearances, content to be the mother and grandmother of a large and successful family of refugee intellectuals. The task, to pronounce on the reliability of John Smith in light of his Hungarian and Transylvanian adventures, started off as a minor research assignment. Yet, the figure of the oft-doubted Smith and the task of vindicating him triggered an unexpectedly strong response in Laura, followed by a spectacular resurgence of her creative and professional energies. There is no doubt that, with the combination of her language skills and background in Hungarian history, she was the perfect choice for the job. Conversely, it was the perfect vehicle for her own, long-dormant intellectual and academic ambitions; and once she had become convinced of Smith's credibility, the task of restoring Smith's reputation became inseparable from Laura's own professional vindication.

It was a task that gave her a chance to validate the ambitions and promises of those early years. It also allowed her to reconstruct, in retrospect, her professional life as one in which the first period of academic success was presented not as an unrequited promise but as preparation for the crowning achievement of the late years.

To examine the connections between her education and early years in Hungarian academia and the achievements of her later years in its American counterpart, we have to revisit the beginnings, in the last years of the 19th century. Looking back on her path to academia, Laura claimed to belong to the first group of girls to attend university.[3] Technically, she was in fact in "the first group of girls which invaded the holy halls"[4] but, as she was well aware, a small number of women had been allowed to enroll at the faculties of arts and medicine since 1896, ahead of her group.[5] Did she start her account with this snappy opening to highlight her achievement? Rather, she did it to underscore her pride in and loyalty to the small cohort of women, her high-school class, that was the first one graduating from a properly accredited girls' high school.

Laura was almost certainly the only one in her group who had a mother with a high-school diploma. Cecile's diploma from Vilna's Mariinski' higher girls' school in 1878, preserved among the family's documents, testified to a surprisingly wide breadth of education that made her unique in her generation.[6] Yet, despite the curriculum's impressive offering of academic subjects, it was obviously geared to provide young women, mainly daughters of the Russian nobility and upper-middle class with a suitable set of drawing-room skills rather than to prepare them for university studies.[7]

Laura's *alma mater*, the Girls' High School of the National Association for Women's Education, on the other hand, matched the rigorous academic standards of boys' gymnasia, the university preparatory high schools of the period. It provided students with a curriculum tipped towards the humanities and languages, yet balanced with sciences, mathematics, and a sprinkling of art. The final examination, the *matura*, the only prerequisite of university admittance, consisted of written and verbal exams in eight subjects.[8] With the exception of physics, in which she only achieved a passing grade, Laura received "outstanding" marks (the equivalent of A) in five subjects and "good" in two, graduating with a "good" overall result.[9]

The diploma also listed her teachers by name and qualification. With one exception, all of them had a doctoral degree, which highlights the exceptionally high calibre of the school's faculty. Two of her teachers were among the leading Hungarian academics of the time and held chairs at Budapest University while also teaching at the Girls' High School. Zsolt Beöthy, the girls' idolized teacher of Hungarian Literature and Philosophy was the leading literary historian of the period.[10] His university and high-school textbooks raised generations in the nationalistic tradition.[11] Regardless of the merits of his literary theories, he was a champion of women's access to higher education. So too was Manó Beke, a mathematician of international renown and a university professor, who later even joined the Association of Feminists. These scholars taught at the girls' gymnasium to prove that, given equal chances, young women were capable of reaching the highest levels of learning.

The president of the graduation examination board was Henrik Marczali, member of the Hungarian Academy and professor at Budapest University.[12] It was an auspicious meeting between the period's leading historian and the young Laura (if not necessarily one under the best of circumstances; in History, she received only "good," the equivalent of B); for Marczali was to become Laura's professor in her university years and, in time, her doctoral supervisor and mentor.

The most influential and prolific Hungarian historian of the period, Marczali was also a fascinating personality whose rise in turn-of-the-century Hungarian academia showcased the liberal values of the era.[13] The son of a rabbi, he was raised according to the principles of Pestalozzi, the famous Swiss educator of the late 18th-early 19th century who advocated the child's right to follow his own pace. He received home schooling until the age of 10 and graduated from high school at 14.[14]

Marczali was instrumental in the modernization of the Hungarian university and high-school history curricula in the 1880s and 90s. His versatility and productivity became legendary: he published highly original monographs on such diverse topics and periods as the Emperor Joseph II, the first medieval Hungarian dynasty, the Árpáds, the Hungarian 18th century, and a biography of Maria Theresa, among others. He edited and wrote six volumes of world history, published between 1898 and 1905, and edited many volumes of Hungarian historical sources of the 18th and 19th centuries.

Laura attended the Faculty of Arts of Budapest University for four and a half years. Within this period, the number of women students grew steadily, from 45 to 132.[15] Still, they comprised only a small fraction of the student body that averaged 1,602 students during these years.[16] The National Association for Women's Education set up a residence for women students (named after the liberal minister of education, Gyula Wlassics who in 1895 codified women's access to post-secondary education) as well as a University Women's Room, a study room to withdraw to between classes.[17]

Laura's university registration book provides valuable information on her university life. In addition to her personal data, it lists the courses she took, along with the names and signatures of her professors and her exam results.[18] When Laura married in 1904, her name change to Mrs. Sándor Stricker, née Laura Pollacsek, was noted. This is, to my knowledge, the only document known referring to the Magyarization of the family name from Pollacsek to Polányi in 1912.[19]

The course list of her first year reads like a who's who of the history of humanities in Hungary, from Bernát Alexander, the leading philosopher of the era and mentor to a whole generation of young philosophers, including Lukács, through Marczali and Beöthy, to Pál Gyulai, the great literary historian. Laura's courses spanned a wide assortment of fields from philosophy, psychology and aesthetics to Hungarian literature and linguistics, Hungarian and world history, classical literature, and art history. Her second-year courses weighed heavily towards Hungarian history, with six courses (lectures as well as seminars), although in the second semester Laura added Roman history and art, as well as five classes of French literature.

In her third and fourth years, the course load was reduced by approximately half and from then on, history, Hungarian literature and language dominated her studies, although she continued to attend Alexander and Beöthy's philosophy and aesthetics classes. Beöthy must have remained one of her favourite professors, just as during the high-school years, and she took at least one but more often two of his courses in each semester. She also took at least one course a year taught by Marczali. The topics, covering Hungary's history from the earliest times through 16th-century historical sources to its economic history in the 14th to 16th century, to Joseph II and the 1848 revolution, are further evidence of his versatility as a historian.

Finally, the registration book also listed Laura's grades and exam results as overwhelmingly "outstanding" and "excellent," and the information that, as a result, she was exempt from tuition in almost each of her semesters. The fact that for most of her university years, she worked part-time at the Statistical Library and prepared, with her cousin Ervin Szabó, the *Bibliographia Economica Universalis*, gives some indication of young Laura's energies and ambitions. It also helps explain the shock her family and friends must have felt upon her sudden marriage and the interruption of her studies in 1904.[20]

In 1909, she defied expectations again and returned as a full-fledged academic, successfully defending her doctoral thesis in History, with Aesthetics and English Literature as subsidiary subjects. The doctoral diploma was issued in May 1909;[21] there is no information on how long she had worked on her thesis whose shortened version was published in the *Közgazdasági Szemle* [Economic Review] in the same year.[22] The requirements for a doctoral degree, compared to today's North American academic standards, were perhaps less strenuous (there was no course requirement and the size of the dissertation was considerably smaller), yet it was still a significant measure of academic excellence. In that place and age where titles (be they based on birth or merit) were taken very seriously and students of law and medicine earned the doctorate on graduation, a doctorate in history would certainly suggest one's ambition geared toward an academic career.

The suggestion for the topic, the economic policy of Charles III (Charles VI as Habsburg Emperor) almost certainly came from Marczali who had a long-standing interest in both economic history and Hungary's early-18th-century history. Laura's wide-ranging interests in the humanities, reflected in her choice of university courses, seemed to predestinate her for a topic with a more universal appeal. Yet her work experience in the Statistical Library and the editing of the *Bibliographia* demonstrated that she was drawn to the clarity and objectivity of economics and statistics. At a time when economic history was in its infancy, this experience also made her singularly well suited to the task.

Charles III was not among the most popular Hungarian rulers. He came to the throne following the repression of the Rákoczi-uprising, led by the Transylvanian prince who united anti-Catholic, anti-Habsburg and anti-feudal forces. Rákóczi's defeat was followed by the revival of the Counter-Reformation in Hungary and the redistribution of estates to pro-Habsburg nobles. The most striking aspect of Laura's dissertation is the objectivity with which she treats the Emperor's economic policies, without a hint of the nationalistic rhetoric rampant in contemporary Hungarian historiography. True, others before her, most importantly Marczali, had prepared the field. Hungarian historians of the late 19th century had begun to separate the Habsburgs' economic policies from their religious and political decrees and proved that Habsburg-led efforts for Hungary's economic modernization were frustrated by the Hungarian nobility's selfish clinging to their feudal privileges.[23]

To this two-dimensional picture, which presented the ruler's intentions on the one hand and the opposing Hungarian nobles' interests on the other as diametrically opposing, her study added new depth. The more complex model she outlined took into consideration the initial economic conditions found in the Hungarian lands, the devastation brought on by the Turkish occupation, as well as the compromises of the dynastic policy itself. The sum of these factors, she concluded, reinforced the initial differences in the two, Austrian and Hungarian halves of the Habsburg Empire. Paradoxically, by the time of the *Pragmatica Sanctio* (Charles' decree that made the two constitutionally indivisible), the economic development of the Austrian and Hungarian parts became irreversibly divergent.[24]

Laura's dissertation, a solidly researched and convincingly argued study, conveyed its author's maturity as an historian. The choice of a highly quantifiable topic and her emphatically objective treatment of it (as if she wanted to demonstrate that women were capable of serious scientific work) provided further proof that she was able to stand up to a field entirely occupied by men. Contrary to her expectations, however, it was an achievement that remained on paper and failed to translate into a faculty position. I have not found any documentary evidence proving that the University did in fact change its policy regarding women's habilitation that year as Laura stated in her 1957 letter; but if it did, it would have certainly fit well into the trend of a rising backlash against women's gains in higher education.

The next couple of years in Laura's life represented a period of self-reflection when, with the academic avenue blocked, she searched for a new intellectual challenge. The months following the completion of her doctorate were spent with long walks, "digesting," taking time off for herself and the children, who provided her with "new experiences on which to ponder."[25] It was during this period, in October 1910, that she went to see Freud in Vienna. She asked for a recommendation to Sándor Ferenczi, the Hungarian psychiatrist whose reputation was just emerging. "The most beautiful and interesting female patient of my first office hour wants to undergo a thorough cure with you. I don't need to recommend Dr. Stricker to you," wrote Freud to his Hungarian disciple.[26] Freud's comment indicates that Laura may have met Ferenczi socially before; in any case, she seems to have changed her mind and never went through with the cure, nor even looked up Ferenczi. (As a disappointed Ferenczi reported to Freud two months later, "instead of the patient with the beautiful eyes whom you sent me ... but who didn't come,"[27] it was Cecile who went to see him.[28]

Laura's hesitation seems to indicate that she was considering going into therapy. Three years later she did in fact go through some sort of nervous breakdown and, at that time, spent a few months at the Bircher-Brenner clinic, the same establishment where Cecile had previously taken a short course in psychoanalysis.[29] At the same time, as a young mother of two, she had a personal and professional interest in this new and promising field; it had so much to say about children's development and the long-term impact of mistakes parents make in raising them. By the spring of 1911, only months after her visit to Freud, she was ready to embark on a new project, an experimental kindergarten, that would provide her with an intellectual and practical challenge while, at the same time, would ensure that her own children received the best possible early education.

Laura's interest in education went back to her university years, no doubt sparked by her own position in the vanguard of women's education. She quickly developed a reputation as an expert on educational issues, especially those concerning young women. In 1905 she participated in a debate on the necessary skills for young women of the educated middle class at a Freemason meeting[30] and in 1908 was elected a member of the National League for Public Education.[31] These engagements contributed to legitimizing her expertise in the public eye. Ferenczi's letter to Freud in February 1912 reported among the latest successes of their movement that "the beautiful Frau Dr. Stricker (who once looked you up in Vienna) is going to give the teachers a lecture on Ostwald, Payat (?), and you. In so doing, she is advertising her private school, in which teaching is being done according to your principles, and at the same time nudism and love of art are being advanced."[32]

Preoccupied with the success of the psychoanalytic movement, Ferenczi apparently failed to take note of his own important role in inspiring Laura to open her kindergarten. He was in fact the first to apply the Freudian principles to education. In his 1908 lecture at the First International Psychoanalytical Conference in Salzburg he gave a brilliant and highly influential lecture on the topic "What Practical Tips for the Rearing of Children Come from Freudian Experiences?" published in both German and Hungarian in the same year under the title "Psychoanalysis and Education."[33]

The advertisement for Laura's kindergarten outlined her venture's mission as a double task: to fill the gap before the beginning of public education at age six and to provide a broadly defined, non-religious moral education for young children. She relied heavily on Ferenczi's argument that present-day education, including moral education based on repression, literally acts as a breeding ground for various neuroses.[34] The alternative, a non-dogmatic moral education, based on honesty and tolerance, would result in the raising of healthier adults and, consequently, a healthier society.[35] Laura's articles borrowed liberally from the Ferenczi article; but where Ferenczi wrote "non-dogmatic," clearly referring to the harmful effects of religious indoctrination, Laura went a step further to define her goal (and using the expression as an alternate name for her kindergarten) as "Secular Moral Education."[36]

It would be tempting to trace the origins of Laura's kindergarten back to the German kindergarten movement of the 19th century.[37] Early childhood education was a topic frequently discussed in the Hungarian bourgeois feminist press and the liberal tradition of women taking their children's education into their own hands must have been an inspiration to Laura. However, in a departure from the educational philosophy of Froebel that inspired the German kindergarten movement, her pre-school was primarily envisaged as an attempt to apply Freudian psychology to pedagogical practice. Despite the international influences, her experiment was rooted in turn-of-the-century Hungary, reflecting the faith of

Laura's generation that education and the alternative institutions of the counterculture community were to produce a morally, politically and socially conscious, progressive middle class in Hungary.

In a 1912 lecture given at the Miskolc branch of the Sociological Society, Laura used the occasion not only to promote her pedagogical experiment but also to outline the connection between her school and the wider aims of their reform movement.[38] Every political and ideological movement realized, she said, that the key to the future was in the education of the young generation. The indoctrination of the young was a priority from the Catholic-Protestant struggles to the late 19th-century French state's efforts for a secular civic education. In their fight for the future Hungary, the forces of progression ought to focus their efforts on the education of the young.[39]

According to the documents of the kindergarten, carefully preserved in the family archives, Laura opened the school in the fall of 1911 and kept it in operation for two school years. The publicity, preceding the opening, demonstrated for the first time Laura's considerable public relations skills in promoting her projects and causes. The advertising campaign that included newspaper ads, lectures at the Freemasons and the Sociological Society, as well as word of mouth, was kicked off in *The Woman and Society*, the bulletin of the Association of Feminists. At the time, in 1911, Laura already had reservations about the feminist programme and leadership. She must have realized, however, that the Association's membership provided the only potential clientele for her school. Putting her qualms aside, Laura took advantage of an educational conference, organized by the Association of Feminists in May 1911. As the newsletter reported, she gave "an attractive and interesting lecture to point out what we should refrain from if we want to assure the young child's healthy physical and mental development. She emphasized that the child's self-awareness and personality remains the same during his/her entire adult life; thus he/she will carry the same almost unchanged notions that had been imprinted on his/her memory at the beginning of her mental life."[40] In September of the same year, she followed up on her lecture with an article, trying to convince her "fellow feminists" that "they also have to strive to create a new type of mother."[41] This new, "conscious mother" should raise her children with the benefit of the new child psychology and in the company of other children whose parents think along the same lines.[42]

Laura herself was the model of the "conscious mother." In the above-cited article she referred to Freud's advice: "we have to avoid the extreme and frequent outwardly signs of our love for the child, such as kisses, hugs, etc. According to Freud's theory, this will raise in the child an excessive expectation towards sexual life."[43] A passage of Eva Zeisel's memoirs provides a glimpse into the workings of the Freudian principles in the raising of Laura's children: "we were not a family where physical contact was usual."[44]

The second part of Laura's article, as well as separate information sheets provided detailed information on her pedagogical plans.[45] Since the children were able to complete the regular school curriculum in 2-3 hours, the schoolday—3-4 hours in total, five days a week—also included instruction in gymnastics, music and dance. In these, Laura relied on the methods introduced by the period's most progressive, fashionable pedagogical movements—gymnastics according to Mensendieck and Dalcroze's eurythmics. In addition, the school offered lessons in German, French, and English, as well as clay modeling and pastel painting.[46] A declaration, to be signed by each parent secured the parents' co-operation in the school's programme as well as in financial, hygienic and pedagogical matters. On these documents, the school's name was already indicated as "Co-operative Private Education," the "private" referring to the quality of the care these children were used to (habitually, they would have been privately educated at home until about the age of 10) and the "co-operative," to the aim of fulfilling the children's need for socialization as well as the co-operation between parents, children and school.

Judging from the number of pupils—according to the surviving documents and photographs, it never rose over 12 in each of its two years of operation—we can assume that the school was not a financially profitable enterprise. The fee, 250 crowns per semester (in comparison, Laura's university tuition fee a few years earlier was 76 crowns per semester) should have covered most of the operating costs,[47] and Laura could also rely the financial backing of her husband, if the need arose.

The kindergarten operated from the family's residence, under 83 Andrassy ut. The building was just a few blocks down from no. 2 of the same street, where the Pollacseks had lived in their most prosperous period, before 1900. Laura and her family occupied one of the spacious flats on the main floor and had the use of the small city garden, itself overlooking the park-like section of the boulevard called Octogon.

The small group of children was easily accommodated in the single classroom that was most probably set up in the Strickers' apartment. The layout of the room was traditional, with the blackboard in the front, and the pupils' desks in neat rows, but the children's relaxed posture, the flower arrangements, the abundant natural light, and, most of all, the small number of students made all the difference. Weather permitting, the class moved into the garden. While properly although far from uniformly dressed in the classroom, outside, in the idyllic setting of trees and trellises, the children would sit around a large table, in short black leotards and barefooted. "Aunt Mausi" conducted the lesson, with another teacher at a side table taking the minutes.[48]

The regular elementary-school subjects: arithmetic, reading, writing were taught by József Migray, an old friend of Adolf Polanyi. As an avowed anarchist, he must have been barred from teaching in the state school system.[49] In the second year, Laura hired a young Swiss woman from Geneva to teach eurythmics at the kindergarten. *Mlle* Jeanne recalled her memories of Budapest 66 years later, along with the humility the Polanyis often inspired in outsiders:

> Dear Sir,
>
> In the spring of 1913, Mausi hired me in Geneva to teach rythmique in the kindergarten she had established for her young children in Budapest. In the fall, I returned to Budapest to also teach at the lyceum that Cecilia founded on top of a modern apartment building where Michael and his mother lived next to a beautiful courtyard.
>
> I would often eat with the family that was very close, with Cecilia's children who adored her, often visiting. Karly was the most brilliant of them all, exceptionally talented in every field. In the middle of the debates on Kant's "Critique of Pure Judgment" in Hungarian and German ... I often felt lost![50]

Among the documents preserved by Laura Polanyi there are dozens of crayon drawings made by her pupils under the tutelage of Dezsö Czigány, an outstanding artist and member of the leading modernist group, the "Eights."[51] Laura herself gave the lessons of "secular moral education."[52] Attesting to the relaxed spirit of the school, the children addressed by her family nickname, as "Aunt Mausi."

The minutes of the lessons reveal the topics covered, ranging from the origins of life to sexual reproduction, the current Socialist strikes, the moral of the caveman and everything else in between. The questions, gently but firmly raised by Laura, were clearly pointed at all those "taboos," whose repression would make the children vulnerable, later in life, to neuroses. Compared to the accepted pedagogical practice of the period, the classroom discussions were extremely liberal and democratic, allowing every child to freely express themselves in a time when in a regular classroom or even in polite company, children were forbidden to speak to adults without being asked. At the same time, the lessons were carefully structured and even the most-innocent-sounding questions were loaded with psychological meaning. There is not one instance of Laura letting herself derailed from her set course by the spontenous and at times truly amusing turns of discussion; it is obvious that she took her pedagogical and Freudian principles seriously, maybe a touch too earnestly.

She also prepared progress reports, based on the minutes and the questionnaires, to be filled out by the parents, for the regular parent-teacher conferences. These fit well into the school's philosophy that prescribed an unusual degree of parent participation in its life. In sharp contrast to regular schools where parents had no choice but to comply with the school's authority, the parent-teacher meetings of Laura's school became discussion groups, where parents were asked to voice their concerns and generally participate in the decisions concerning the curriculum.[53] Both the questionnaires and the meetings reported unqualified success, revealing the expectations and values of the parents who would send their children to an experimental school. The minutes of the parents' meeting are full of praise for the children's progress, independence and creativity, and the honesty and truthfulness of the school's philosophy.[54]

Two of the kindergarten's pupils went on to become famous artists and the minutes of the classes provide sometimes amusing sometimes eerie signs of their future careers. One of them, Laura's own daughter is shown on a classroom picture sitting in the first row— "always in the first row, naturally," she would point out with her self-deprecating humour in an interview[55]—foreshadowing the self-assurance with which she went on to her trailblazing life and career. Responding to the obligatory question of the teacher, "What are you going to do in the summer vacation?" she would reply without hesitation: "I am going to paint."[56] As for little Arthur Koestler, he would sit with a brooding expression in the last row. Whenever the discussion became animated, he frequently had to be reminded to let the others put a word in edgewise.[57] To the question: "Why are we studying?" followed by the other children predictable reply, "So that we become more intelligent," Koestler would promptly answer with a less conventional: "So that we become more famous," revealing his later, notorious ambition.[58] And with the discussion veering to the Titanic's disaster and how people learn about events like that, little Arthur would hint at his future calling when pronouncing: "because the journalist always travels and sees things."[59]

In Chapter 1 I already quoted Koestler's memories of the kindergarten in a different context. There, he set Laura's "somewhat confused pedagogical ideas" straight.[60] In his memoirs, Koestler then went on to describe, in his habitual sarcastic vein, the "extremely stimulating lessons."[61]

> One day we heard stories about 'primitive man'—a near-gorilla who lived in caves,
> wore animal skins, and hunted wild beasts with clubs; the next, we were given
> coloured crayons and told to express our feelings by drawing anything that came into
> our heads while a gramophone played 'Santa Lucia' and the Barcarole from 'The Tales
> of Hoffman.' On still another memorable day, Mrs. Lolly [Mausi's fictional name in
> Koestler's memoirs] startled us all by explaining that her two children (both of whom
> attended the class) had come out of her own tummy, where she was now hatching a
> third, and that this was the way all children were born. This, indeed, was food for
> thought. It led me to ask my mother for more explicit information during a family
> *jour*—and to my abrupt withdrawal from the school.[62]

In addition to being the only eyewitness account of Laura's kindergarten,
the above passage serves as an example of the mixture of truth and fiction literary
memoirs are made of. As for the topics discussed, Koestler's memories proved to
be remarkably correct; the documents support him in every little detail. He is
curiously mistaken, however, when it comes to much more substantial facts; as
the documents show, he in fact started the kindergarten in September 1911, not
1910, as he stated a few paragraphs later. While that may have been an honest
mistake, the story of his withdrawal from the kindergarten is difficult to explain
as a lapse of memory; according to a fair number of documents, he stayed
enrolled, happily chatting away in the classes until the end of the school year,
June 1912.[63] In September 1912, he started grade one.

As for Koestler's motives to alter the history of his school career, there
may have been several. In recalling his earliest memoires of sexual nature, among
them the fascination with one of the little girls in his class, he may have wanted to
shorten the time spent in her company in order to exaggerate the impact. At the
same time, the fictitious description of his mother's reaction served the purpose
of presenting her as overly stern and prudish, in contrast to his own emerging
voracious sexual appetite.

Incidentally, this short passage in Koestler's autobiography within the
context of the documents of the kindergarten also adds a strong argument to the
recent debate concerning Koestler's Jewish identity. In Koestler's recent, much
praised and debated biography, his Jewishness was presented as the "key to his
personality and life story."[64] According to his biographer, that was especially the
case for his childhood. Recalling his childhood memories, Koestler consistently
repressed and downplayed this part of his identity, denied his encounters with
Jewish religious tradition and anti-Semitism.[65] His claims that he and his family
were assimilated, says the biographer, were born out of his later denial and

repression of his Jewishness and should not be taken at face value.[66]

True, the documents of the kindergarten helped to catch Koestler in the act of shifting dates, even changing important details of his childhood when it served the various motives of his adult, autobiographer self. At the same time, those same documents proved him right in characterizing his upbringing and environment as emancipated. In the minutes of the lessons, there was not a single reference to Jewish religion or religion of any kind. In the discussions about the origins of life, the children's questions were answered according to the latest scientific position, translating the terms of Darwinism into images more accessible for children (hence the frequent references to "cavemen").

These children obviously came from secular families, with parents who knowingly sent them to a secular environment. Two of the names on the class list, both well-known intellectuals, one an artist, the other a leading Socialist journalist, indicate the socio-economic background of the families whose needs the kindergarten served. For these progressive, by all accounts mostly Jewish, assimilated intellectuals and artists, the kindergarten filled an important void, providing a substitute for religious indoctrination, as a sort of alternative Sunday school.[67] Koestler's mother may have been prudish when it came to early sexual education, even if she did not take little Arthur out of school. But had she been part of the traditional, non-assimilated, religious Jewish world Koestler's recent biographer insists on putting her, she would have never enrolled him, not even for a few weeks, at a school that proudly advertised as its aim to substitute dogmas with a "secular moral education."

The kindergarten was a true synthesis of Laura's theoretical interest in pedagogy and psychoanalysis and her practical need to provide her own children with expert but personalized care and education. In her interpretation, as one of the key missions of the democratic counterculture, it also fulfilled a crucial public service. Finally, the balancing act of juggling different tasks and intellectual levels, providing her 5-6-year-old charges with carefully structured "secular moral education" lessons, analyzing them for the parents, promoting her school to possible clients and explaining its significance to her wider intellectual community kept her, literally and figuratively, on her toes.

If psychoanalysis was first discovered by the mother, pedagogy was initially the daughter's field of expertise. Inspired perhaps by the success of Laura's kindergarten, Cecile launched her own pedagogical entreprise in September 1912. In August, she published a full-page ad in *The Woman and Society*, announcing the opening of a Women's Lyceum.[68] The ad revealed lofty ambitions: the Lyceum was to be a "post-graduate scientific course for Hungarian women" with "regular lectures in physics, chemistry, biology, musicology, art history, French literature, German literature, psychology, pedagogy, sociology, economics, technology, hygiene, and art" and seminars as well as additional lectures in "law, electricity, monism, literature, aesthetical methods, design, psychological questions, nutrition, etc."[69] Operating out of in Cecile's apartment, the Lyceum's preliminary list of invited lecturers was a virtual who's who of modern Hungarian arts, literature and sciences; one can almost picture Cecile making sure that "everybody who counts" got on her list.

. The final, detailed programme of the Lyceum's first school year was printed in a 22-page brochure, and contained a much reduced but still impressive list of intellectual luminaries.[70] On the copy preserved by the family, however, many of the names and titles were crossed out with Cecile's unmistakable handwriting. In the end, it seems that of the 36 originally advertised courses and lecturers only 17 remained. Even Laura's course on Pedagogy was, apparently, cancelled. The first year of the Lyceum's existence was also its last. From the fall of 1912, Cecile also advertised a Dalcroze course either as a desperate measure to boost enrollment or, more likely, to make use of the expertise of Swiss teacher Laura had hired for her kindergarten.[71]

From its beginnings, the Women's Lyceum was a barely disguised takeoff on the Free School for Social Studies, the popular open university of the Sociological Society, copying much of the latter's programme and faculty, without its resources and clearly thought-out curriculum. Besides, Cecile's entreprise had no obvious, specific audience since her target, "the scientifically and esthetically highly cultured Hungarian woman,"[72] was already accomodated by the courses of the Free School. Or, if this hypothetical woman was more conservatively inclined, she could attend the lectures of the Christian Socialist Open University that also targeted women. Finally, if she belonged to the younger generation, the Galileo Circle, the leftist students' organization founded in 1908 also held courses and lectures which were popular with young university student women, both as students and instructors.

It just may be that if the Lyceum did not have any obvious function to fulfill (and given that its establishment was timed conspicuously close to Laura's pedagogical experiment), its only genuine purpose was to allow Cecile to share some of the limelight enjoyed by her children. With her daughter at the peak of her creative activities, respected for her intellect as much as admired for her beauty, and with her son Karl becoming the leader of the progressive students, Cecile may have felt the need to prove her worth. Perhaps it was just another coincidence that as soon as Laura and her family moved to Vienna, leaving the kindergarten behind, Cecile did not continue with her own pedagogical experiment. The Lyceum, if it ever had any students, ceased to exist after its first year.

The Strickers' move to Vienna in 1913 brought an end to Laura's association with the kindergarten, even if, as she claimed in her 1957 letter, it went on to function.[73] The Strickers' third child was born in November 1913, only a few months before the war and the end of an entire era.

In her 1957 summary of her life and aspirations, Laura made short shrift of the following decade and its life-shattering events — "War and peace, defeat and occupation, revolutions and inflation supplied us with problems 1914-1924"[74]—to quickly cut to the next station in her professional life, her revival of historical interest and the research into Maria Theresa's mercantilist policies.[75]

As I mentioned in the previous chapter, Laura's study of the Habsburg empress's economic policy, submitted as her eldest son, Michael's doctoral dissertation, complemented the topic of her own doctoral thesis on the economic policy of Charles VI. The approximately 450 type-written pages, preserved in the family's archives, contain the results of preliminary research that largely followed the work she had started in her dissertation.[76] In a questionnaire listing her publications in 1957, she referred to it as "Monograph on Maria Theresa's Economic Policy, Unpublished," indicating the dates of its completion as 1928-32.[77]

In Chapter 3 I described the events that rendered Laura's Maria Theresa-project obsolete, as well as the new project that grew out of her Soviet experience. I also attempted to reconstruct the possible personal and political motives that kept her interest alive in the planned study of the Soviet Union of the early 1930s. Despite the considerable amount of time and effort that went into its research and preparation, it was her one project that never passed the stage of research, although not for lack of trying.

On Laura's death, her daughter found files of bibliography, quotations and references for a survey on the years 1934-35 in the Soviet Union. The main argument of the planned study, in the words of Eva Zeisel, was to show that "Russia is the safeguarder of the Western culture, like the monasteries were the safe-guarders of the heritage of the antiquity."[78] According to Eva Zeisel, her mother had completed her research and organized the material collected in the Soviet Union by 1943. This is confirmed by a letter of Laura to a British friend, Mrs. Armitage in which she described the scope and direction of her planned study:

Ever since I have been in Russia, more precisely, since my arrival to the S.U. in 1934 [in fact, she arrived there as early as 1932] my attention was captivated by the cultural transformation engineered and going on in every field of life. It was the time of the Second Five-Year-Plan and all decent citizens, ambitious specialists, and, really, young and old in the S.U. were primarily interested in the results of production and began reading the papers in checking these numbers. I for my part, realizing that other essential things were going on, too, read editorials, checked the news and tendencies in social relationships, education, revaluation of history, revaluation of man and life, revaluation of emotional and family relationships ...[79]

The letter confirmed that in 1943 Laura still took Stalin's official line at face value as wholeheartedly as she had in 1934-35. While she was in the company of a whole army of Western intellectuals, sympathizers and fellow travelers, very few had her share of close encounters of the Stalinist terror; yet, she did not let these experiences interfere with her decidedly positive view of the Stalinist system, at least in its form before 1936.

It seems clear to me now—she went on in her 1943 letter—that the policy to make a happy family of the Soviet people—nationalities, classes (worker, peasants, intelligentsia, generations, plants and kolkhozes, believers and unbelievers—was not only set but was deemed of such first class importance that not even the consequences of the unforeseen murder of Kirov (in December 1934) could prevent that 1935 was a year devoted to teach the people the pursuit of happiness.[80]

From 1943 on, there were other signs that pointed to Laura's determination to bring her Soviet project to fruition. In a letter to Professor Alexander Baltzly, Laura drew up an ambitious plan of a collective volume that would have included her contribution: "Russia, its life and culture in transition: the time of the Second Five Year Plan" to be written by herself and a co-author, a young Ph.D. graduate recommended by Baltzly.[81] A year later, she reconsidered. Responding to a James Stern, who was referred to her by a mutual friend to assist "on some material you have assembled for a book on the 'latest trends in Russian home politics,'"[82] she cited the latest military and political developments of January 1944 that made her "inhibitions personal and political" even stronger, prompting her to wait, until she can "show the historical trend of a question which for the time being can only be approached by treading on peoples' most sensitive feelings."[83]

Then in November 1946, Laura took up the project one last time, to the point of considering collaboration with yet another young historian. In a letter, dated 7 November 1946, Ronald Thompson acknowledged the receipt of the material Laura sent him through her daughter.[84] The date coincided with Laura's son-in-law, Hans Zeisel's appointment to the University of Chicago Law School and the Zeisels' move to Chicago. Thompson was already acquainted with Laura's niece, Marika Szecsi, who taught economics at the University of Chicago.[85] In the process of completing his degree, Thompson was teaching several courses on Russian and Soviet history. He seemed to continue a previous discussion on co-authoring a book on the Soviet Union. Based on the material collected by Laura, he paraphrased the thesis in the following: "between the difficult days of the First Five-Year Plan and the still more difficult days of the Moscow purge, the period [between January 1934 and December 1936] represents a momentary easing of the situation, a time when 'life was becoming more joyous' and when, *as you so well demonstrate, Soviet humanism was blossoming in all directions.*"[86] There is no sign of further communication between the two, perhaps because Laura never went through with the move from New York to the Zeisels' household in Chicago. The conclusion of Ronald Thompson's letter, however, eloquently expressed his awe, typical of young American scholars, in meeting this family of Old-World erudition. He was also among the first observers to comment on the Polanyis' history as a worthy academic subject.

> I was very pleased to hear your brother, Professor Michael Polanyi, when he spoke at the University here last month. It seems to have been something of an international reunion for the Polanyi family—your brother from England, your daughter from New York, Tomi from the Philippines, Vera from Argentina [Adolf's children], George [Stricker, Laura's son] and Marika as native Chicagoans. And all of you originally from Budapest—there should be quite a history in that family dispersion alone![87]

Despite the time and energy spent on collecting its material, the Russian project never came to realization. The final months of the war and the first months of peace-time were filled with hopes for (or fear of) news from relatives and friends. Further hopes were pinned on the post-war developments in Hungary and the possibility of a democratic outcome. Hungarian émigrés of all persuasions looked at the Soviet Union, the new master of Eastern Europe, with mixed feelings and expectations. The beginning of the Cold War made the position vis-à-vis the Soviet Union even more complicated. These developments clearly advised against the publication of a study on recent Soviet policies, even for someone less diplomatic and conscious of "personal and political inhibitions" than Laura.

The late 1940s pass largely unaccounted for in the intellectual biography of

Laura. The only indication of any work on her part is a reference letter, written for her in 1957 by her brother Karl. It indicated that she had acted as his assistant "in the field of economic history of antiquity, from 1947 to 1951. As director of a project sponsored by the Council for Research in the Social Science, at Columbia University, I was engaged in an inquiry into the origins of economic institutions. During shorter periods, Mrs. Striker was employed as Research Assistant of the Project, but over most of the time she offered her voluntary help which was gratefully accepted."[88]

The participation in Karl Polanyi's research (the work culminated in the publication of his *Trade and Market in the Early Empires* in 1957[89]) was secondary to Laura's main occupation during these years; her enthusiastic participation in the raising of her two grandchildren, Eva's daughter and son, born in 1940 and 1942, respectively. Almost immediately after her arrival in the States, Eva Zeisel had begun teaching at the Pratt Institute in New York as well as building a reputation as one of the leading ceramic artists in the United States. Taking prolonged trips to factories all over America and later to Europe and Japan as well, and with her husband teaching at the University of Chicago Law School, Eva relegated a good part of motherly responsibilities to Laura. With her daughter's whirlwind career in progress, Laura became the stabilizing centre of her grandchildren's life, giving her full attention to the selection of the best possible schools, the organization of birthday parties, and the completion of school projects.

A chance encounter some time during the early 1950s led Laura to a new historical project that was to take over as the passion of her late years.

> During the 1950s, when [Karl] Polanyi was teaching economic history at Columbia University, he received a visit from Bradford Smith, author of a number of popular biographies. Smith said he was in the process of writing a biography of Captain Smith (no relation), founder of the colony of Virginia, the man most widely known for the fact that, when he fell prisoner to an Indian tribe, the chief's daughter Pocahontas saved his life. "John Smith was a prolific autobiographical writer," said Bradford Smith, "but his writings are under a cloud. His reputation is that of teller of tall tales, taking liberties with the truth whenever it suited him. At the core of these accusations are the events recorded in Smith's book *Travels in Hungary and Transylvania*. Written around 1600, it deals with his alleged adventures during the war between the Austrian imperial armies and the Turks. An English historian of Hungarian descent has found this book full of lies. I am not sure he is right and am looking for a second opinion."
>
> "I came to you because your name betrays Hungarian descent, and I thought you might be able to help me find the right expert; I need a historian who knows

Hungarian and reads Latin, the language in which John Smith wrote his book."
    "It so happens I know such a person," was Polanyi's answer. "She has a
doctorate in history, knows Hungarian because that is her mother tongue, and knows
Latin because she went to a European gymnasium. She lives a block from here. She is
my sister."[90]

Much like Captain Smith's adventures in Eastern Europe, Laura Polanyi's
involvement in the Smith scholarship was laced with serendipity. Hans Zeisel's
above quoted, anecdotal retelling of the event and its conclusion: "Bradford
Smith went to see Laura Polanyi Striker and the ensuing conversation changed
her life"[91] aptly captured this fairy-tale-like element.

The first meeting of Laura and Bradford Smith in 1951 November was
preceded by Bradford Smith duly introducing himself by letter, followed by
another letter, outlining the results of his preliminary research and the assignment
he had in mind.[92] At this point, Smith, while clearly impressed by Laura's
qualifications and intellect, regarded her as no more than a potential, if possibly
overqualified, research assistant. As a professional writer who depended on
writing for an income, he stressed in the summary of their first meeting that he
could not afford to pay her according to her "experience and scholarly
attainments" but neither could "he afford to do without them!"[93]

Bradford Smith's "little problem"[94] concerned the veracity of the Captain's
highly picaresque account of his adventures in Eastern Europe. While it was not
an overly complicated problem to solve, it required a special set of skills, namely
the knowledge of Hungarian and Latin, in addition to familiarity with the early
17th-century history of Hungary and Transylvania. American scholarship
concerning the validity of Captain Smith's Eastern European adventures at this
time rested on the verdict pronounced by Lewis Kropf, an English historian of
Hungarian origin. Kropf, in an article serialized in 1890 not only deemed John
Smith's *True Travels* a pseudo-historical romance at best but doubted that its hero
had ever set foot in Eastern Europe.[95] To subsequent American historians,
Kropf's position became the accepted wisdom, since "no American historian
dared take issue with a Hungarian expert on his own ground."[96] Bradford Smith
was the first in more than half a century to consider a second opinion.

It was a decision characteristic of Bradford Smith's open and unbiased
approach; and in addition to contribute to the success of his biography it made
him ideally suited for the collaboration with Laura. The relationship of the two,
eventually, also turned into a great success, though only after a series of initial
mishaps. From the beginning, Smith must have been aware that Laura, with her
credentials and experience, was no ordinary research assistant. While Laura

insisted that she would not accept payment for her work and that she was "working on the condition of full authority on the Hungarian issues"[97] Smith, perhaps thinking that Laura was unaware of the amount of work involved, kept trying to come to a clear business arrangement.[98]

Following their first meeting in November 1951, Laura left New York to spend the winter months, as became her habit from the mid-1940s, in Dunedin, Florida. In one of the many reports she was to send to Karl Polanyi in the following months, she wrote: "On my last day before 70 with all that is left. Karlicsku I just write down for you the plain facts about J. S. in Hungary and Transylvania."[99] The letter indicated that during these first months of familiarizing herself with the Captain's legendary figure, she already realized the potential of her contribution to the Smith-controversy.

In March 1952, Laura broke off her silence and in a letter to Bradford Smith she clarified the nature of her role in what started, to all intents and purposes, as Bradford Smith's project on his own. From here on, she clearly set the tone for the collaboration, proving herself surprisingly apt at staking her territory and negotiating her conditions. She reiterated her initial claim to take charge of the Hungarian material and claim "'sole scholarly responsibility' for the Hungarian issues."[100]

Bradford Smith's response came less than a week later in a good-natured letter, not only accepting all her conditions, but relieved to hand over the responsibility for the Hungarian aspect.[101] Instead of simply crediting Laura for her contribution, he now offered to publish her study as an independent article, appended to his biography. This unusually generous offer was no doubt helped by Laura's polite but unmistakable determination to assert for herself the role of co-author. Almost certainly aware of the reversal of the usual roles, Bradford Smith must have realized the potential benefits not only for himself but also for the Smith scholarship. Finally, he had a deadline looming over his head.

While Bradford Smith was away in England, searching the British archives, Laura set out to work on the Hungarian material. It did not take long for her to discover that Lewis Kropf, the unchallenged authority on the Captain's Hungarian adventures was far from the unbiased expert he made himself out to be. Taking advantage of his access to Hungarian historical sources, out of reach for English and American scholars, Kropf in fact "had disregarded important information available to him in the sources he himself quoted."[102]

Laura's initial survey of contemporary Hungarian sources quickly and firmly established Smith's veracity. Poring over 17th-century maps and documents, published by the Hungarian Academy and familiar to her from her university studies, and considering contemporary, local variations in the pronunciation of names, she successfully identified most geographical locations and personal names in Smith's account. Now she had to present all this new information in a form accessible to the American readership of a popular biography, maintaining a balance between the historiographical background, the demolition of Kropf's opinion, and the presentation of her own findings.

To help with this complex task, Laura enlisted her brother, Karl. He had already played an important part by recruiting her for the project and may have felt responsible for its success. The exchanges between Karl and Laura provide insight into a period of intense collaboration in the research and editing of her final article, with Karl's wife, Ilona's equally keen participation. Manuscript versions traveled between the siblings' respective New York apartments as well as between New York and Pickering, where the Polanyis had just settled. Karl was teaching at Columbia but commuting to and making his home in Canada as Ilona was banned from the U.S. because of her past involvement in Communist and leftist activities.

Karl and Ilona were instrumental in the identification of place names, finding such ingenious sources as "Ilona's secret weapon," a modern railway directory, and the "apocryphal papers, called Bus time-table—all your mysterious battle grounds are in it...."[103] Karl Polanyi's comments, far from being charitable, provided a glimpse of the formidable editor. "Research material, my darling, is NOT a text: it is for the edification of the author, NOT of the reader," he commented on an early version of his sister's essay.[104] At one point, Karl became quite possessive about the project, scolding his sister for "interfering" with the already corrected manuscript, which, he wrote, now became "hopelessly confused and beyond repair. It has ceased to be an argument; it is a mere aggregate of sentences. Also, it is hopeless to 'argue' against Kropf at every street corner: the whole has to be erected into a monument, under which the opponent is crushed and your hero stands vindicated. I was, I think, on the way towards that aim, but your impatience has messed it all up."[105] Then, in the next sentence, Karl suddenly struck a conciliatory note, still stressing his own part in the project: "It's a sad story, but together we'll pull it off in the end."[106]

In June 1952, Bradford Smith returned from his research trip in England and reported to Laura about his findings there, including a short Latin life of Smith by the 17th-century author Henry Wharton, which had been referred to but never translated into English or studied before.[107] Then he raised the inevitable question: "And now I'm eager to know how you are coming along. ... I hope you have got along as you hoped to do."[108] Three weeks later, he inquired again: "I hope you are well along with your account."[109] And, gently turning on the pressure, he added: "I have been trying to write the Turkish chapter, leaving the Hungary chapter until I can see your work."[110]

In the end, Bradford Smith's biography went to the publishers on the last day of 1952, with Laura's separate essay following it in March 1953. In his acknowledgments, the author introduced the essay of his co-author as a "masterpiece of history patiently reconstructed"[111] and, as a sign of genuine appreciation, he dedicated the book "To Laura Polanyi Striker, collaborator and friend."[112] In its final form, Laura's essay justified Bradford Smith's decision to have it appended to his own text. The detailed account of the complex political, military and religious conflicts of early 17th-century Hungary and Transylvania would have overwhelmed the short Hungarian chapter of his biography. Yet it was a necessary backdrop to support her thesis that John Smith's description of 1601-2 Hungary and Transylvania was not only accurate in every aspect but that it could only have been written by a participant of the events.

The publication of *Captain John Smith: His Life and Legend* in September 1953 was followed by generally positive reviews, all of them making note of Laura's valuable contribution.[113] Yet Laura herself seemed to have a difficult time finding closure and accepting that she was not allowed to pour into her essay more of the ideas and material collected in her research. During the editorial process, Bradford Smith had to remind her not to detract from the main points by supplying the reader with too much information: "...the sheet in which you suggest more refutation of Kropf seems to me really unnecessary; you have quite flattened the poor man already!"[114] He suggested that instead of introducing the different versions of the Smith texts in the essay, "it would be far better to write an article on the two texts, using your Hungarian background to make the points you do about them."[115] As for Laura, she vented her frustration over not being able to include her newest "brainwave" in the manuscript that had, in the meantime, gone to the printer, in a letter to Karl.[116] A week later, Bradford Smith had to remind her that "time is rapidly running out when we can hope to keep on altering the text... After that [the manuscript went to the printer] the cost of making any change would be prohibitive."[117]

By September 1953, while Bradford Smith was turning his attention to new projects, Laura, still very much within the John Smith mindframe, summarized her plans and doubts to Karl. "Karlicsku, I think you are right, a number of short experiences should be written up in historical journals: Ferneza, a comparison of the two editions [of John Smith's texts], the personality of Kropf ... etc., yet if one ignores one's age, declining mental capacities, the physical handicaps, the condition of Sándor ... and is dreaming about another true historical essay, perhaps should not waste all the best parts?"[118]

In the course of the next six years, Laura managed to fulfill most of these dreams. Immediately after the publication of the Smith-biography, she began work on Henry Wharton's *The Life of John Smith, English Soldier*. Written in Latin in 1685 and never translated into English before, Wharton's short, laudatory biography of Smith was published with Laura's introductory essay, "Captain John Smith in Seventeenth Century Literature" in 1957 by the University of North Carolina Press.[119] In 1958, *The Virginia Magazine of History and Biography* published her article "The Hungarian Historian, Lewis L. Kropf, on Captain John Smith's *True Travels*."[120] In the process, she became the acknowledged expert on Smith's Eastern European period and took her place in the John Smith legendarium. In a 1958 article in *American Heritage*, Marshall Fishwick placed her alongside Pocahontas, one saving the life, the other the reputation of Smith.

The rehabilitation of John Smith became a veritable obsession of Laura's last years. (In a letter to Karl, she called it "my *Besessenheit*—German for obsession—with J.S."[121]) Beginning in 1951 and ending a week before her death in December 1959, she championed the Captain's cause with a determination and perseverance that compensated for all the failed or aborted plans of an academic career and scholarly success in the past.

What was it in the John Smith project that motivated her to accomplish the remarkable output of the last eight years? The question was already raised by Lee Congdon who, in a 1986 article, argued that Laura's devotion to John Smith sprang from two sources: her admiration for him as the hero of the common people and her belief that children—in the Hungary of her youth as well as in America—needed heroes of humble origin.[122] Congdon had apparently come across Laura's articles and the documents of her kindergarten in the Hungarian National Library's Polanyi Collection. Without considering the context of the experimental school in 1911-12, he drew a straight line from the objectives of her "moral education" classes to her defense of John Smith, as a worthy hero for American schoolchildren. Congdon's article had its merits: it introduced the phenomenon of early-twentieth-century Hungarian counter-culture and the fascinating history of the Polanyis to North-Americans. As for Laura's real motives, they were at once more simple and more complicated than Congdon's suppositions.

One of the most important factors was timing. The Smith project came to

Laura at a point when, after decades of historical and personal emergencies, she was finally settled, her children established in life, and even her grandchildren off to university. While still closely involved in their lives, especially in the case of her daughter's family, for the first time in a long time, she was left with time and the freedom to spend it on herself. Her husband, Sándor Stricker never accommodated himself to American life as fully as the rest of the family, but neither was he a burden. Peacefully slipping into old age, he was relatively healthy and happy with the proximity of his children and grandchildren.

The fact that John Smith found Laura by the "divine intervention" of her brother, Karl, had a particular significance. In their shared youth in pre-war Hungary, Laura was considered as brilliant and promising in her intellectual talents as her brothers. Yet during the following three decades, while Karl and Michael rose into the highest levels of academia, she was preoccupied with academically less productive tasks. First raising her children, then keeping them, as well as her relatives and friends, out of danger consumed the better part of the interwar period. Once the war was over, she chose to help to bring up her grandchildren and advance her daughter's career instead of her own.

As the eldest sister, Laura developed her relationships with her brothers into an art form, always accommodating their vanities and differences with one another. Karl was especially eager to report his successes to his sister and anxious to hear her praise. It was all the more significant when he summarized the meaning of the Smith-project both to Laura and to their relationship:

> My dear Mausi, your decision to not include the gaps of Hungarian historiography in your study has made me very happy. ... It is an extraordinary gift from life. Of course I had my share in it by being able to encourage you all the way, since I realized what it would mean for you to complete it. The more deeply I was moved to see your perseverance in the last, difficult stage. When it seemed that it is *impossible* to finish; at least not without serious reduction. Yet you have built it. ... What curious miracle ties connect my late accomplishment with yours. Never had I made it this far, here, on the path of research if not for your help.[123]

Karl's remark on his own late accomplishment was a reference to the 1940s when he had been teaching at Bennington Heights and Columbia. Back then, Laura was always at hand to cheer him on and to help Karl with his projects at Columbia, but strictly in a subordinate role. Laura showed an uncharacteristic dependence on Karl's advice when the roles were reversed and she was writing her first essay on John Smith followed from this earlier arrangement. Traces of this unusual lack of confidence were erased only after her eventual success. The fact that this came so late in life tinged it with a little sadness. As her old friends, the family physician Gyula Holló and his wife congratulated "the great historian," he wrote: "In the afterlife, you will sit on the right side of John Smith but John Smith can wait a little longer."[124] The wife, more tactfully, added: "My Dear Mausi, of course you are a great historian. But I could raise the question: Oh why this late, when the leaves are falling, and the geese are leaving![125] I could but will not because I know the answer."[126]

More than any other of her previous scholarly interests, the Smith-project was a perfect fit for Laura's background and skills: the languages, Hungarian and Latin, and the time period, only slightly earlier than that of her doctoral thesis. Moreover, partly because the project came to her so late in life, she was finally ready to delve into a controversy, free from all her previous cautions and inhibitions. For the Captain's figure provoked much contention and, as Laura wrote in the opening of her essay, had become the object of a veritable "scholarly battle which has raged over his veracity."[127]

Bradford Smith's biography offered new evidence in the Captain's favour but also looked into the century-old scholarly debate over his battered character and at the making of the legend that made him, against all odds, one of the first and best-loved American heroes. By pronouncing on the reliability of the Captain's Hungarian adventures, Laura became part of a truly American tradition as well as one of a few Hungarians who joined in this intellectual lineage. She found herself in good company. The side of the defense included Hungarian scholars such as Ferenc Pulszky who, as a member of the exiled Kossuth cabinet, came to America in 1858 and was consulted for an earlier Smith-biography.[128] Another Hungarian among Smith's defenders was Antal Szerb, the brilliant literary historian of the interwar period.[129] An anglophile and lover of literary and historical curiosities, Szerb wrote a short article, published in 1940 both in Hungarian and English in which he pointed out the *True Travels'* potential value as a source for Hungarian history.[130]

But the Hungarian scholar with the most decisive and lasting influence over American historiography was Lewis L. Kropf. An engineer by training, Kropf immigrated to England in the 1870s and, as an amateur historian, began to contribute small articles on English-Hungarian relations to British and Hungarian historical journals. His devastating opinion of John Smith as a braggart and a liar quickly became accepted, for

... he was Hungarian by birth, familiar with the country, its geography, and its history. As a historical researcher, Kropf enjoyed official recognition from the Hungarian Historical Society and the Hungarian Academy of Arts and Sciences. To these bodies he was elected as a member and corresponding member respectively. His publications appeared in leading English, American, and Hungarian periodicals.[131]

The irony of the situation could not have escaped Laura: here she was, another Hungarian historian, claiming her expertise sixty years after Kropf, without many of the latter's credentials. The parallels between the two of them were inescapable. As Bradford Smith pointed out:

> Just as every scholar was afraid to attack Kropf because they couldn't handle Hungarian materials, so they'll be afraid to tackle you. And your thesis is so demonstrably thorough and so supported with references and documentation that no one would have the temerity to attack it, or the time to follow up on your work to see if you had slipped. So don't expect anything but the admiration you have been getting.[132]

The above letter also provides a hint as to why Laura kept making additions to her publications after they were submitted, pestering her editors to insert just one last snippet of documentary evidence; as if she felt she needed to prove her expertise beyond any doubt. The article she wrote on Kropf is another case in point. Published in 1958 in *The Virginia Magazine of History and Biography*, her study was made up of two distinct parts. It was a psycho-biographical portrait of Kropf, as well as a rehashing of the main arguments of her defense of John Smith. In the first, Laura looked at Kropf's background and scholarly output to show that, although a prolific writer, he was not a proper historian by training or approach. She argued that as an engineer, he had no consideration for the human factors, only concrete measurements and data. "He had a predilection for setting others right and making an impression with his findings"[133] and, most of all, "a propensity for exposing flaws in beloved traditions and time honored conceptions."[134] In the second part of the article, Laura went on to show how Kropf's selective treatment of Hungarian sources robbed the Captain of his good reputation.

And here was another hint at the source of Laura's passion for the rehabilitation of John Smith. She sympathized with the commoner who had to fight social conventions and rely solely on his abilities but, most of all, identified with him because of the tremendous odds he had to face, both in his life and after his death. Her short preface to the translation of Wharton's manuscript remained unpublished, perhaps because Laura felt it revealed too much of the personal attachment she developed to her hero. (Or, perhaps, because it was not written by her; both the Shakespeare reference and the style points to Karl Polanyi as its possible author.) In this short piece, Laura (or Karl) presented the posthumous fight for Smith's honour as a chain of events, ranging from natural disasters to human errors, accidents and political catastrophes. "The first documents in defense of his word went down to the bottom of the sea, in prey of Shakespeare's tempest. The last documents to prove his veracity went up in flames at the Budapest Archives during the 1956 Revolution."[135] This unfortunate series of events was extended to the Wharton manuscript whose earlier American translation was hindered by the intended translator's sudden death in 1824. "Against such odds did the commoner soldier of the seventeenth century, and I, a historian in search of the truth 350 years later, try to establish his honor,"[136] went the conclusion, pointing to the bond between the American hero and his Hungarian rescuer; their share of and ability to withstand historical disasters.

In her remaining years Laura continued to champion the Captain's cause with a vigour that not only belied her age and declining health but also demonstrated her remarkable talent for public relations. Exercised earlier in the interests of her children and grandchildren as well as in her efforts to rescue relatives and friends during the war, she now used it for her own benefit and that of John Smith.

A few examples of her "somewhat aggressive championing"[137] of the Captain's cause highlight the breathless pace of these last years. In 1957, she turned the 350th anniversary of Jamestown's foundation into an "occasion to clear definitely the controversy about John Smith's integrity."[138] She offered copies of the reprint of her Smith-essay for display and sale, and arranged for the printing and sale at the festivities of a "Congratulatory Poem" from 1684 that she had found in the British Museum.[139] She sent her translation of the Wharton Life, with the related reviews attached, to the American Ambassador in London, asking him to forward it to the Queen, who was to visit Virginia on the occasion.[140] In August 1957, she sought Bradford Smith's advice about a "daydream" of hers: to put together a memorial lecture, accompanied with slides, to be held either at Bennington (where Bradford Smith was on faculty) or William and Mary.[141]

In 1958, she contacted Oscar Handlin, the editor of the *Harvard Guide to American History*, sending him the Kropf-article and taking issue with the Guide's 1954 edition that still referred to Kropf's article as the last word on Smith's credibility.[142] Handlin took her polite but firm criticism graciously and replied: "You have certainly effectively disposed of Mr. Kropf. I am sure the next issue of the Harvard Guide will take ample account of your criticism."[143]

The last item on Laura's list of future projects was a study of the Smith-controversy itself. She tentatively titled the planned study "The Affaire Smith" in obvious reference to the Dreyfus affair. It may be not entirely coincidental that her idea followed the publication of a book by the Polanyis' close friend, the Hungarian journalist Miklós (Nicholas) Halász, on the original "affaire,"[144] dedicated to Karl Polanyi. Her ambitious undertaking never got past the initial stage of planning. Perhaps because the project was to involve "sensitive areas of American history,"[145] Laura reverted to her old cautious ways and set out to find an American historian with whom to share the authorship.[146] When she asked Allan Nevins of Columbia University to help find her a potential collaborator, she had already failed in her first such attempt a year earlier. Her correspondence from June-July 1957 depicts the series of misunderstandings with her designated co-author, Marshall Fishwick of Washington and Lee University, later a prolific author in American Studies.[147] It seems that while Fishwick was interested in summarizing the material Laura had sent him and use it in his own articles and books—and was offering to credit her as a source—he had no intention of a closer collaboration.[148] In the end, he even referred to "the language barrier" as the reason for their misunderstandings; quite uncalled for given Laura's standing in academia, not to mention her nearly perfect written and spoken English.[149] To his credit, a year later Fishwick generously praised Laura's contribution to the Smith-scholarship in his article and coined the epithet, "Hungarian Pocahontas."[150]

The Smith-project enabled Laura to enjoy in her last years the life of an independent academic, with almost yearly research trips and newly built or re-established professional ties in Hungary and Austria. Her visits with her son and his family in Budapest were now coordinated with research at various Hungarian archives. She built a working relationship with Kálmán Benda, the leading expert of 17th-century Hungarian history, and had him review her essay in the Bradford Smith biography.[151]

Back in 1953, Laura had enlisted the help of an Austrian archivist, Dr. Franz Pichler of the Central Archive in Styria, Graz. Checking the Styrian Archive for evidence of Turkish-Austrian military skirmishes and traces of John Smith as he passed through Graz on his way to Transylvania, Pichler quickly became another champion of the Captain and was instrumental in identifying the names in Smith's account. In addition, he hired the local boy scouts for a re-enactment of the 1601 battle, complete with pyrotechnics, described in Smith's *True Travels*. Pichler summarized his findings in a 1957 article for *The Virginia*

Magazine of History and Biography, translated from the German by Laura herself.[152]

Her visits to Europe through the 1950s represented the highlights of Laura's last years. While in many ways she remained the centre of gravity in the lives of her daughter, son, and grandchildren, the European trips were the most visible signs of the well-rounded and independent life she finally achieved. She refused to give in to the inevitable: age and declining health. After suffering a broken hip in 1958, she could walk with difficulty; pictures taken in her last year all show her with a cane. Yet she shrugged off her "fading pedestrian capabilities"[153] and toured the Tuscan towns, researched the archives of Budapest and Graz, and visited with her son's family in Hungary and her brother in Manchester to the end. The European trips also brought her into closer contact with the political events of the day, a "politico-ideological experience" she thoroughly enjoyed.[154]

In a rare moment of self-reflection, Laura pondered the significance of the Smith-project in her life in a letter to her oldest surviving friend, Recha Jászi. She reported on her daughter and grandchildren— "my nearest family" —away in Germany, her son in New York— "working from morning till night, and ... call every Sunday evening here" —and her recent two-months-long visit in Europe with her son and "his very nice two daughters and perfectly charming little son." Then she went on:

> However, I don't want to be ungrateful to life. The friend of my seventies has, of course, made my seventies as exciting and, I must concede, happy as nothing else could have done. I mean, of course, Captain John Smith. Please read the few pages of this reprint just as a friendly interest in my life in these last seven years. I, of course, overrate the importance of my mission, but for me it is enough. It really was my main concern, even much excitement, during the last years.[155]

She could not have found a more fitting legacy than that of the Hungarian historian who contributed to the vindication of America's hero, and, in the process, bridged her country of origin with her country of choice.[156]

On her last European trip in the fall of 1959, Laura revisited the itinerary of her youthful travels in Italy, accompanied by her daughter, then ended with visits with her family and friends in Budapest and Vienna. Back in New York, she was dictating the results of her latest findings in the archives of Hungary and Austria until the day she was admitted to Columbia-Presbyterian Hospital. She died nine days later, on 23 December 1959, following an operation to remove a tumor in the liver.[157]

As if by design, the last article with her name, as co-author of Bradford Smith, titled "The Rehabilitation of Captain John Smith," appeared almost three years after her death.[158] It provided Bradford Smith with the chance to demonstrate, one last time, his magnanimity to Laura by by including her as co-author; he may have used the notes she had left behind but the article was entirely his work. It summarized the latest scholarly evidence that had accumulated in John Smith's favour since 1953, including new research on the Captain's Russian adventures. And it highlighted, one more time, the friendship and mutual service, over the gulf of three and a half centuries, between the American hero and the Hungarian refugee.

Laura's dignified parting at the close of 1959, at age 77, however premature and painful for her family, was as graceful and composed as the rest of her life. To the end, an adoring family surrounded and comforted her. The academic triumph of her last years that restored her rightful place among her brilliant brothers, brought her satisfaction, yet she must have felt an equal pride in her other accomplishment, her successful and flourishing offspring. It was a balance she had been striving for all her life and achieved only near the very end.

As a member of the first generation of women that struggled with the confrontations, compromises and dilemmas that came with "wanting to have it all," Laura Polanyi's life offers valuable lessons to generations of women who came after her. But she was also confronted with unique choices. As an intellectually promising member of a family that valued intellectual achievement above all, she showed a quietly independent spirit by setting her own pace and postponing her professional career in exchange for starting a family early. Later in life, she showed extraordinary strength of character and demonstrated that she valued moral and family obligations over a comfortable lifestyle.

Her life, with its compromises, belated successes and unfulfilled expectations, also raises questions about the way we measure achievement. Without the chance encounter with the legendary Captain and Laura's perseverance in bringing the project to fruition, she would not have earned the recognition that had eluded her for so long. And without this belated success, her remarkable accomplishments as daughter, eldest sister, wife and mother, in keeping her extended family together and helping friends in times of crisis, all that ultimately made her life successful and complete, would have remained unheralded.

Notes

Introduction

1. See fig. 31. In 1986, on the centennial of Karl Polanyi's birth, a modest exhibition was organized in Budapest, concurrent with the publication of a thin volume of documents, Erzsébet Vezér, ed., *Irástudó nemzedékek: A Polányi család dokumentumai*, vol. 7, Archivumi füzetek (Budapest: MTA Filozófiai Intézet Lukács Archivum, 1986). The family tree on fig. 31. follows the one published on page 12 of the above volume but also corrects its omissions.

2. György Litván, *Szabó Ervin, a szocializmus moralistája* (Budapest: Századvég, 1993), 19. In a statement typical of the myths surrounding the family, the Polanyis' first historian, Erzsébet Vezér, suggested that the Polanyis represented a unique case within the assimilating Jewish middle class; instead of increasing material well-being, they "chose the way of the intellect, with a truly puritan lifestyle." Erzsébet Vezér, "The Polanyi Family," Kari Polanyi-Levitt, ed., *The Life and Work of Karl Polanyi* (Montreal, New York: Black Rose Books, 1990), 18.

3. Laura Fermi, *Illustrious Immigrants: The Intellectual Migration from Europe, 1930-41* (Chicago: University of Chicago Press, 1968, revised edition 1971), 111.

4. Ibid. 113-14.

5. The exception to this rule is the pathbreaking study of Lee Congdon, *Exile and Social Thought: Hungarian Intellectuals in Germany and Austria, 1919-1933* (Princeton, N.J.: Princeton University Press, 1991) that highlighted the crucial influence of the turn-of-the-century Hungary's social and intellectual milieu on émigré intellectuals on the development of their thought in the 1920s.

6. A series of conferences had been held and multiple volumes of essays devoted to the legacy of Karl Polanyi by the Karl Polanyi Archive at Montreal's Concordia University. The most recent is Kenneth McRobbie and Kari Polanyi Levitt, eds., *Karl Polanyi in Vienna: The Contemporary Significance of The Great Transformation* (Montreal, New York, London: Black Rose Books, 2000). Linda McQuaig, *All You Can Eat: Greed, Lust and the New Capitalism* (Toronto, London, New York: Viking by Penguin Books, 2001) is a recent example of the continuing influence of Karl Polanyi's thought. The scholarly legacy of Michael Polanyi continues to generate an entire network of societies and journals, such as *Tradition and Discovery* and *Polanyiana*, among others. As well, several doctoral dissertations and scholarly biographies on Karl and Michael Polanyi are rumoured to be in preparation.

7. The only exception is Ilona Duczynska, Karl Polanyi's wife, whose captivating life has been the subject of a biography and a number of articles. György Dalos, *A cselekvés szerelmese* (Budapest: Kossuth, 1984) and "Part Two: Karl Polanyi and Ilona Duczynska," in McRobbie and Polanyi Levitt, *Karl Polanyi in Vienna*, 255-293.

8. Fermi, *Illustrious Immigrants*, 113.

9. Erzsébet Vezér, "A Polányi család," *Irástudó nemzedékek*, 8-11; Ilona Duczynska, "I First Met Karl Polanyi in 1920...," *Karl Polanyi in Vienna*, 303-307.

10. Vezér, "A Polányi család," 12.

11. I thank Professor Franca Iacovetta of the University of Toronto for bringing this aspect, only marginally explored my study, to my attention.

12. Literally: Twentieth Century, the journal was launched in January 1900 and was published until the spring of 1919.

13. For an assessment of the programme and scholarly achievement of the circle, see György Litván and László Szücs, eds., *A szociológia elsö magyar mühelye: a Huszadik Század köre*, vols. 1-2 (Budapest: Gondolat, 1973) and György Litván's introductory essay, "Bevezetés," ibid., 5-46.

14. György Litván, "Introduction: Oscar Jászi (1875-1957)," idem, ed., *Oszkár Jászi, 1875-1957, Homage to Danubia*, States and Societies in East Central Europe (Lanham, Md.: Rowman & Littlefield, 1995), xi.

15. On the conflict outside and within the Sociological Society and its broader implications, see Litván, "Bevezetés," 7-28.

16. On the motives of this rediscovery and the changing meanings of turn-of-the-century Hungarian political culture, see the introduction of György Litván to his selected essays, *Októberek üzenete* (Budapest: Osiris, 1996), 5-10.

17. Péter Hanák was the editor of the grand synthesis of *Magyarország története 7, 1890-1918* (Budapest: Akadémiai, 1978) and the author of several pathbreaking essay collections, moving from the political to the social and cultural history of Hungary in the Monarchy. *Magyarország a Monarchiában* (Budapest: Gondolat, 1975); *A Kert és a Mühely* (Budapest: Gondolat, 1988), in English: *The Garden and the Workshop. Essays on the Cultural History of Vienna and Budapest* (Princeton, N.J.: Princeton University Press, 1998); *Ragaszkodás az Utópiához* (Budapest: Liget, no date).

18. See, among others, the articles in Éva Somogyi, ed., *Polgárosodás Közép-Európában: Tanulmányok Hanák Péter hetvenedik születésnapjára* (Budapest: MTA Történettudományi Intézete, 1991). Originally from the small towns on the Monarchy's periphery, members of the circle of the Twentieth Century came together in the emerging metropolis, Budapest. On the city, see Károly Vörös, *Egy világváros születése* (Budapest: Kossuth, 1973); Thomas Bender and Carl E. Schorske, eds., *Budapest and New York: Studies in Metropolitan Trasnformation, 1870-1930* (New York: Russell Sage Foundation, 1994); András Gerö and János Poór, eds., *Budapest: A History from Its Beginnings to 1998*, Social Science Monographs (Boulder, Co., distributed by Columbia University Press, 1997). The role of Jewish entrepreneurs and bankers in Hungary's economic modernization as well as the preponderance of Jews in the urban middle class and the professions was recognized as a consequence of Hungary's semi-feudal social and political structure. Ever since the seminal essays of István Bibó, published between 1945 and 1949, such crucial issues of Hungarian social history as the lopsided modernization and the role of Jewish middle class in it, as well as a critical analysis of anti-Semitism and the Holocaust in Hungary were declared taboo. Bibó's "Zsidókérdés Magyarországon 1944 után," first published in 1948 in the journal *Válasz*, vol. 8, nos. 10-11, 778-877, was re-published in 1984 in Péter Hanák, ed., *Zsidókérdés, asszimiláció, antiszemitizmus* (Budapest: Gondolat, 1984), 135-294. Other important contributions to the problems of Jewish assimiliation in the Hungarian context are,

among others, György Litván, *Magyar gondolat, szabad gondolat* (Budapest: Magvetö, 1978); Péter Hanák, "Problems of Jewish assimilation in Austria-Hungary in the nineteenth and twentieth centuries" in Pat Thane, Geoffrey Crossick, and Roderick Floud, eds., *The Power of the Past: Essays for Eric Hobsbawm* (Cambridge, N.Y.: Cambridge University Press, 1984), 235-250; and Ferenc Fejtö, in collaboration with Gyula Zeke, *Hongrois et Juifs: Histoire millénaire d'un couple singulier (1000-1997)* (Paris: Balland, 1997). In Hungarian: *Magyarság, zsidóság* (Budapest: História, MTA Történettudományi Intézete, 2000).

19. Gábor Gyáni, *Hétköznapi Budapest: Nagyvárosi élet a századfordulón* (Budapest: Városháza, 1995); idem, *Az utca és a szalon* (Budapest: Uj Mandátum, 1999).

20. William O. McCagg, Jr., *Jewish Nobles and Geniuses in Modern Hungary*, East European Monographs (Boulder, Co.: distributed by Columbia University Press, 1972, reprint 1986); György Lengyel, *Vállalkozók, kereskedök, bankárok. A magyar gazdasági elit a 19. században és a 20. század elsö felében* (Budapest: Akadémiai, 1989).

21. Litván, *Szabó Ervin*. His biography of Oszkár Jászi was in preparation at the completion of this manuscript.

22. Two of the most important examples of the genre are Lajos Hatvany, *Urak és emberek* (Budapest: Szépirodalmi, 1980) and Anna Lesznai, *Kezdetben volt a kert...* (Budapest: Szépirodalmi, 1966).

23. Gyáni, *Hétköznapi Budapest*, 12-27.

24. Litván, *Szabó Ervin*, 98-100.

25. Judit Szapor,"Les associations féministes en Hongrie, XIX-XXe siècle," *Pénelope*, no. 11 (Fall 1984): 169-73; idem, "Mit akarnak a radikális asszonyok?": Nöi politikusok az 1918-as demokratikus forradalomban" in Beáta Nagy, ed. *Magyar nök a politikában* (Debrecen: Csokonai, forthcoming) and the articles in idem and Margit S. Sárdi, eds., *Szerep és alkotás* (Debrecen: Csokonai, 1997).

26. Erzsébet Vezér, editor of the first collection of documents on the Polanyis, gave this title to her introductory essay to the volume, *Irástudó nemzedékek*.

158

The Hungarian Pocahontas

Chapter 1: Literate Generations

1. Fig. 2. Hanák, ed., *Magyarország története*, illustration 146.

2. On the construction of the grand boulevards, see Hanák, "Polgárosodás és urbanizáció," *A Kert és a Műhely*, 17-62. and Károly Vörös, ed. *Budapest története*, vol. 4 (Budapest: Akadémiai, 1978), 396-98.

3. Here and further, I will use Polanyi, the Magyarized version of the family name (but in its Anglicized spelling), when it applies to Laura and her siblings.

4. Ilona Duczynska, "Polányi Károly (1886-1964)," *Századok*, vol. 106, no. 1 (1971): 89-90, described Cecile's family background based on her husband, Karl Polanyi's memories. The versions of Vezér, in an introductory essay, "A Polányi család," 7, as well as idem, "The Polanyi Family" in Polanyi-Levitt, *The Life and Work of Karl Polanyi*, 19, closely follow Duczynska's outline.

5. For the information on Wohl's exact date of birth and his appointment as Vilna's Jewish censor, I thank Jean Richards, Laura Polanyi's granddaughter, who has shared with me the results of her recent inquiries in the former Soviet Union.

6. See, for example, Lucy S. Davidowicz, ed., *The Golden Tradition: Jewish Life and Thought in Eastern Europe* (New York: Holt, Rinehart and Winston, 1967), L. Rau, *Jerusalem in Lithuania: Illustrated and Documented*. 3 vols. (New York: Vilno Album Committee, 1974) and Henri Minczeles, *Vilna, Wilno, Vilnius: La Jérusalem de Lituanie* (Paris: Editions de la Découverte, 1993).

7. John Doyle Klier, *Imperial Russia's Jewish Question, 1855-1881* (Cambridge, New York: Cambridge University Press, 1995), especially Part 2. Wohl's activities are mentioned on pages 171 and 173.

8. Fig. 7 and notes of Laura Polanyi on the Polanyi ancestors, 212/268, Polanyi Collection, Manuscript Division, Széchényi National Library, Budapest, Hungary (heretofore: OSzK PC).

9. Vezér, "A Polányi család," 7. The letter of A. Wohl to Cecile Wohl on 2 (14) December 1892, OSzK PC, 212/2 lists the addresses of Lazar Wohl at the Moscow and St. Petersburg branches of the International Commerce Bank.

10. See, among others, A. Wohl to Cecile Wohl, 9 (21) March, no year, OSzK PC, 212/2, my translation. A possible explanation, if correct, is mentioned in a recently published version of Ilona Duczynska's reminiscences, namely that about the time Cecile graduated from high school, the previously widowed A. Wohl married his non-Jewish housekeeper. Ilona Duczynska, "'I first met Karl Polanyi in 1920...'," 303.

11. Linda Edmondson, *Feminism in Russia, 1900-1917* (Stanford, Calif.: Stanford University Press, 1984), 17-19.

12. Laura Polanyi to István Erdös, 20 February 1939, London, OSzK PC 212/77. Why Warsaw? Perhaps as a compromise between the in-laws or because it was more accessible for the Wohls in the winter.

13. Marsha Rosenblit, *The Jews of Vienna 1867-1914: Assimilation and Identity* (Albany, N.Y.: State University of New York Press, 1983), 21; William McCagg, Jr., "Vienna and Budapest around 1900:

the problem of Jewish influence" in György Ránki, ed., *Hungary and European Civilization* (Bloomington, Ind.: Indiana University Press, 1986), 244-5.

14. Klier, *Imperial Russia's Jewish Question*, 171 refers to Sh. Kliachko (sic!), the state rabbi of Vilna who in 1866 sat on a government-appointed special commission of "Jewish Experts" with A. Wohl.

15. Ilona Duczynska, "Polányi Károly," 90-91, my translation.

16. Leon Trotsky, *My Life: An Attempt at an Autobiography*, with the introduction of Joseph Hansen (London: Penguin Books, 1975), 239.

17. Erich Haberer, *Jews and revolution in nineteenth-century Russia* (Cambridge, New York: Cambridge University Press, 1995), 52-56.

18. Litván, *Szabó Ervin*, 18.

19. Laura Polanyi remembered that, as a child, she visited the vineyards in Ungvár (today: Uz'horod in the Ukraine) that had been in the family "since old times" and she linked their ownership to a patent issued by Joseph II. "Some facts and hear-says about our family, recorded as remembered," manuscript in the possession of Eva Zeisel.

20. Ibid.

21. Adolf Pollacsek was one of the signatories of a lease in 1868 of steam-mills and distilleries. OSzK PC 212/6. The official record of the founding of the Steam-Mill Co. of Ungvár in 1871 was excerpted in and enclosed with Laura Polanyi's letter to István Erdös on 20 February 1939 (OSzK PC 212/77), to be returned, but is no longer among the family documents.

22. The following account of Mihály Pollacsek's accomplishments is based on his documents at OSzK PC 212/9 and Vezér, "A Polányi család," 6-7.

23. Vezér, "A Polányi család," 7.

24. *Pester Lloyd*, 11 January 1905, quoted in the letter of Laura Polanyi to István Erdös, 20 February 1939, OSzK, PC, 212/77.

25. See, among others, Litván and Szücs, *Szabó Ervin levelezése*, vol. 1, 296-7, 302-3.

26. "We spent Christmas the same way you did with the difference that under the pretext of midnight Mass we did not party or ate stuffed cabbage, only chicken, English roast, bacon and other simple dishes at aunt Lujza." Letter of Lajos Kiss to Laura Polanyi, 30 December 1899, OSzK PC 212/139, my translation.

27. Litván and Szücs, *Szabó Ervin levelezése*, vol. 1, 20-21, records the request for an overcoat from Károly Pollacsek's wardrobe for Lujza's youngest son, Ervin Szabó.

28. László Katus, "Magyarország gazdasági fejlödése (1890-1914)," in Hanák, *Magyarország Története 1890-1918*, chapter 4, 264-65.

29. Ibid., 376 and chart 38.

30. Ibid., 376 and fig. 12; György Kövér, *Iparosodás agrárországban* (Budapest: Gondolat, 1982), 78 and fig. VIII/b.

31. Katus, "Magyarország gazdasági fejlödése (1890-1914)," 380.

32. Károly Vörös, "A fövárostól a székesfövárosig," *Budapest története*, vol. 4, esp. 387-417.

33. William McCagg, *Jewish Nobles and Geniuses* (Bloomington: Indiana University Press, 1972), reprint edition 1986, 27. His estimate is likely overstated.

34. McCagg, ibid., 37-39, argues that the majority of the newly ennobled Jewish elite had no longstanding roots in Hungary.

35. See letter of Karl Polanyi to Mihály Pollacsek, 1899, OSzK PC 212/328.

36. The apartment, under no. 9, was located on the second floor, third, if counting the main floor. According to Ilona Duczynska, it occupied the entire floor of "a palatial building." Duczynska, "'I first met Karl Polanyi in 1920...'," 303. The building at the cross of the busy intersection of Andrássy ut and Váci körut was frequently photographed and a contemporary photo is reproduced here.

37. Duczynska, "Polányi Károly," 90.

38. Adolf Polanyi to Laura Polanyi, 30 March 1899, OSzK PC 212/171.

39. Letters of A. Wohl to his grandchildren, OSzK PC 212/2.

40. Lajos Kiss to Laura Polanyi, 21 June 1897 (?), OSzK PC 212/139, my translation.

41. Idem, 30 December 1899, my translation.

42. Laura Polanyi's high school graduation certificate, OSzK PC 212/72.

43. Litván and Szücs, *Szabó Ervin levelezése,* vol. 1, 76-81.

44. Duczynska, "Polányi Károly," 90.

45. E.g. Oszkár Jászi, "Emlékiratok (1953-55)" in György Litván and János F. Varga, eds., *Jászi Oszkár publicisztikája* (Budapest: Magvetö, 1982), 558.

46. A. Wohl to Cecile Wohl on 31(18) May 1900, OSzK PC 212/2.

47. Eva Brabant, Ernst Falzeder and Patrizia Giampieri-Deutsch, eds., *The Correspondence of Sigmund Freud and Sándor Ferenczi* vol. 1 (Cambridge, Mass.: Belknap Press of Harvard University Press, 1993), 237.

48. Judit Szapor, "Egy Szabad Egyetemért: A Társadalomtudományok Szabad Iskolája," *Medvetánc* 1985/4-86/1: 125-158.

49. Jászi, "Emlékiratok (1953-55)," 559.

50. Litván and Szücs, *Szabó Ervin levelezése,* vol.1, 56, 57, 63, 152, and others and Litván, *Szabó Ervin,* 34-36.

51. University registration book of Laura Polanyi, OSzK PC 212/74.

52. Letters of Ilona Vargha to Laura Polanyi in 1898 and 1899, OSzK PC 212/212.

53. Letters of Géza Molnár to Laura Polanyi, OSzK PC 212/164.

54. Géza Molnár to Laura Polanyi, 11 August 1901, OSzK PC 212/164, my translation.

55. University registration book of Laura Polanyi, OSzK PC 212/74.

56. OSzK PC 212/264/1 and 212/263.

57. For Szabó's beginnings as a visionary librarian, see Litván, *Szabó Ervin*, 45-49.

58. Litván and Szücs, *Szabó Ervin levelezése*, vol. 1., 245, 246 and 293.

59. Ervin Szabó to Laura Polanyi, 12 July 1903, ibid., 300-1.

60. Letters of Sámuel Glöckner to Laura Polanyi, OSzK PC 212/115.

61. Oszkár Jászi to Szabó, 12 July 1903, Litván and Szücs, *Szabó Ervin levelezése*, vol.1. 298, my translation.

62. Laura Polanyi to Szabó, 10 July 1903, ibid., 296-7, my translation.

63. Laura Polanyi to Szabó, 18 July 1903, ibid., 302, my translation.

64. Laura Polanyi to Szabó, 27 November 1903, ibid., 394-5.

65. Szabó to Laura Polanyi, January 1904, ibid., 412, my translation. On the Museum's mandate, see ibid. 395, note 2.

66. Szabó to Laura Polanyi in April 1904, ibid., 472-3.

67. Laura Polanyi to Szabó on 23 August 1904, ibid., 560, my translation.

68. Karl Polanyi (mistakenly attributed to Cecile Wohl) to Sándor Stricker, 21 August 1904, OSzK PC 212/31, my translation.

69. Henrik Marczali to Laura Polanyi, Riva, Italy, 8 September 1904, OSzK PC 212/159.

70. Margit Kunwald to Laura Polanyi, 27 August 1904, OSzK PC 212/147.

71. Oszkár Jászi married (and later divorced) the artist and writer Anna Lesznai, and the marriage of Pál and Valéria Dienes (he a mathematician, she also a mathematician and philosopher) was a legendary marriage of equals.

72. She also mentioned that her mother planned to have beautiful children, a sign of the eugenic consciousness of the time. Interview with Eva Zeisel, New York, March 1994.

73. In her handwritten notes, probably from her last years, Laura Polanyi carefully documented the achievements of the Stricker ancestors. An uncle of Sándor Stricker was Salomon Stricker, 1834-1898,

the pioneering professor of pathology and founding director of the Institute of Experimental Pathology at the Vienna School of Medicine. OSzK PC 212/268.

74. Karl Polanyi was in fact to work for his uncle in 1907-1908.

75. Adolf Polanyi to Laura Polanyi, 27 July 1905, OSzK PC 212/172.

76. Károly Pollacsek to Laura Polanyi, 22 January 1917, OSzK PC 212/325.

77. Sophie married Egon Szécsi, Adolf's brother-in-law in 1910. Michael Polanyi to Laura Polanyi, 9 August 1910, courtesy of Eva Zeisel.

78. Károly Pollacsek to Laura Polanyi, 22 January 1917, OSzK PC 212/325.

79. Sándor Stricker opened his own textile factory in 1907 in the Bohemian town Königenhof an Elbe. Letters of Laura Polanyi to Sándor Striker, OSzK PC 212/88.

80. *Szabad Gondolat*. A Budapesti Napló melléklete, no. 17 (19 January 1907): 12.

81. Ibid., no. 19 (22 January 1907).

82. Ibid. no. 10 (11 January 1907): 13.

83. University registration book of Laura Polanyi, OSzK PC 212/74.

84. Official copy of doctoral diploma, dated 5 April 1917, in the possession of Eva Zeisel.

85. *Közgazdasági Szemle*, 1909, Budapest, 1-54.

86. Letter of Laura Polanyi to Marshall Fishwick, 13 April 1957, OSzK PC 212/768.

87. See my article, "Les associations féministes en Hongrie, XIXe-XXe siècle", *Pénelope*, no. 11 (Fall 1984): 169-73. The documents of the Association of Feminists are under Font P 999 at the Hungarian National Archives, Budapest.

84. On the women writers and artists of the period, see Erzsébet Vezér, *Kaffka Margit* (Budapest: Szépirodalmi, 1976) and idem, Lesznai Anna élete (Budapest: Kossuth, 1979) as well as Gábor Sánta "Schneider Fáni (Lux Terka Budapestje)", Judit Kádár, "'A legerotikusabb magyar írónö': Erdös Renée", and Csilla E. Csorba, "A kisérletezéstöl az önmegvalósitásig, magyar nö-fotográfusok a századfordulón" in Nagy and Sárdi, eds., *Szerep és alkotás*, 93-100, 117-124 and 101-116.

85. A detailed account of the confrontation within the Sociological Society is provided in Litván, "Bevezetés," esp. 15-22. On the polarization between the nationalists and the progressives, see idem, *"Magyar gondolat - szabad gondolat. "* Note that "radicals" or "bourgeois radicals" were the terms used by the Jászi-circle itself to identify their democratic socialist political program and their party, founded in 1914.

86. For a complete list of the courses offered, see Judit Szapor, "Egy szabad egyetemért," 144-156.

87. On the suffrage as a dividing issue between European social democrats and bourgeois feminists, see Richard Evans, *Comrades and Sisters: Feminism, Socialism, and Pacifism in Europe 1870-1945* (Brighton, Sussex: Wheatsheaf Books; New York: St. Martin's Press, 1987), esp. 1-13 and 37-65. On

the same division in Hungary, Judit Szapor, "Sisters or Foes: Women's Emancipation and Women's Movements in Hungary" in Sylvia Paletschek and Bianka Pietrow-Ennker (eds.), European *Women's Movements in Europe 1870-1918: A Comparative Perspective* (Stanford, Calif.: Stanford University Press, 2004).

88. Invitation to the meeting of the masonic lodge "Könyves Kálmán" on 15 February 1908, in the possession of Eva Zeisel.

89. Letter of Vilma Glücklich, general secretary of the Association of Feminists to Laura Polanyi, 9 November 1909, OSzK PC 212/116.

90. Ferenc Nagy to Laura Polanyi on 3 April 1911, OSzK PC 212/166.

91. OSzK PC 212/75.

92. *A Nö és a Társadalom*, June 1911, 1.

93. I only included engagements for which I found documentary evidence. In her curriculum vitae in 1957 Laura Polanyi wrote: "Lecturer on History and problems of Pedagogy, Adult Education Association, Budapest and all over the country, 1904-1913." OSzK PC 212/76.

94."On the origins of the Russian revolution." Lecture at the "Vorwärts" Workers' Cultural Association. In German. Reprint in Széchényi National Library, Budapest. In Hungarian: "Az orosz forradalom elötörténete" in *Irástudó nemzedékek*, trans. Erzsébet Vezér, 26-37.

95. "Világi erkölcstanitás", *Szabadgondolat* no. 1 (May 1911), 43-45.

96. Programme of the Women's Lyceum for the years 1912/13, OSzK PC 212/264/8.

97. Arthur Koestler, *Arrow in the Blue* (London: W. Collins and H. Hamilton, 1954), 56.

98. *Szabadgondolat* no. 1 (May 1911): 43-45.

99. Kernstok was the second husband of Laura's sister-in-law, the sculptor Gina Stricker.

100. Communication of Eva Zeisel.

101. OSzK PC 212/51 and 212/28.

102. The original document is in the possession of Eva Zeisel.

103. OSzK PC 212/76.

104. Suzannah Lessard, "Profiles: The Present Moment," *New Yorker*, 13 April 1987: 37.

105."Mit akarnak a radikális asszonyok" [What do the Radical women want], OSzK PC 212/264/2. The manuscript of an electoral speech with the proposed list of women candidates is in the possession of Eva Zeisel.

106. Laura Polanyi's letter to Oszkár Jászi in 1942 (no date), in the possession of Eva Zeisel.

107. Lessard, "The Present Moment," 37.

108. Adolf held a position at the Ministry of Commerce while Ernö Seidler, a Polanyi-cousin held the rank of commissar (cabinet minister) in the Hungarian Soviet government. Ervin Szabó who died just prior to the Hungarian October revolution, was canonized by the Republic of Councils as one of the forefathers of the Communist revolution.

109. Litván, "Introduction," in *Homage to Danubia*, esp. X-XV.

110. In Stefan Zweig's memoirs, the bureaucratic restrictions on travel, imposed during and after WWI, came to symbolize the general relapse in civil rights and the triumph of xenophobic nationalism. *The World of Yesterday: An Autobiography* (London: Cassell, 1987), 308.

Chapter 2: The "Radical Women"

1.Thomas Hine, "Lines of the times," *Inquirer*, 26 November 1995, 27.

2. http://www.@artdirect.com/zeisel on 13 December 1995. The website has been since discontinued.

3. Ibid. According to her private communication, Eva Zeisel never considered herself a feminist.

4. The Hungarian Association of Feminists was part of the international network of bourgeois women's organizations and its aims and methods showed remarkable similarities with those of its Western counterparts. Linda Edmondson was the first to point out the striking similarities between the Western and Eastern European feminist movements, defying all explanations based on social or economic development, education or ideology. Edmondson, *Feminism in Russia*, 1.

5. Jane Rendall, "Women and the Public Sphere," *Gender and History*, 11, no. 3 (November 1999): 477.

6. Mary Ryan, *Cradle of the Middle Class: The Family in Oneida County, New York, 1790-1865* (Cambridge, England, New York: Cambridge University Press, 1981).

7. Nancy A. Hewitt, *Women's Activism and Social Change: Rochester, New York, 1822-1872* (Ithaca, N. Y.: Cornell University Press, 1984) and Leonore Davidoff-Catherine Hall *Family Fortunes: Men and Women of the English Middle Class 1780-1850*, (London: Hutchinson, 1987).

8. Examples of this trend can be found, for instance, in the articles of the volume by Nanette Funk and Magda Mueller, eds., *Gender Politics and Post-Communism: Reflections from Eastern Europe and the Former Soviet Union* (New York: Routledge, 1993).

9. This is not to exclude the possibility that future research will be able to come up with local equivalents of the cult of domesticity. One could start with unearthing the virtually unknown history of the Hungarian conservative women's associations in the second half of the 19th century. 10. The editors of a comparative Western women's history warned of "the pitfalls of discourse" and stressed the need to deconstruct traditional stereotypes. Despite the efforts of theorists to distinguish between public and private by equating each sphere with each sex, "spheres and sexes intersected and overlapped, their boundaries vague and fluctuating." Geneviève Fraisse and Michelle Perrot, eds., *A History of Women in the West, vol. 4, Emerging Feminism from Revolution to World War* (Cambridge, Mass., London, England: The Belknap Press of Harvard University Press, 1993), 321.

11. In his comparative studies on the European first-wave women's movements, Richard Evans argued for a more widely defined public sphere, one that includes women's struggle to enter the professions, universities, as well as political life per se. Richard J. Evans, *Comrades and Sisters*, 5.

12. Karen Offen, Ruth Roach Pierson, Jane Rendall, eds., *Writing Women's History* (Bloomington, Ind.: Indiana University Press, 1991), Introduction, xxxii-xxxiii.

13. Barbara Einhorn, *Cinderella Goes to Market: Citizenship, Gender and Women's Movements in East Central Europe* (London, New York: Verso, 1993), 6.

14. Ibid.

15. Ibid.

16. Ibid.

17. In English: Jürgen Habermas, *The Structural Transformation of the Public Sphere: An Inquiry into a Category of Bourgeois Society*, translated by Thomas Burger with Frederick Lawrence (Cambridge, Mass.: Cambridge Univ. Press, 1989).

18. Ibid., 30 and Dena Goodman, "Public Sphere and Private Life: Toward a Synthesis of Current Historiographical Approaches to the Old Regime," *History and Theory* 31, no.1 (1992): 1-2.

19. For Habermas's reception and the recent revival of his early work in the English-speaking world, see Harold Mah, "Phantasies of the Public Sphere: Rethinking the Habermas of Historians," *The Journal of Modern History* 72 (March 2000): 153-182.

20. Susan P. Conner, "Women and Politics" in Samia I. Spencer, ed., *French Women and the Age of Enlightenment* (Bloomington: Indiana University Press, 1984), 50.

21. Ibid.

22. An example is Jean Cohen and Andrew Arato, eds., *Civil Society and Political Theory* (Cambridge, Mass.: MIT Press, 1992).

23. *Feminists read Habermas: Gendering the Subject of Discourse*, edited and with an Introduction by Johanna Meehan (New York and London: Routledge, 1995). The "idealization of the universal public conceals the way in which women's (legal and constitutional) exclusion from the public sphere was a constitutive not a marginal or accidental feature of the bourgeois public from the start," charged Joan Landes in "The Public and the Private Sphere: A Feminist Reconsideration," ibid., 98. More recently, Jane Rendall revisited Habermas and dismissed his work as one of the "simple models of the public sphere or of the public/private contrast ... now limiting our understanding of the vocabulary and practices of eighteenth or nineteenth-century women." Jane Rendall, "Women and the Public Sphere," 483.

24. In an earlier article, Dena Goodman defended Habermas's model as one flexible enough to incorporate the more recent gains of women's history. Dena Goodman, "Enlightenment Salons: The Convergence of Female and Philosophic Ambitions," *Eighteenth Century Studies*, 1989: 329-350. In a subsequent article, she refuted Joan Landes's critique as one based on a misrepresentation of Habermas's model. "Public Sphere and Private Life: toward a synthesis of current historiographical approaches to the Old Regime," *History and Theory*, no. 6 (1992): 1-20.

25. Ibid., 20.

26. Ibid., 16.

27. Ibid.

28. Jürgen Habermas, *A társadalmi nyilvánosság szerkezetváltozása*, trans. Zoltán Endreffy (Budapest: Gondolat, 1971).

29. On the Wohl salon, see Mihály Lackó, *Halál Párizsban, a történész Grünwald Béla művei és*

betegségei (Budapest: Magvető, 1986), 154-6.

30. Ibid., 157-8 and Henrik Marczali, "Emlékeim," *Nyugat*, 22 (1929), no. 3: 224-5.

31. Olwen Hufton, *The Prospect Before Her: A History of Women in Western Europe* (London: Harper&Collins, 1995), 430.

32. Ibid. 431.

33. Ibid.

34. Ute Frevert, *Women in German History: From Bourgeois Emancipation to Sexual Liberation*, trans. Stuart McKinnon-Evans (Oxford, Hamburg, New York: Berg, 1989), 55.

35. Ibid. The best-known study on Rahel Varnhagen is Hannah Arendt, *Rahel Varnhagen: The Life of a Jewish Woman*, trans. Richard and Clara Winston (London: East and West Library, 1957).

36. *Rahel Varnhagen: A Portrait*. Translated from the Swedish by Arthur G. Chater, with an introduction by Havelock Ellis, (New York and London: G. P. Putnam's Sons, 1913), reprint edition (Westport, Conn.: Hyperion Press, 1976).

37. Litván and Varga, *Jászi Oszkár publicisztikája*, 558-59, my translation.

38. On the traditional women's organizations, see Judit Szapor, "Les associations féministes," *Pénelope*, no. 11 (Fall 1984): 169-174, the manuscript of Janka Gergely, Hungarian National Archives, Section P, no. 999, file 19, item 33, 1-2, and Kornélia Burucs, "Nők az egyesületekben," *História*, 15, no. 2 (1993): 15-18.

39. Letter of Cecile Pollacsek to Michael Polanyi, 6 December 1928, transl. Erzsébet Vezér in *Irástudó nemzedékek*, 47-48.

40. Georg Lukács to Leó Popper, Budapest, July 1909, in Éva Fekete and Éva Karádi, eds., *Lukács György levelezése, 1902-1917* (Budapest: Magvető, 1981), 139.

41. Cecile Polanyi (sic) to Georg Lukács, Budapest, 17 May 1910, Vezér, *Irástudó nemzedékek*, 40.

42. Cecile to Lukács on 2 March 1912, ibid., 41-42, complains about not being taken seriously by Lukács and the young generation. A letter of Edit Hajós to Lukács gives further indication that Cecile's complaint was justified: "Cecile insists on lake Starmberg. It's just like her: to go there so that she can have something to talk about at her parties... I feel sorry for Karli. It's much more practical to have a dull but goodhearted and honest mother." Edit Hajós to Lukács, 16 June 1909, LAK (Lukács Archives and Library), copy at the KPA, box 1.

43. Cecile Pollacsek to Lukács, 17 May 1910, Vezér, *Irástudó nemzedékek*, 40-41.

44. Invitation to the lecture of Cecile Pólányi-Pollacsek, OSzK PC 212/10.

45. Vezér, *Irástudó nemzedékek*, 47-48.

46. *Neue Pester Journal*, December 1924, *Pester Lloyd*, 19 December 1927.

47. OSzK PC 212/68.

48. "The History of the Russian Revolution," lecture at the *Vorwärts* Workers' Cultural Association, reprint in the Széchényi National Library, trans. Erzsébet Vezér, *Irástudó nemzedékek*, 26-37.

49. Ibid., 37, my translation.

50. Ibid.

51. A postcard that Cecile sent to Eva, her then 3-year-old granddaughter, shows the main building of the Bircher-Benner Sanitorium. OSzK PC 212/30.

52. Eva Brabant, Ernst Falzeder and Patrizia Giampieri-Deutsch, eds., *The Correspondence of Sigmund Freud and Sándor Ferenczi*, vol. 1 (Cambridge, Mass.: Belknap Press of Harvard University Press, 1993), 237. Italics in the original.

53. Ibid., 238.

54. Ibid.

55. Edit Rényi, a member of Lukács's Sunday Circle and Juliska Láng, the wife of Karl Mannheim, were among the first trained analysts in Hungary.

56. Vezér, "A Polányi család," *Irástudó nemzedékek*, 9.

57. Cecile to Georg Lukács, 2 March 1912, Ibid., 41.

58. Vezér, "The Polanyi family," *The Life and Work of Karl Polanyi: A Celebration*, 21.

59. On the history of the Association, see Szapor, "Les associations féministes," 169-17; "Sisters or Foes: The Shifting Frontlines of the Hungarian Women's Movement" and Susan Zimmermann, "Frauenbestrebungen und Frauenbewegungen in Ungarn Zur Organizationsgeschichte der Jahre 1848 bis 1918," in Nagy and Sárdi, *Szerep és alkotás*, 171-204.

60. J[anka] G[ergely], manuscript, Hungarian National Archives, Section P, no. 999, The documents of the Association of Feminists, file 19, item 33.

61. Ibid.

62. On the history of the international women's rights organizations, see Leila J. Rupp, *Worlds of Women: The Making of an International Women's Movement* (Princeton, New Jersey: Princeton University Press, 1997), especially 14-26.

63. It is an important point on which, at least as far as the Hungarian feminist movement is concerned, the portrait of the international leadership drawn by Leila J. Rupp needs to be corrected. Rupp talks about the pervasive Christian spirit and sometimes manifest anti-Semitism of the international leadership as well as the Jewish members' repressed Jewishness in Rupp, *Worlds of Women*, esp. 52-60.

64. Strickerné Pollacsek Laura, *Néhány szó a nöröl s nönevelésröl* (Budapest, 1906), reprint in the Széchényi National Library. Vezér, *Irástudó nemzedékek*, 49-60. The text suggests that it was written for a debate, the specifics of which I was not able to find out; most likely a debate at the headquarters of the Association of Feminists.

65. See, among others, the articles of Andor Máday, "Feminism as class struggle" and Rózsa Bédy-Schwimmer, "The Role of Women in the Transformation of Society" in the feminist bulletin *A Nö és a Társadalom* [The Woman and Society], vol. 1 (1907), 18 and 115, respectively.

66. Laura Polanyi, "*Néhány szó a nöröl,*" in Vezér, *Irástudó nemzedékek*, 51.

67. See the letter of Vilma Glücklich to Laura Polanyi, Budapest, 9 November 1909, in which the former ends her letter with the rather official greeting: "Looking forward to your prompt reply, with comradely regards." OSzK PC 212/116.

68. "Az értelmiségi középosztály asszonya," *Szabad Gondolat, a Budapesti Napló melléklete*, 19 January 1907, 12.

69. Harkányi Ede, "A házasság csödje," *Szabad Gondolat*, a *Budapesti Napló* melléklete, no. 18, 11 January 1907, 12. Harkányi published two volumes, *A holnap férfiai*, 1904 and *A holnap asszonyai*, 1905 ([Men of Tomorrow] and [Women of Tomorrow]), both in the series The Library of Social Sciences (Budapest: Grill Karoly).

70. Ede Harkányi to Laura Polanyi, 13 September 1909, OSzK PC 212/124. The daily *Világ* (literally: Light) was in fact launched in 1910 with the financial backing of the Freemasons and became the main forum of the radicals; there is no sign, however, that Laura Polanyi ever published in it.

71. See Evans, *Comrades and Sisters*, 87-88.

72. Sz. G., "A feminista mozgalom," *Huszadik Század*, vol. 14 (July-December 1913): 72, my translation.

73. Ibid, my translation.

74. Ibid., 73.

75. Document in the possession of Eva Zeisel.

76. For the range of individual reactions to the war among Hungarian intellectuals, see Congdon, *Exile and Social Thought*, 3-27. On page 5, Congdon raises an important point which explains—if does not excuse—the pro-war position of the intellectuals, namely that Hungarians anti-Russian sentiment was justifiable because of Russia's role in crushing the 1848-1849 Hungarian revolution.

77. For the ideological connection between feminism and pacifism, see Evans, "Women's Peace, Men's War?" in *Comrades and Sisters*, 121-156 and esp. 122-124.

78. For a detailed account of Schwimmer's activities during the war, see Anne Wiltsher, *Most Dangerous Women: Feminist Peace Campaigners of the Great War* (London, Boston and Henley: Pandora, 1985.

79. Ilona Duczynska, "I first met Karl Polanyi in 1929...," 308.

80. Karl Polanyi to Laura Polanyi, September 1915, OSzK PC 212/325, in Hungarian, my translation.

81. OSzK PC 212/76, page 1.

170 The Hungarian Pocahontas

82. Anne Wiltsher, *Dangerous Women*; Johanna Alberti, *Beyond Suffrage: Feminists in War and Peace, 1914-28* (London: Macmillan, 1989); Richard Evans, *Comrades and Sisters*.

83. Wiltsher, *Dangerous Women*, 127.

84. Ibid., 162. On the history and failure of the Peace Ship expedition, *Ibid.*, 154-174.

85. Lessard, "The Present Moment," 36-37.

86. The diplomatic world was not ready for a woman, let alone a Jewish woman ambassador. There were financial and communication problems as well as relentless intrigues from her old-school collegues; she resigned within two months. The correspondance of Count Károlyi provides details of Schwimmer's valiant battle. György Litván, ed., *Károlyi Mihály levelezése*, vol. 1., 1905-1920 (Akadémiai: Budapest, 1978), nos. 287, 291, 298-9, 307, 308, 340-342, 345, 348, 350-351, 355-6, 373, 380, 383. About the circumstances of Schwimmer's resignation, see ibid., note to no. 383, pp. 388-390.

87. Lessard, "The Present Moment," 37 and www.@artdirect.com/zeisel, December 13, 1995.

88. Interview with Eva Zeisel, New York, March 1995.

89. Vezér, *Irástudó nemzedékek*, 12.

90. "Mit akarnak a radikális asszonyok?," OSzK PC 212/264/2.

91. "Mit akarnak a radikális asszonyok?," in the possession of Eva Zeisel.

92. Mária M. Kovács, "The Politics of Emancipation in Hungary," in Andrea Pető and Mark Pittaway, eds., *Women in History - Women's History: Central and Eastern European Perspectives*, CEU History Department Working Papers Series 1 (Budapest: Central European University, 1994), 81-85.

93. Strickerné Pollacsek Laura, *Néhány szó a nöröl s nönevelésröl* in Vezér, *Irástudó nemzedékek*, 49-60.

94. The numbers, impossible to confirm, seem to be inflated for the sake of her argument. Zimmermann, "Frauenbestrebungen und Frauenbewegungen," 202-203, estimates the membership in 1917 at approximately 4000.

95. For a more detailed discussion of the Hungarian political context, see Judit Szapor, "Feministák és 'radikális asszonyok:' Nöi politikusok az 1918-as demokratikus forradalomban," in Beáta Nagy, ed., *Magyar nök a politikában* (Debrecen: Csokonai, forthcoming).

96. Kovács, in "The Politics of Emancipation in Hungary," discusses the emergence of a post-1919 conservative women's rights groups, without acknowledging their pre-war origins within or outside of the mainstream bourgeois feminist movement.

97. The writer Tibor Déry described the guests as a mix of "a few significant men and their snobbish entourage" in his memoirs *Itélet nincs*, (Budapest: Magvető and Szépirodalmi, 1979), 336.

98. Ernö Glatz, "Prologue," manuscript in the possession of Eva Zeisel.

99. Those who turned Communist though, as for instance Lukács did, were offered another chance after the Second World War.

100. Litván, *Károlyi Mihály Levelezése*, vol. 1, 562.

101. Laura Polanyi to Oszkár Jászi, 16 February 1945, draft of letter in the possession of Eva Zeisel.

102. Oszkár Jászi to Laura Polanyi, n. d., in the possession of Eva Zeisel.

103. Laura Polanyi to Oszkár Jászi, 16 February 1945, in the possession of Eva Zeisel.

Chapter 3: "The Hungarian Jug was Shattered, Scattered into a Hundred Pieces"

1. Karl Mannheim, "Letter from Heidelberg I," in Éva Gábor, ed., *Mannheim Károly levelezése 1911-1946* (Budapest: Argumentum, MTA Lukács Archivum, 1996), 233, my translation.

2. Oszkár Jászi to Róbert Braun on 30 August 1919, in Litván and Varga, *Jászi Oszkár levelezése*, 227, my translation. Jászi left Hungary in May 1919, in protest against the Bolshevik dictatorship that itself fell on August the 1st.

3. Karl Mannheim to Oszkár Jászi, Frankfurt am Main, 25 April 1933, Gábor, *Mannheim Károly levelezése*, 60, my translation.

4. Jászi to Mannheim, 11 February 1933, Ibid., 56.

5. Mannheim to Jászi, 25 April 1933, Ibid., 60.

6. The degree of displacement is well illustrated by the Polanyis' family tree. Out of the 23 family members of the second and third generations, 19 changed their country of residence between 1919 and 1942.

7. See Laura Polányi's notes on Egon Szécsi, in the possession of Eva Zeisel.

8. According to the verbal communication of György Litván, Adolf was accused by his fellow exiles of embezzling party funds.

9. Interview with Ruth Danon, Adolf Polanyi's granddaughter, New York, April 2001.

10. "The news from Adolf really are better; if it's true and stays that way, Adolf now makes close to 24,000 lira which is quite a nice income." Karl Polányi to Laura Polányi, Vienna, 1 November 1922, OSzK PC 212/325.

11. Letter of Cecile Pollacsek to Michael Polanyi, 6 December 1928, Vezér, *Irástudó nemzedékek*, 47; Márta Vágó, *József Attila* (Budapest: Szépirodalmi, 1975), 115 and 119; Interview with Ruth Danon, New York, April 2001.

12. An excellent short biography of Duczynska, Dalos, *A cselekvés szerelmese*, was published in Hungarian, and Kenneth McRobbie is said to be working on her biography as well.

13. Kenneth McRobbie, "Ilona Duczynska: A Sovereign Revolutionary," in McRobbie and Polanyi-Levitt, *Karl Polanyi in Vienna*, 254.

14. "From Central Europe, Three Friends Remember: Eva Czjek, Erzsébet Vezér, György Litván," in McRobbie and Polanyi-Levitt, *Karl Polanyi In Vienna*, 283.

15. Ibid. 287.

16. György Dalos, "The Fidelity of Equals: Ilona Duczynska and Karl Polanyi," in Polanyi-Levitt, *The Life and Work of Karl Polanyi*, 42.

17. Dalos, *A cselekvés szerelmese*, 97.

18. Dalos, "The Fidelity of Equals," 38.

19. See Richard Stites, *Revolutionary Dreams: Utopian Vision and Experimental Life in the Russian Revolution* (New York, Oxford: Oxford University Press, 1989) and Edmondson, *Feminism in Russia,* 9-10.

20. Interview with Ruth Danon, April 2001.

21. Felix Schiffer, "Vorgartenstrasse 203: Extracts from a Memoir," in McRobbie and Polanyi-Levitt, *Karl Polanyi in Vienna,* 340.

22. "From Central Europe, Three Friends Remember: Eva Czjek, Erzsébet Vezér, György Litván," 282.

23. Ilona Duczynska, "I first met Karl Polanyi in 1920...," 305.

24. Ibid. 304-5.

25. Ibid. 304. Duczynska's reminiscences, extensively quoted in various versions of the family's history, became an important source of the myths surrounding the Polányis.

26. According to Laura's daughter, Eva Zeisel, buying the garden and marrying her mother were her father's "two bursts of vision." Lessard, "The present moment," 50.

27. Interview with Eva Zeisel, March 1995. Her memories of the Whites "taking rich Jews to the Danube" may reflect later events, namely the atrocities committed by Hungarian Fascists 25 years later, during WWII. Or they may be coloured by the memory of the political murder of Béla Somogyi, the respected editor of the Social Democratic daily *Népszava* in January 1920—his and his assistant's body were indeed found in the Danube.

28. Lessard, "The Present Moment," 37.

29. The actual numbers of those killed have been contested by the opposite political sides for the last eighty years. I follow the numbers quoted by a recent, excellent English-language survey of Hungarian history: László Kontler, *Millennium in Central Europe: A History of Hungary* (Budapest: Atlantisz, 1999), 338-342.

30. As Károlyi recounted in his memoirs, his wife, the eternal optimist, predicted their exile to last for three months, himself, the eternal pessimist, a year. It was to last twenty seven years. Mihály Károlyi, *Hit illuziók nélkül,* Hungarian translation by György Litván (Budapest: Európa, 1977), 179.

31. OSzK PC 212/268.

32. Kontler, *Millennium in Central Europe,* 352.

33. Litván, *Károlyi Mihály levelezése,* vol. 1, 559, 647.

34. János Jemnitz and György Litván, *Szerette az igazságot* (Budapest: Gondolat, 1977), 212.; Litván, *Károlyi Mihály levelezése,* vol. 1, 560-61.

35. Litván, *Károlyi Mihály levelezése,* vol 1, 559, 575, 647, 649.

174 *The Hungarian Pocahontas*

36. An anecdote about the escape of Georg Lukács, People's Commissar of Education during the Bolshevik dictatorship, is highly illustrative of the fine lines these women trod. In the fall of 1919, Lukács, with a price on his head, was hiding in the attic of the studio of Olga Máté. She was the widow of the philosopher Béla Zalai who died as a prisoner of war in Russia, and an acclaimed photographer in her own right. Following a denunciation, the police came to search her studio and found Lukács's personal belongings in her closet. Without a moment's hesitation, she slipped into the role of the war-widow and snapped at the policemen: "'Don't dare to touch them! They're all that remain of my husband's things!" Upon which the men searching the house saluted the martyr's widow and left. Fekete and Karádi, *György Lukács: His Life in Pictures and Documents*, 116-7.

37. Recent English overviews of Hungary's history that provide balanced interpretations of the interwar period: Péter Hanák, ed., *The Corvina History of Hungary: From the Earliest Times until the Present Day*, translated by Zsuzsa Béres (Budapest: Corvina, 1991), esp. 175-203, and Kontler, *Millennium in Central Europe*, 325-364.

38. Bethlen's concept of "conservative democracy" included the re-introduction of public voting outside the capital and the largest urban centres, a measure unparalleled in contemporary Europe, the decrease in the number of women eligible to vote, and the legalization of the Social Democratic Party only in exchange for its foregoing the organization of public servants and agricultural workers. For an overview of the changes in the suffrage of the period, in a European comparative perspective, see Gábor Gyáni and György Kövér, *Magyarország társadalomtörténete a reformkortól a második világháboruig* (Budapest: Osiris, 1998), 334-337.

39. 425,000 families received 8.5% of the arable land, still leaving nearly half of the peasantry (20% of the population) landless, and maintaining the concentration of 30% of the country's arable land in the hands of four hundred landowning families. Kontler, *Millennium in Central Europe*, 347.

40. Ibid., 358, rightly stresses the continuity of the cleavage, but neglects to mention the changed dynamics between the two sides.

41. Kontler somewhat understates the case when he writes that "the intellectual climate did not favour the modernist and progressive trends." Ibid.

42. Kontler, *Millennium in Central Europe*, 359.

43. For an analysis of the populist movement and the cleavage between the "urban" and "populist" intellectuals, see the essays of Miklós Lackó in *Válságok-választások* (Budapest: Gondolat, 1975) and *Sziget és külvilág* (Budapest: MTA Történettudományi Intézete, 1996).

44. Katalin N. Szegvári, *Numerus clausus intézkedések az ellenforradalmi Magyarországon* (Budapest: Akadémiai, 1988); Kovács, "The Politics of Emancipation in Hungary," in Pető and Pittaway, *Women in History - Women's History*, 81-89; and Viktor Karády, "A numerus clausus és a zsidó értelmiség," *Iskolarendszer és a felekezeti egyenlötlenségek Magyarországon (1867-1945)* (Budapest: Replika, 1997), 235-245.

45. The number of Hungarian-Jewish students studying abroad, according to various estimates, was approximately equal to those attending university in Hungary and 70-90% of the Hungarian students abroad were Jewish. Viktor Karády, "Egyetemi antiszemitizmus és érvényesülési kényszerpályák: Magyar zsidó diákság a nyugat-európai föiskolákon a *numerus clausus* alatt," in *Iskolarendszer és a felekezeti egyenlötlenségek Magyarországon*, 253-4.

46. In the late 1920s, the University of Vienna was still Hungarian students' first pick, along with Charles University of Prague, especially its medical school. A smaller number went to German universities. From the mid-1930s, following the rise of Nazism, these switched to the universities of Italy and France. Ibid., 247-266.

47. Ibid., 254.

48. Manès Sperber, *All Our Yesterdays, Vol. II., The Unheeded Warning, 1918-1933*, Translated by Harry Zohn (New York, London: Holmes & Meier, 1994), 47.

49. The description is based on the memoirs of two of his friends from Vienna and Berlin, Arthur Koestler and Manès Sperber. Manès Sperber, *All Our Yesterdays, Vol. II., The Unheeded Warning, 1918-1933*, Translated by Harry Zohn (New York, London: Holmes & Meier, 1994), 69-71; Arthur Koestler, *The Invisible Writing, The Second Volume of an Autobiography: 1932-40* (New York: First Stein and Day Editions, 1984), 61-62.

50. Curriculum Vitae, Dr. Hans Zeisel, in the possession of Eva Zeisel and Paul F. Lazarsfeld, "An Episode in the History of Social Research: A Memoir," Donald Fleming and Bernard Bailyn, eds., *The Intellectual Migration: Europe and America, 1930-1960* (Cambridge, Mass.: The Belknap Press of Harvard University Press, 1969), 275.

51. Lessard, "The Present Moment," 37.

52. Ibid., 38; Lucie Young, "Still Ahead of the Curve," *New York Times*, 14 August 1997, C6.

53. Lessard, "The present moment," 38.

54. Ibid., 39.

55. Ibid.

56. Ibid.

57. Eva Zeisel, Memoirs, Unpublished manuscript, 69.

58. Ibid., 68.

59. Congdon, *Exile and Social Thought,* xi.

60. Ibid.

61. Lessard, "The Present Moment," 40.

62. Victor Weisskopf, *The Joy of Insight: Passions of a Physicist* (New York: Basic Books, 1991), 45. Weisskopf also described Eva's parties in an interview given to Leó Szilárd's biographer. William Lanouette with Bela Silard, *Genius in the Shadows: A Biography of Leo Szilard, The Man Behind the Bomb* (New York: C. Scribner's Sons, Toronto: Maxwell Macmillan Canada, New York: Maxwell Macmillan International, 1992), 78-79.

63. Eva Zeisel, Memoirs, 68.

64. Ibid., 68-69.

65. Interview with Hilde Striker, New York, March 1995. When I met her in her Central Park West apartment in 1995, she was near 90, still working at the office every day.

66. Karády, in "Egyetemi antiszemitizmus," *Iskolarendszer és a felekezeti egyenlötlenségek Magyarországon*, 256, terms it a "new culture of emigration."

67. Lessard, "The Present Moment," 39.

68. *Esti Kurir*, 11 April 1931.

69. A copy of the dissertation, in Eva Zeisel's possession, bears Michael's name. According to Michael Striker's sister-in-law, Barbara Stricker, Michael received his doctorate in economics. Barbara Striker, "Re: Judit Szapor, 'Laura Polányi 1882-1959: Narratives of a Life'", *Polanyiana*, vol. 8 nos. 1-2 (1999), 83. It is also possible that he submitted the dissertation for his doctorate in law, a degree we know he possessed and for which academic requirements were notoriously lax.

70. Gyáni and Kövér, *Magyarország társadalomtörténete a reformkortól a második világháboruig*, 244.

71. In her correspondence, a letter from a fellow historian of 18th-century Habsburg economic history referred to the forthcoming publication of her study on Maria Theresa and Charles IV. Ödön Málnási to Laura Polányi, Eger, 22 March 1934, OSzK PC, 212/156.

72. Lucie Young, "Still Ahead of the Curve," C6.

73. See ibid., as well as Lessard, "The Present Moment" and others.

74. Karen E. Steen, "The playful search for beauty," *Metropolis*, January 2001, 85.

75. Koestler expressed hope that she would eventually change her mind. Arthur Koestler to Eva Zeisel, London, 17 January 1977, letter in the possession of Eva Zeisel.

76. An example of this ambiguity is the introductory essay to the catalogue of her exhibition at Montreal's *Musée des Arts Décoratifs* that skips her imprisonment entirely and glosses over her exit from the Soviet Union in the following short passage: "Like many foreign experts, she was removed from her position. In September, 1937, she left the Soviet Union and sought refuge in Vienna where her aunt and younger brother were living." *Eva Zeisel, Designer for Industry*, catalogue essay by Martin Eidelberg, Le Château Dufresne, Inc. Musée des Arts Décoratifs de Montréal, distributed by the University of Chicago Press and in Canada by Macmillan of Canada, 1984, 28.

77. Introducing her memoirs, Eva Zeisel provided the disclaimer: "none of it is true, but I shall be precise reporting my memories." Memoirs, 1.

78. Lessard, "The present moment," 42.

79. Ibid., 70.

80. Ibid.

81. Alexander Weissberg, *The Accused*, Translated by Edward Fitzgerald, with a preface by Arthur Koestler (New York: Simon and Shuster, 1951), 157.

82. Koestler, *The Invisible Writing*, 67. For a more detailed description of the Kharkov Institute in the context of the international network of physics, see my article, "A Matter of Life or Death: Western Physicists at the Ukrainian Physico-Technical Institute in the 1930s," in A. de Graaf and A. Ninetto (eds.), *Migrant Scientists in the Twentieth Century* (New York: Palgrave, forthcoming).

83. Lessard, "The Present Moment," 40.

84. During a recent interview, she denied when asked if it was ever a consideration. Interview with Eva Zeisel, April 1995.

85. Koestler, *The Invisible Writing*, 67.

86. Lessard, "The Present Moment," 40.

87. Ibid., 40-41.; Eva Zeisel, Memoirs, 73, 75, 81-82. On a lighter note, Victor Weisskopf referred the story of their group, including Eva, visiting a collective farm in the Ukraine at the time of the famine. *The Joy of Insight*, 55-58.

88. Eva Zeisel, Memoirs, 78.

89. Ibid., 77.

90. Ibid., 73.

91. Ibid., 80., Lessard, "The Present Moment," 43.

92. Eva Zeisel, Memoirs, 101.

93. In an interview, he modestly added that he was "just one day earlier" than most, having taken the train from Berlin to Vienna on the day after the Reichstag burned. Leo Szilard, "Reminiscences," in Fleming and Bailyn, *The Intellectual Migration*, 95, 97.

94. Ibid. , 96.

95. Gábor, *Mannheim Károly levelezése*, 53-54 and 56-58.

96. Ibid., 59-61.

97. Koestler, *The Invisible Writing*, 182. An almost identical description of the conversation is provided in Weissberg, *The Accused*, 212-13.

98. Koestler, *The Invisible Writing*, 182-3.

99. Ibid. 195.

100. The date is indicated on their divorce decree, dated from April 1938, in the possession of Eva Zeisel.

101. Lessard, "The Present Moment," 44.

102. Lessard, "The Present Moment," 44.

103. According to the widow of Michael's younger brother, Hevesi was at the time head of the Soviet Film Industry. Interview with Barbara Stricker, Budapest, December 1997.

104. Eva Zeisel, Memoirs, 22.

105. His letters from Moscow, describing mostly positive impressions, were published by Endre Kárpáti, "Madzsar József moszkvai leveleiből," *Századok*, vol. 105, no. 1 (1971): 105-134.

106. Melissa A. Biggs, "Spirited Touch," *Metropolis*, November 1994, 42. Examples of Eva Zeisel's work in the Soviet Union were exhibited at the Knoxville Museum of Art, February 20-June 20, 2004 and are reprinted in the exhibition's catalogue, Karen L. Kettering and Knoxville Museum of Art, "The playful search for beauty," (Knoxville, Tenessee: 2004).

107. Lessard, "The Present Moment," 44.

108. Interviews with Eva Zeisel, March 1995 and April 2001.

109. The June 1936 decree reversed the previous, 1920 regulation and banned abortion, except in medically necessary cases. It remained in force until 1955. Endre Kárpáti, "Madzsar József moszkvai leveleiből," 121.

110. Laura Polanyi to Mrs. Armitage, 27 July 1943, OSzK PC, 212/80.

111. Ervin Sinkó, *Egy regény regénye: Moszkvai naplójegyzetek 1935-1937* (Ujvidék: Forum, Budapest: Magvető, 1988), 148-49, 158-59.

112. Ibid. 166-67.

113. It is worth recalling the fact, however, that Michael Polanyi, Laura's brother, needed only a short visit in the Soviet Union to arrive at a devastating critique of the Soviet system. In his *USSR Economics: Fundamental Data, System, and Spirit* (Manchester: University of Manchester Press, 1936), he lamented the lack of free entreprise and the fundamental shortcomings of central planning.

114. Interview with Eva Zeisel, April 2001.

115. Alexander Orlov, *The Secret History of Stalin's Crimes* (New York: Random House, 1953).

116. See, among others, Robert Conquest, *Stalin and the Kirov Murder* (New York, Oxford: Oxford University Press, 1989), 109-112.

117. Orlov, *The Secret History*, 107.

118. Ibid., 107-109. Eva Zeisel also refers to this passage of Orlov's book in her interview for the *New Yorker*. Lessard, "The Present Moment," 46.

119. Young, "Still Ahead Of the Curve," C6.

120. A further argument against Eva Zeisel's suggestion that she was to play a key role in the Zinoviev-Kamenev trial is based on common sense: were that the case, the NKVD would have never released her; many people disappeared for knowledge much less dangerous.

121. Memoirs, 51.

122. Lessard, "The Present Moment," 44.

123. Memoirs, 65 and Lessard, "The Present Moment," 46.

124. Ibid. 46.

125. As an example, "an April 1935 Soviet law made children down to the age of twelve subject to all the same penalties as adults—a law that was later to be used to put pressure on arrested oppositionists in blackmailing them into confessions by threats against their young offspring. On June 1935, a complementary law was published which, for the first time, held family members responsible even if ignorant of their relations' crimes." Conquest, *Stalin and the Kirov Murder*, 78.

126. Lessard, "The Present Moment," 46.

127. Ibid.

128. Weissberg, *The Accused*, 103.

129. Arthur Koestler, Preface to Weissberg, *The Accused*, xi.

130. Alexander Weissberg to Hans Zeisel, London, 22 March 1948, in the possession of Eva Zeisel.

131. Ibid.

132. "*Die letzte Aktion, die wir gemeinsam unternahmen, war die, die ins am meinsten einanden nahe brachte; der Kampf um Deine Befreidung.*" Alex Weissberg to Eva Zeisel, Hamburg, 22 February 1960, in the possession of Eva Zeisel.

133. Ibid.

134. Interview with Eva Zeisel, March 1995. As for the possible impact of these references on Eva's release, one should consider the fact that by the time Eva was released, most if not all of their authors had been arrested as well.

135. "During the spring and early summer of 1937 the pressure upon investigators, procurators, and judges to find, prosecute, and punish 'wreckers' and 'traitors' responsible for the catalogue of ills cited by Molotov mounted continuously. ... Moreover, Vyshinskii also made it clear to regional procurators that a low rate of prosecutions for political offenses would be considered as a sign of poor performance." Peter H. Solomon, Jr., *Soviet Criminal Justice under Stalin* (Cambridge, U. K., New York: Cambridge University Press, 1996), 241.

136. "By the summer of 1937 it was hard for any justice official to withstand the pressure to join rank and lay political charges wherever possible. For, once the Purge went into high gear and judges and procurators themselves were registered among its victims, pursuing the vigilance campaign became a matter of life and death for Soviet legal officials." Ibid., 242.

137. Ibid., 247.

138. Koestler, Preface to Weissberg, *The Accused*, xi.

139. Eva Zeisel, Memoirs, 66.

140. Ibid., 85-86.

141. He arrived at 9 million, which in 1951, at the time of his autobiography's publication, was as good as any other known estimate. See Koestler's Preface to Weissberg, *The Accused*, xv.

142. The exact date of Michael Stricker's return is given in Weissberg's book. He received a package from Laura in October 1937 and in it, sewn into a pair of fur gloves, in the best romantic traditions, was a small piece of paper. The message read: "Ena [Eva] is free and in Austria. Vicki [Misi] too. He has been in Vienna for a month now. We expect you soon, but be careful. Make a halt in Prague on your way back and get in touch with us from there. Because of your arrest everyone knows that you're a Communist—including the police." Weissberg, *The Accused*, 351.

143. Ibid., 338-39.

144. Weissberg gave power of attorney to his brother, Samuel Weissberg, an attorney in Vienna, to proceed with the divorce in his absence. The document is in the possession of Eva Zeisel.

145. Barbara Striker, "'This is the voice of Radio Schutzbund'," Kenneth McRobbie and Kari Polanyi Levitt, *Karl Polanyi in Vienna*, 272.

146. Ibid, 273.

147. Ilona Duczynska, "I first met Karl Polanyi in 1920," 311.

148. Barbara Striker, "'This is the voice of Radio Schutzbund'," in *Karl Polanyi in Vienna*, 272-74.

149. McRobbie, "Ilona Duczynska: Sovereign Revolutionary," 257.

150. Endre J. Nagy, "After Brotherhood's Golden Age: Karl and Michael Polanyi," Kenneth McRobbie, ed., *Humanity, society and commitment: On Karl Polanyi* (Montréal, New York: Black Rose Books, 1994), 98-99.

151. Interviews with Eva Zeisel, March 1995, April 2001.

152. Letter of Dr. Endre Stricker to Laura Polányi, 14 August, no year, in the possession of Eva Zeisel.

Chapter 4: The Odyssey of the Polanyis

1. Dr. Endre Stricker to Laura Polanyi, Kolozsvár (Cluj), 14 August 1939, in the possession of Eva Zeisel, my translation.

2. Ibid.

3. Polgár was an official of the war-time Jewish self-administration in Budapest. Randolph L. Braham, *A magyar Holocaust* (Budapest: Gondolat, Wilmington: Blackburn International Corporation, 1988), vol. 1, 75, 357. He was in a group of prominent Hungarian Jews that the SS released to Switzerland in 1944 in a deal negotiated by the Hungarian Zionist leaders. Laura's niece, Lili Radvanyi and her husband, the psychiatrist Lipót Szondi, were also in this group. On the controversial deal, see Braham, *A magyar Holocaust*, vol. 2, chapter 29, 285-310, and, from an American perspective, David S. Wyman, *The Abandonment of the Jews: America and the Holocaust, 1941-1945* (New York: Pantheon Books, 1984) 243-45.

4. György Polgár to Laura Polanyi, Geneva, 25 November 1945, OSzK PC 212/174, my translation and emphasis.

5. See e. g. Laura Fermi, *Illustrious Immigrants*, 113-14.

6. This overview is not aspiring to fulfill the need for a long-overdue survey of the literature on the refugee intellectuals. The author of a relatively recent, excellent history of the New School for Social Research offers a critique of the American scholarship up to the mid-1990s. Claus-Dieter Krohn, *Intellectuals in Exile: Refugee Scholars and the New School for Social Research*, translated by Rita and Robert Kimber (Amherst, Mass.: The University of Mass. Press, 1993), 1-11.

7. Maurice R. Davie, *Refugees in America: Report of the Committee for the Study of Recent Immigration from Europe* (New York, London: Harper and Brothers, 1947; Donald Peterson Kent, *The Refugee Intellectual: The Americanization of the Immigrants of 1933-1941* (New York: Columbia University Press, 1953).

8. Peter Gay, "Weimar Culture: The Outsider as Insider," in Fleming and Bailyn, *The Intellectual Migration*, 12.

9. W. Rex Crawford, Introduction, Franz L. Neumann, Henri Peyre, Erwin Panowsky, Wolfgang Köhler, and Paul Tillich, *The Cultural Migration: The European Scholar in America* (University of Philadelphia Press, 1953, New York: Barnes & Co., Perpetua Edition, 1960), 1.

10. Peter Gay, in his essay "Weimar Culture: The Outsider as Insider," Fleming and Bailyn, *The Intellectual Migration*, 11-93, applied Neumann's line of argument to Weimar culture to conclude that the dazzling creativity of Weimar stemmed, to a large degree, from the outsider position of its creators.

11. Fleming and Bailyn, *The Intellectual Migration*; Robert Boyers, ed., *The Legacy of the German Refugee Intellectuals* (New York: Schocken, 1972), especially the essay of Henry Pachter, "On Being an Exile: An Old-Timer's Personal and Political Memoir"; Jarrell C. Jackman and Carla M. Borden, eds., *The Muses Flee Hitler: Cultural Transfer and Adaptation, 1930-1945* (Washington D. C.: Smithsonian Institution Press, 1983). An example of a similar approach in a different genre is the insightful survey of

Fermi, *Illustrious Immigrants.*

12. Roger Daniels, *Coming to America: A History of Immigration and Ethnicity in American Life* (New York: HarperCollins, 1990) and idem, "American Refugee Policy in Historical Perspective," in Jackman and Borden, *The Muses Flee Hitler*, 61-77; Henry L. Feingold, *The Politics of Rescue: The Roosevelt Administration and the Holocaust, 1938-1945* (New Brunswick, N. J.: Rutgers University Press, 1970); Saul S. Friedman, *No Haven for the Oppressed: United States Policy Toward Jewish Refugees, 1938-1945* (Detroit: Wayne State University Press, 1973); David S. Wyman, *Paper Walls: America and the Refugee Crisis, 1938-1941* (Amherst, Mass.: The University of Mass. Press, 1968, revised edition New York: Pantheon Books, 1985); and idem, *The Abandonment of the Jews: America and the Holocaust, 1941-1945* (New York: Pantheon Books, 1984).

13. Cynthia Jaffee McCabe, "'Wanted by the Gestapo: Saved by America'—Varian Fry and the Emergency Rescue Committee," Jackman, Borden, *The Muses Flee Hitler* (Washington, D.C.: Smithonian Institution Press, 1983), 79-91.

14. Andy Marino, *A Quiet American: The Secret War of Varian Fry* (New York: St. Martin's Press, 1999). It was, however, followed closely by another, popular biography, Sheila Isenberg, *A Hero of Our Own: The Story of Varian Fry* (New York: Random House, 2001) as well as a feature film, produced by HBO.

15. The *exiles + emigrés: The Flight of European Artists from Hitler* exhibition and its catalogue, Stephanie Barron with Sabine Eckmann, eds., Los Angeles County Museum of Art, 1997, is an outstanding example of the latter.

16. Recent examples are Peter Gay, *My German Question: Growing Up in Nazi Berlin* (New Haven, Conn.: Yale University Press, 1998); Herbert Strauss, *In the Eye of the Storm* (New York: Fordham University Press, 1999); Lotte Strauss, *Over the Green Hill: A German Jewish Memoir, 1913-1943* (New York: Fordham University Press, 1999); and the part memoir, part generational portrait of Walter Laqueur, *Generation Exodus: The Fate of Young Jewish Refugees from Nazi Germany* (University Press of New England for Brandeis University Press, 2001).

17. An example of this sometimes arbitrary compartmentalization is Hartmut Lehmann and James J. Sheehan, eds., *An Interrupted Past: German-Speaking Refugee Historians in the U.S. after 1933* (Washington, D.C. German Historical Institute, Cambridge, New York: Cambridge University Press, 1991).

18. Pachter, in his essay "On Being an Exile," Boyers, ed., *The Legacy of the German Refugee Intellectuals*, already warned of the dangers of simplistic classification of this kind, citing the example of such subgroups as White Russians, Red Spaniards and Hungarian Communists.

19. Andreas Lixl-Purcell, ed., *Women of Exile: German-Jewish Autobiographies since 1933* (New York, Westport, Conn.: Greenwood Press, 1988.

20. John Bodnar, in his *The Transplanted: A History of Immigrants in Urban America* (Bloomington, Ind.; Indiana University Press, 1985) provided the model of such study in the case of working-class immigrant networks.

21. Fermi, *Illustrious Immigrants*, 111; Congdon, *Exile and Social Thought.*

22. Studies dealing with the experience of intellectual refugee women are few and far between. The best

is the collection of essays by Sibylle Quack, ed., *Between Sorrow and Strength: Women Refugees of the Nazi Period* (Washington, D.C.: German Historical Institute and Cambridge University Press, 1995). It has an especially relevant chapter on women refugee professionals in the U.S. Lixl-Purcell, *Women of Exile* and Mark M. Anderson, ed., *Hitler's Exiles: Personal Stories of the Flight from Nazi Germany to America* (New York: New Press, 1998) recycle some of the same, previously published material, and sample from the refugee autobiographies commissioned by Harvard University and the Leo Baeck Institute during the war.

23. Anderson, *Hitler's Exiles*, includes accounts by German woman physicians, fighting an uphill battle against the combined challenges of immigrant hardship and social conventions.

24. Peter Gay provides an account of the reaction of his own family of secular, assimilated German Jews and their refusal "to be Jews by Nazi edict." Gay, *My German Question*, 110.

25. Lessard, "The Present Moment," 49.

26. Mrs. Bruce's letters to Eva and Laura had been preserved among Laura's documents. An indication of Eva's gratitude is that she named her own daughter after Mrs. Bruce's Jean.

27. Felix Schaffer, "Vorgartenstrasse 203: Extracts from a Memoir," in *Karl Polanyi in Vienna*, 333, met up with Egon Szécsi in the Buchenwald concentration camp.

28. Laura Polanyi to the American Consul in London, draft, 27 September 1938, in the possession of Eva Zeisel.

29. Laura Polanyi to the American Consul in London, draft, 27 September 1938, in the possession of Eva Zeisel.

29. Ibid. Originally a physicist, Leibowitz was an acquaintance of Leo Szilard. William Lanouette with Bela Silard, *Genius in the Shadows*, 120-21. It was probably Szilard who secured Leibowitz's assistance in Michael Stricker's immigration.

30. When Michael Striker and his family moved to a considerably grander apartment, it remained in the family and has served over the years as Karl Polanyi then Eva Zeisel's apartment.

31. Letters of Michael Striker to Laura Polanyi, New York, 27 April 1938, 2 May 1938, and 19 May 1938, in the possession of Eva Zeisel.

32. Lederer, the husband of Laura's cousin, was a professor at the New School. Lazarsfeld, Hans Zeisel's friend and collaborator in Vienna, had stayed on in America when his Rockefeller scholarship expired in 1934. Paul F. Lazarsfeld, "An Episode in the History of Social Research: A Memoir," in Fleming and Bailyn, *The Intellectual Migration*, 275-76.

33. Michael Striker to Laura Polanyi, 10 May 1938, in the possession of Eva Zeisel.

34. Sándor Stricker to Laura Polanyi, Budapest, 24 April 1938, in the possession of Eva Zeisel.

35. Fragment of a letter, from unknown, Budapest, 22 June 1938, in the possession of Eva Zeisel.

36. Michael Polanyi to Eva Stricker, 28 June 1938, in the possession of Eva Zeisel.

37. Laura Polanyi's biographical draft about Egon Szécsi, in the possession of Eva Zeisel.

38. Postcard of Laura Polanyi to Michael Polanyi, 30 August 1938, in the possession of Eva Zeisel.

39. Postcard of Laura Polanyi to Eva Stricker, 28 August 1938, in the possession of Eva Zeisel.

40. Postcard of Laura to Michael Polanyi, 10 August 1938, in the possession of Eva Zeisel.

41. Michael Polanyi to Laura, Manchester, 2 August 1938, in the possession of Eva Zeisel.

42. Interview with Barbara Stricker, Budapest, December 1997.

43. Máriusz Rabinovszky to Eva Stricker, Budapest, 19 September 1938, in the possession of Eva Zeisel; Lili Radványi to Eva Stricker, Budapest, no date, in the possession of Eva Zeisel.

44. In her interviews, Eva often refers to the mirror images of their imprisonment and their bond forged by the act of saving each other's life. Interview with Eva Zeisel, March 1994, Suzanne Lessard, "The Present Moment," 49-50.

45. Mrs. Bruce to Eva Stricker, Kent, 12 September 1938, in the possession of Eva Zeisel.

46. Neither Eva Zeisel nor Kari Polanyi-Levitt could recall who suggested the idea of contacting them. Interviews with Eva Zeisel, March 1994, March 1995, interview with Kari Polanyi-Levitt, Montreal, April 1998.

47. In a letter to Laura, Eva makes a coded but obvious reference to a *friend*, underlined in the original, an acquaintance of her uncle Karl, soon to call on Laura in Vienna. Eva Stricker to Laura Polanyi, London, no date, in the possession of Eva Zeisel.

48. In the same letter, Mrs. Bruce is referred to as "a *friend* too." Ibid. Another clue points to Michael Polanyi as the source for the Quaker connection. Mrs. Bruce had a sister in Manchester, who was Michael Polanyi's neighbour there.

49. The Quakers' heroic efforts in rescuing Jews and other persecuted from the Nazis have never been widely publicized. David Wyman consulted the archives of the American Friends Service Committee for his books, *Paper Walls* and *The Abandonment of the Jews*. He specifically notes that the Friends' representatives in Vienna and Berlin had good working relations with the American consuls there. Wyman, *Paper Walls*, 161.

50. Phyllis Richards to Eva Stricker, 12 September 1938, in the possession of Eva Zeisel.

51. As a sign of gratitude, Eva named her first-born daughter Jean Richards—after Mrs. Bruce's daughter and Mrs. Richards. The families stayed in touch in later years. In 1943, Phyllis Richards wrote to Laura: "I have asked Hans and Eva to send me a snapshot of Jean, as I long to see what she is like. I hope you got the letter I wrote in answer to yours, in which you told me about her birth and christening. I was so touched to think she had been named after me..." Phyllis Richards to Laura Polanyi, no date, in the possession of Eva Zeisel.

52. Telegram of Laura Polanyi, 22 September 1938, original in German, in the possession of Eva Zeisel, my translation.

53. Laura Polanyi to Andor Németh, London, 23 December 1938, in the possession of Eva Zeisel.

54. Ibid., my translation.

55. Telegram of Eva and Hans Zeisel to Laura Polanyi, 24 December 1938, in the possession of Eva Zeisel. A letter from Laura's niece that reached her in London also recalled the memory of old Christmases. Lili Szondi to Laura Polanyi, Budapest, no date, OSzK PC 212/205.

56. Red Star Line, Passenger Traffic Manager to Laura Polanyi, 10 March 1939, in the possession of Eva Zeisel. Ella Bruce to Laura Polanyi, 25 March 1939; 15 June 1939, in the possession of Eva Zeisel.

57. Ella Bruce to Laura Polanyi, 25 March 1939, in the possession of Eva Zeisel; Susan Zuccotti, *The Italians and the Holocaust: Persecution, Rescue, and Survival* (New York: Basic Books, 1987), 41.

58. Michael Polanyi to Laura Polanyi, January 1938, in the possession of Eva Zeisel.

59. In Hungary, decree no. IV/ 1939, the so-called "second Jewish law" further limited the number of Jews in the professions and employed by companies, and established racial criteria instead of the previous religious ones. Michael Polanyi's reaction: "Since according to Hungarian law I am a Jew, I expect to be fired soon." Michael Polanyi to Laura Polanyi, Manchester, 11 December 1938. Original in Hungarian, my translation. In the possession of Eva Zeisel.

60. Michael Polanyi to Laura Polanyi, 16 February 1939; notes of Laura Polanyi on Egon Szécsi, in the possession of Eva Zeisel.

61. As the legendary Hungarian essayist Ignotus wrote to her, "I was really delighted to hear that you caught the last pre-war steamer..." Ignotus to Laura Polanyi, 17 February, 1940, OSzK PC 212/130. Getting out of Europe on the "last ship" or "last train" as well as "catching the last ship" were among the most commonly used phrases in the émigré mythology. Eva Zeisel "caught one of the last trains out," in March 1938, according to Lessard, "The Present Moment," 49. Leo Szilard took the last train to Vienna, following the burning of the Reichstag that was not stopped and searched at the border. Leo Szilard, "Reminiscences," Fleming and Bailyn, *The Intellectual Migration*, 96-97, and so on.

62. Michael Polanyi to Laura Polanyi, Manchester, 8 September 1939, in the possession of Eva Zeisel.

63. Irma Pollacsek to Laura Polanyi, no date (probably November 1938), OSzK PC 212/247.

64. Photocopy in the possession of Eva Zeisel.

65. Sándor Vince to Laura Polanyi, Chicago, 30 November 1939, OSzK PC 212/213.

66. Recha Jászi to Michael Polanyi, 26 September 1939. OSzK PC 212/134.

67. "I can already see them as future American millionaires," she quipped. Irma Pollacsek to Laura Polanyi, 5 August 1939, OSzK PC 212/170.

68. Anderson, *Hitler's Exiles*, 201.

69. The friendship of the two women preceded WWI and Recha's marriage to Jászi.

70. Odyssey was a reference frequently used by this most literate cohort of refugees. See e.g. Hannah Arendt, "We Refugees," in Anderson, *Hitler's Exiles*, 260.

71. Recha Jászi to Laura Polanyi, Oberlin, 7 November 1939, OSzK PC 212/134.

72. Ibid., in Hungarian, my translation.

73. Arthur Rundt, the well-known director of the Viennese *Volksbühne*, was Recha's first husband.

74. Recha Jászi to Laura Polanyi, 7 November 1939, Oberlin, OSzK PC 212/134. Victor Weisskopf, Eva Zeisel's physicist friend from Vienna and Berlin, described this common experience in a darkly humorous vein: "[It was] a period when you were asked if you were expecting children, and you said, 'No, first we expect parents.' It was literally so. Of what little money we had, we had to pay the way of my mother, my brother, and my little sister coming over. They were facing death and they had to come over." Charles Weiner, "A New Site for the Seminar: The Refugees and American Physics in the Thirties," in Fleming and Bailyn, *The Intellectual Migration*, 222.

75. Their correspondence in OSzK PC consists of mainly Recha's letters with copies of only a few of Laura's.

76. To submit the necessary paperwork was one thing, to have Sándor obey the instructions was another. In December 1939, instead of checking on the status of his August application, he went ahead and submitted a new one then blamed the boys for failing to inform him. Máriusz Rabinovszky to Laura Polanyi, Budapest, 2 February 1939; István Rudó to Michael Striker, Budapest, 1 December 1939, in the possession of Eva Zeisel.

77. Máriusz Rabinovszky to Laura Polanyi, 6 January 1939, OSzK PC 212/175; Wyman, *Paper Walls*, 170.

78. Alexander (Sándor) Vince to Laura Polanyi, 30 November 1939, OSzK PC 212/213.

79. Ralph E. Church to Alexander Vince, Washington, D.C., 20 February 1940, in the possession of Eva Zeisel.

80. According to the Declaration of Intention, in the possession of Eva Zeisel, he finally reached the U.S. on 18 August 1941.

81. Karl Polanyi congratulated with these words his nephew. Karl Polanyi to Michael Striker, Washington D.C., 8 August 1941, OSzK PC 212/325. The itinerary of Sándor Stricker is in the possession of Eva Zeisel.

82. Adolf Polanyi to Laura Polanyi, Rio de Janeiro, 16 February 1942, OSzK PC 212/172.

83. Laura Polanyi to Karl Polanyi, 26 April 1944, KPA, box 14.

84. Sophie Szécsi to Laura Polanyi, October 1938, in the possession of Eva Zeisel.

85. Arthur Rényi to Laura Polanyi, Budapest, 25 February 1940, OSzK PC 212/178.

86. Arthur Rényi to Laura Polanyi, Budapest, 10 March 1941, OSzK PC 212/178.

87. Michael Polanyi to Ilona Duczynska, 30 July 1941, KPA, box 14.

88. Recha Jászi commented: "What a blessing that Sofie's son is gone, what a relief for her! Or have the Nazis sent him off in their humanitarian fashion?" Recha Jászi to Laura Polanyi, Oberlin, Ohio, 21

March 1942, OSzK PC 212/134.

89. Even if they could keep the fragile lines of communication open, it would have taken a miracle to get her out. "In October [1941] legal exit from Nazi territory ended. Escapes took place throughout the war, but for most victims of Nazi terror the closed borders formed an almost insuperable barrier." Wyman, *Paper Walls*, 205.

90. Arthur Rényi to Laura Polanyi, Budapest, 31 August 1946, OSzK PC 212/178, my translation.

91. Recha Jászi to Laura Polanyi, 14 February 1943, OSzK PC 212/134.

92. László Radványi to Laura Polanyi, Le Vernet, 15 August 1940 and to Ottó Stricker on 18 November 1940, in the possession of Eva Zeisel. Radványi and Anna Seghers were eventually sent out of Marseilles by Varian Fry. Marino, *A Quiet American*, 259. They survived the war in Mexico.

93. Recha Jászi to Laura Polanyi, 14 February 1943, OSzK PC 212/134.

94. Adolf Polanyi to Laura Polanyi, Rio de Janeiro, 29 July 1941, OSzK PC 212/172.

95. In an article, "Laura Polanyi (1882-1959): Narratives of a Life," *Polanyiana*, vol. 6, no. 2. (1997): 41-47, I related the story of Adolf's sons. The following account includes the information provided by Thomas Polanyi, in his reaction to that article, *Polanyiana*, vol. 8, nos. 1-2, (1999): 85-86.

96. Ibid.

97. Laura Polanyi to Lionello Venturi, 31 May 1941, in the possession of Eva Zeisel.

98. Laura Polanyi to Michael and Thomas Polanyi, 1 June 1941, Laura Polanyi to Lionello Venturi, 31 May 1941, in the possession of Eva Zeisel.

99. Wyman, *Paper Walls*, 195.

100. Eric D. Frankel to Laura Polanyi, 30 June 1941, in the possession of Eva Zeisel.

101. Laura Polanyi to Michael and Thomas Polanyi, 1 June 1941, in the possession of Eva Zeisel, her emphasis, my translation.

102. Just as Laura was warned, on her arrival, by her friend Recha of anti-Semitism in the U.S. "Things in America look easy over there [in Europe]," Recha wrote. They don't know how antisemitic America already is." Recha Jászi to Laura Polanyi, Oberlin, 7 November 1939, OSzK PC 212/134.

103. Michael Polanyi to Ilona Duczynska, 30 July 1941, KPA, box 14.

104. A. M. Warren, State Department, Washington D. C., to Michael Striker, 18 December 1941, in the possession of Eva Zeisel.

105. Adolf Polanyi to Laura Polanyi, Rio de Janeiro, 29 July 1941, OSzK PC 212/172.

106. Ibid.

107. Adolf Polanyi to Laura Polanyi, Rio de Janeiro, 1 November 1941, OSzK PC 212/172.

108. Ibid.

109. Karl Polanyi to Laura Polanyi, New York, 12 November 1941, OSzK PC 212/325.

110. Karl Polanyi to Laura Polanyi, New York, 5 January 1942, OSzK PC 212/325.

111. Thomas Polanyi to Laura Polanyi, 31 December 1943, in the possession of Eva Zeisel.

112. In Arendt's parable, Mr. Cohn, the 150 percent German patriot becomes an instant 150 percent patriot in every country he flees to for he simply cannot come to terms with simply being a Jew. Hannah Arendt, "We Refugees," Anderson, *Hitler's Exiles*, 253-262.

113. If they came into contact with it, it was an encounter reminiscent of Eva's first impression of the *shtetls* she accidentally passed in the Ukraine. See Chapter 3.

114. Richard Plant, "Being Gay, Becoming Jewish," Anderson, *Hitler's Exiles*, 311.

115. Letter of John H. Lathrop to Laura Polanyi, 28 December 1944, in the possession of Eva Zeisel.

116. Interview with Jean Richards, New York, March 1995.

117. Ibid. The minister thanked Laura for her gift, a book of Michael Polanyi and "for giving me some insight into the rare intellectual atmosphere of your family."

118. Koestler, *The Invisible Writing*, 501-503.

119. "It took two months to get this present letter," wrote Michael Polanyi to his niece on 30 May 1938. Michael Polanyi to Eva Zeisel, in the possession of Eva Zeisel.

120. "The joint protest of the French Nobel-laureates, supported by a simultaneous letter from Einstein to Stalin, was never acknowledged or answered, but seems nevertheless to have influenced Alex's fate. ... Once higher quarters recognised the significance of the case, his bare life at least was safe." Koestler, *The Invisible Writing*, 501.

121. "My Dear Mausi! Pikler Ilus received the following news that you should forward to Evi: 'Befreit, verständiget Weisskopf, Placzek, Ruhemann. Bezoget Einreise erlaubniss neutralen Landes' Alex Weissberg, Krakau, ulica Dietla 75/14." Telegram of Irma Pollacsek to Laura Polanyi, 11 April 1940, in the possession of Eva Zeisel.

122. A young Polish-Jewish woman met and befriended Weissberg there. Halina Nelken, *And Yet, I Am Here* (Amherst, Mass.: University of Mass. Press, 1999).

123. Alex Weissberg to Eva Zeisel, Krakow, 11 April 1940, 18 June 1940, 25 June 1940, 29 July 1940, Alex Weissberg to Arthur Rényi, 14 May 1940, in the possession of Eva Zeisel.

124. Eva Zeisel to Georg Placzek, New York, 21 May 1940, in the possession of Eva Zeisel.

125. Eva Zeisel to Albert Einstein, New York, 17 July 1940, in the possession of Eva Zeisel. At the beginning of her letter, she referred to her uncle, Michael Polanyi, who had already contacted Einstein in a separate letter.

126. "Dear Mr. Liebmann:

A very good friend of mine, Mr. Michael Polanyi, Professor at the University of Manchester, brings attention to the fate of a young physicist, Mr. Alexander Weissberg. I have heard of him before and I should like to help him in this emergency situation. I understand that you are one of the few persons who is able to save him in this desperate situation.

Mr. Weissberg was recently released from a German concentration camp after three years of imprisonment with the notice that, that he would be brought back again, if he cannot obtain immediately an immigration visa for an oversea country. His numerous friends in this country are trying to obtain a non-quota visum for him (as University Professor) but this will not be possible in the short time he is given by the German authorities. Would it be possible that Mr. Weissberg gets some visa through your help in the meantime?

I understand that his friends here are able and willing to support him. But in addition to that he is a specialist in the field of refrigeration [low-temperature physics] technique and will prove to be an asset for any country which will accept him.

I should greatly appreciate if you could help me to save Mr. Weissberg. If there is such a possibility, please communicate with Mr. Rudolph Modley, Director of Pictorial Statistics in New York. He is an old friend of Mr. Weissberg and will be glad to provide you with all the necessary information.

Very sincerely yours,

Professor Albert Einstein. Albert Einstein to Mr. Charles Liebmann, Knollwood, Saranac Lake, N.Y., 22 July 1940, in the possession of Eva Zeisel.

127. See, among others, Daniels, *Coming to America*, 297-298; Weiner, "A New Site for the Seminar," in Fleming, Bailyn, *The Intellectual Migration*, 214.

128. He may have had the required teaching experience; his curriculum vitae in Laura Polanyi's handwriting, photocopy in the possession of Eva Zeisel, listed his employment at the Charlottenburg *Technische Hochschule* as assistant between 1927 and 1930; however, there is no sign of a position waiting for him in the U.S.

129. Isaac L. Asofsky, executive director of HIAS to Laura Polanyi, New York, 10 September 1940, in the possession of Eva Zeisel.

130. Weiner, "A New Site for the Seminar," 190-234, provides a thorough analysis of the internationalization of the field and the quick reaction of the scientific community to come to the aid of the refugees.

131. Szilard, "Reminiscences," 91-151.

132. Telegram of Alexander Weissberg to Eva Zeisel, Stockholm, 23 April 1946, in the possession of Eva Zeisel.

133. Gina Kernstok to Laura Polanyi, Budapest, 6 May 1946, OSzK PC 212/137.

134. *Magyar Jövö - Hungarian Daily Journal*, 13 July 1944.

135. On Jászi's position, see György Litván, "Egy barátság dokumentumai: Károlyi Mihály és Jászi

Oszkár levelezéséből," in *Októberek üzenete* (Budapest: Osiris, 1996), 256-58.

136. Laura Polanyi to Oszkár Jászi, draft of letter, no date, [March 1945], in the possession of Eva Zeisel.

137. Ibid.

138. Jászi to Laura Polanyi, no date [February-March 1945], in the possession of Eva Zeisel.

139. Ibid.

140. For a summary of Hungary's political development in the years immediately following WWII see Kontler, *Millennium in Central Europe*, 389-407.

141. Letters of Gina Kernstok to Laura Polanyi, OSzK PC 212/137.

142. Laura Polanyi to Karl and Ilona Polanyi, 14 August 1951, KPA, box 14.

143. Adolf Polanyi to Laura Polanyi, Sao Paolo, 1 November 1946, OSzK PC 212/176.

144. In an uncharacteristic departure from her usual modesty, she reported her success to Karl and Ilona. Laura Polanyi to Karl and Ilona Polanyi, 14 August 1951, KPA, box 14.

145. Notes on the Stricker ancestors, in the possession of Eva Zeisel.

146. Laura Polanyi to Eva Carocci, 25 September 1957, OSzK PC 212/82.

147. Ibid.

148. Michael Polanyi sent her some family documents addressed to "the custodian of the family's traditions." Michael Polanyi to Laura Polanyi, 11 August 1957, in the possession of Eva Zeisel.

Chapter 5: "The Hungarian Pocahontas"

1. Laura Polanyi to Marshall W. Fishwick, 13 April 1957, OSzK PC 212/768.

2. Lee Congdon, "The Hungarian Pocahontas: Laura Polanyi Striker," *The Virginia Magazine of History and Biography* 86 (1978): 280. The analogy was first used by Marshall W. Fishwick, in his article, "Was John Smith a Liar?" *American Heritage* 9 (October) 1958: 33 and 110.

3. Laura Polanyi to Marshall W. Fishwick, 13 April 1957, OSzK PC 212/768.

4. Ibid.

5. For a detailed discussion of women's access to higher education in Hungary, see Chapter 2.

6. OSzK, PC 212/8/a. The diploma specified the results of her examination at the end of her graduation year, grade 7: Catechism, no grade (presumably, Jews were exempt from taking the subject); Russian Language and Literature, good; Composition in Russian, satisfactory; French Language, good; German Language, excellent; Arithmetic, excellent; Geometry, excellent; Algebra, good; Geography, excellent; Russian and World history, excellent; Physics, excellent; Pedagogy, excellent. It also listed the rest of the courses she had completed, namely calligraphy, drawing, singing, dancing, and physical education.

7. Cecile's high-school diploma indicated the student's social class. Cecile was listed as a daughter of *meshan'in* or middling sorts. Ibid.

8. In Laura's case, these were: Hungarian language and literature, Latin language and literature, Greek language and literature, Classic literature, German language and literature, History, Mathematics, and Physics. OSzK PC 212/72.

9. Ibid. Her graduation diploma also contained the final grades for subjects taken during her last year of high school but not required as examination subjects: Religious Studies, Geography, Philosophy, Natural history and, finally, Drawing.

10. A letter written by Laura's classmate describes the students' impromptu after-school visit to Beöthy—without a "*garde de dame*"!—and the students' adulation of him in terms typical of all-girl schools to this day. Margit Belgráder to Laura Pollacsek, OSzK PC 212/236.

11. Beöthy's theory of "genuine Hungarian values" was justly criticized, e.g. Antal Szerb's *Magyar Irodalomtörténet*, Fifth edition (Budapest: Magvető, 1972), 410-411.

12. OSzK PC 212/8/a.

13. Marczali was among the Hungarian historians of Jewish origin in the late 19th century whose contribution "to this 'most Hungarian' of disciplines was entirely spectacular. They were instrumental in the creation of modern history writing that became the carrier of Hungarian national identity for several generations." Ferenc Fejtő, "A zsidók és a modern magyar kultura," *História*, Budapest, 22 No. 8 (August 2000): 15.

14. For Marczali's life and works see Péter Gunst's introduction, "Marczali Henrik (1856-1940)" in

Henrik Marczali, *Világtörténelem - Magyar történelem*, Történetirók Tára (Budapest: MTA Történettudományi Intézet, Gondolat, 1982), 5-26.

15. *Magyar Statisztikai Évkönyv*, Uj Folyam 18 (1910), Budapest: Magyar Királyi Statisztikai Hivatal, 1911: 389.

16. Ibid.

17. Interview with Valéria Dienes, one of the first women to graduate with a Ph. D. in Philosophy, in Rózsa Borus, ed., *A század nagy tanui* (Budapest: RTV Minerva, 1978), 13-14.

18. Hungarian universities, to this day, do not provide transcripts. All pertinent information is entered in the registration book and it is the student's responsibility to keep it up-to-date.

19. The name change was authorized by order no. 168649/1912 of the Ministry of the Interior. This contradicts the persistent family myth that assign the Magyarization of the family name of the children to Laura's father, Mihály Pollacsek. See, among others, Vezér, "The Polanyi family," 19; Duczynska-Polanyi, "'I First Met Karl Polanyi in 1920...'," 303-4.

20. For more on Laura's extracurricular activities and marriage, see Chapter 1.

21. Certified copy of doctoral diploma, in the possession of Eva Zeisel.

22. Laura Pollacsek, "III. Károly gazdaságpolitikájáról hazánkban," *Közgazdasági Szemle*, 1909: 1-55.

23. Ibid., 50.

24. Ibid., 54.

25. Laura Polanyi to Michael Polanyi, 26 August 1909, my translation, in the possession of Eva Zeisel.

26. Freud to Ferenczi, 2 October 1910, Brabant, Falzeder, and Giampieri-Deutsch, *The Correspondence of Freud and Ferenczi*, vol. 1, 216.

27. Ferenczi to Freud, 2 December 1910, Ibid., 237.

28. See also Chapter 2, 34-35.

29. Interview with Eva Zeisel, March 1995 and letter of Laura Polanyi to unknown, London, 17 May 1939, in the possession of Eva Zeisel.

30. Sister's work at the Könyves Kálmán lodge on 17 December 1905, The Documents of the Association of Feminists, Hungarian National Archives, font 999, file 6, package 2.

31. Election to the Országos Közoktatás Ligája, OSzK PC 212/75.

32. Brabant, Falzeder, and Giampieri-Deutsch, *The Correspondence of Freud and Ferenczi*, vol. 1, 350.

33. "Psychoanalysis and Education," Sándor Ferenczi, *Selected Writings*, edited and with an introduction of Julia Borossa (London: Penguin Books, 1999), 25-30. In Hungarian: "Psychoanalizis és pedagógia," *Gyógyászat*, 1908, reprinted in Dr. Adorján Linczényi, ed., *Lelki problémák a psychoanalizis tükrében: Válogatás Ferenczi Sándor müveiböl* (Budapest: Magvetö, 1982), 41-49. Both the German and Hungarian originals use "pedagogy" in the title.

34. Ferenczi, *Selected Writings*, 25.

35. Ferenczi, "Psychoanalysis and Education," *Selected Writings*, 28-29, 46, 49.

36. It was also the title of another article, written by Laura for *Szabadgondolat*, no. 1. (May 1911): 43-45.

37. A good summary of the movement is Ann T. Allen, "Spiritual Motherhood: German Feminists and the Kindergarten Movement, 1848-1911," *History of Education Quarterly* vol. 22 no. 3 (Fall 1982): 319-39.

38. OSzK PC 212/256.

39. "The future Hungary" was a favourite metaphor used by the circle of the Twentieth Century to describe both their aim, the new, democratic, industrialized, modern Hungary and the coalition of progressive forces fighting for it.

40. *A Nö és a Társadalom*, June 1911, my translation.

41. Ibid., September 1911.

42. Ibid.

43. Ibid.

44. Lessard, "The Present Moment," 44.

45. OSzK PC 212/258.

46. Ibid.

47. Ibid.; Laura Polanyi's university registration book, 212/74.

48. See illustrations. An additional photograph, not reproduced here, shows the class with an assistant sitting on the side and taking the minutes. Courtesy of Eva Zeisel.

49. Minutes of parent-teacher conference, OSzK PC 212/259; Litván, *Szabó Ervin*, 71.

50. Mme Jeanne Chambaud to William Scott, 6 February 1979, OSzK PC 212/749, original in French, my translation.

51. OSzK PC 212/262 and in the possession of Eva Zeisel.

52. Minutes of the classes, OSzK PC 212/259.

53. Ibid.

54. Ibid.

55. Interview with Eva Zeisel, March 1994.

56. Minutes of 7 June 1912, p. 2, OSzK PC 212/259.

57. Minutes of 3 May 1912, ibid.

58. Minutes of 23 April 1912, ibid.

59. Minutes of 3 May 1912, p. 6, ibid.

60. Koestler, *Arrow in the Blue*, 56.

61. Ibid.

62. Ibid.

63. OSzK PC 212/259.

64. David Cesarini, *Arthur Koestler: The Homeless Mind* (London: Heinemann, 1998), 5.

65. Ibid., 5, 7.

66. Ibid., 22-23.

67. *Tempora mutantur*: three decades later, as a grandmother living in Manhattan, Laura insisted that her grandchildren regularly attend Sunday school at a Brooklyn Unitarian church.

68. *A Nö és a Társadalom*, August 1912.

69. Ibid., my translation.

70. OSzK PC 212/264/8.

71. *A Nö és a Társadalom*, November 1912.

72. OSzK PC 212/264/8, my translation.

73. "I left the school in the care of one of the highly qualified teachers who led it for many decades." Laura Polanyi to Marshall W. Fishwick, 13 April 1957, OSzK PC 212/768. It may have been the Mrs. Domokos, whose experimental school she praised in her 1918 political speech. See Chapter 2.

74. Laura Polanyi to Marshall Fishwick, 13 April 1957, OSzK PC 212/768.

75. Ibid.

76. OSzK PC 212/808 and 809.

77. OSzK PC 212/76.

78. Eva Zeisel to George Stricker, December 1959, in the possession of Barbara Stricker.

79. Photocopy of letter of Laura Polanyi to Mrs. Armitage, 27 July 1943, OSzK PC, 212/80.

80. Ibid.

81. Laura Polanyi to A. Baltzly, 13 May 1943, OSzK PC 212/81.

82. James Stern to Laura Polanyi, 18 January 1944, OSzK PC 212/192.

83. Draft of letter of Laura Polanyi to James Stern, February 1944, ibid.

84. OSzK PC 212/208. The author of the letter did not fail to notice the significance of the date, the anniversary of the October revolution.

85. Ibid. Marika Szécsi was Sophie's eldest daughter. The correspondance does not mention the fact that Thompson had demonstrated the kind of experience Laura needed. She was most likely to be aware of the fact that he had helped to organize the papers of Samuel Harper, his former professor at the University of Chicago. They were published as *The Russia I Believe In: The Memoirs of Samuel N. Harper, 1902-1941* (Chicago, Ill.: University of Chicago Press, 1945), edited by Paul V. Harper, with the assistance of Ronald Thompson.

86. Ibid., my italics.

87. Ibid.

88. Karl Polanyi's reference letter, 22 February 1957, OSzK PC 212/325.

89. Karl Polanyi, H. Arensberg, and H. Pearson, eds., *Trade and Market in the Early Empires* (New York: The Free Press, 1957).

90. Hans Zeisel, "In Memoriam," *The Life and Work of Karl Polanyi*, 243.

91. Ibid.

92. Bradford Smith to Laura Polanyi, 15 October 1951, OSzK PC 212/774.

93. Bradford Smith to Laura Polanyi, 8 November 1951, Ibid.

94. Ibid.

95. Lewis L. Kropf, "Captain John Smith of Virginia," *Notes and Queries*, IX, 7th series (1890), 1-2, 41-43, 102-04, 161-62, 223-24, 281-82.

96. Laura Polanyi Striker, "Captain John Smith's Hungary and Transylvania," in Bradford Smith, *Captain John Smith: His Life and Legend* (Philadelphia, New York: Lippincott, 1953), 312.

97. Laura Polanyi to Bradford Smith, 18 March 1952, OSzK PC 212/774.

98. Bradford Smith to Laura Polanyi, 8 November 1951, OSzK PC 212/774..

99. Manuscript in possession of Eva Zeisel. Laura's 70th birthday fell on February 12, 1952.

100. Laura Polanyi to Bradford Smith, 18 March 1952, OSzK PC 212/774.

101. Bradford Smith to Laura Polanyi, 24 March 1952, OSzK PC 212/774.

102. Laura Polanyi Striker, "The Hungarian Historian, Lewis L. Kropf, on Captain John Smith's *True Travels*: A Reappraisal," *Virginia Magazine of History and Biography* vol. 66, no. 1 (January 1958): 24.

103. Karl Polanyi to Laura Polanyi, 17 August 1952, in the possession of Eva Zeisel.

104. Karl Polanyi to Laura Polanyi, no date, KPA, box 14.

105. Ibid.

106. Ibid.

107. Bradford Smith to Laura Polanyi, 6 June 1952, OSzK PC 212/774.

108. Ibid.

109. Bradford Smith to Laura Polanyi, 30 June 1952, ibid.

110. Ibid.

111. Bradford Smith, Captain John Smith; *His Life and Legend*, 9.

112. Ibid., 5.

113. See, among others, Meager, William, "Acclaiming an American Hero," *Christian Science Monitor*, 1 October 1953, 11; Ellen Hart Smith, "The Many Lives of Capt. John Smith," *New York Herald Tribune Book Review*, 4 October 1953, 4.

114. Bradford Smith to Laura Polanyi, 5 March 1953, OSzK PC 212/774.

115. Ibid.

116. Laura Polanyi to Karl Polanyi, 24 March 1953, OSzK PC 212/780/a.

117. Bradford Smith to Laura Polanyi, 1 April 1953, OSzK PC 212/774.

118. Laura Polanyi to Karl Polanyi, September, no year, KPA, box 14, my translation.

119. *Henry Wharton, The Life of John Smith English Soldier*, translated from the Latin manuscript (1685) with an essay on "Captain John Smith in Seventeenth Century Literature" by Laura Polanyi Striker (Chapel Hill: published for the Virginia Historical Society by the University of North Carolina Press, 1957).

120. *The Virginia Magazine of History and Biography*, vol. 66, no. 1 (January 1958): 22-43.

121. Laura Polanyi to Karl Polanyi, no date, OSzK PC 212/780.

122. Lee Congdon, "The Hungarian Pocahontas: Laura Polanyi Striker," 275-280.

123. Karl Polanyi to Laura Polanyi, 7 April 1953, OSzK PC 212/325.

124. Gyula and Elza Holló to Laura Polanyi, 24 January, no year, OSzK PC 212/129.

125. Allusion to a famous Hungarian poem.

126. Ibid.

127. Polanyi Striker, "Captain John Smith's Hungary and Transylvania," 311.

128. Laura"s multiple connections to the Pulszky family went back to the late 19th century and were discussed in Chapter 2. Pulszky, like herself, was an exile. Following his return to Hungary, his salon in late nineteenth-century Pest had the young Henrik Marczali among its guests. His son was a founder of the Sociological Society and his daughter the president of the Association for the Education of Women.

129. Antal Szerb (1901-1945), novelist, essayist and literary historian, was killed in the Holocaust.

130. Antal Szerb, "Az első amerikai Erdélyben," *Magyar Nemzet*, 12 September 1940; "Captain John Smith in Transylvania," *Hungarian Quarterly*, VI (1940), 734-741.

131. Polanyi Striker, "The Hungarian Historian, Lewis L. Kropf," 23-4.

132. Bradford Smith to Laura Polanyi, 13 November 1953, OSzK PC 212/774.

133. Polanyi Striker, "The Hungarian Historian, Lewis L. Kropf," 26.

134. Ibid., 27.

135. "To the Reader," manuscript, KPA, box 14. The typewritten manuscript is the Karl Polanyi Archives and Karl's authorship is supported by both its style and the Shakespeare reference that would have come more naturally to him.

136. Ibid.

137. Laura Polanyi to Parke Rouse Jr., 12 September 1957, OSzK PC 212/778.

138. Laura Polanyi to William H. Smith, 29 May, 1957, OSzK PC 212/795.

139. Laura Polanyi to Parke Rouse Jr., Virginia 350th Anniversary Commission, 12 September 1957, OSzK PC 212/778; Laura Polanyi to William H. Smith, 29 May 1957, OSzK PC 212/795.

140. Laura Polanyi to the Honorable John Hay Whitney, the American Ambassador in London, 24 September 1957, OSzK PC 212/771.

141. Laura Polanyi to Bradford Smith, 26 August 1957, OSzK PC 212/774.

142. Polanyi Striker, "The Hungarian Historian, Lewis L. Kropf," 22.

143. Oscar Handlin to Laura Polanyi, 28 March 1958, in the possession of Eva Zeisel.

144. Nicholas Halasz, *Captain Dreyfus: The Story of a Mass Hysteria* (New York: Simon & Schuster, 1955).

145. Laura Polanyi to Marshall Fishwick, 28 February 1957, OSzK PC 212/768.

146. Laura Polanyi to Allan Nevins, 13 May 1958, in the possession of Eva Zeisel.

147. OSzK PC 212/768. It was probably Fishwick's earlier book, *American Heroes: Myth and Reality* (Washington: Public Affairs Press, 1954) that prompted Laura to contact him.

148. Marshall Fishwick to Laura Polanyi, 29 June 1957, OSzK PC 212/768.

149. "All along I knew that the language barrier was creating difficulties, but I had not anticipated this." Ibid.

150. Marshall Fishwick, "Was John Smith a Liar?" *American Heritage* 9 (October) 1958: 33 and 110.

151. Kálmán Benda, "Bradford Smith, Captain John Smith, His Life and Legend," *Századok*, Budapest 98 (1954): 708-709.

152. Franz Pichler, "Captain John Smith in the Light of Styrian Sources," *Virginia Magazine of History and Biography*, vol. 65 no. 3 (July 1957): 332-354.

153. Laura Polanyi to Recha Jászi, Dunedin, Florida, 16 March 1958, OSzK PC 212/134.

154. "Each day of my European trip served up not only a touristic but a political event as well," wrote Laura Polanyi to her niece in Italy in the fall of 1957. Laura Polanyi to Eva Carocci, OSzK PC 212/82. The political events Laura referred to in her letter were the Hungarian Uprising of 56 and the Suez crisis.

155. Laura Polanyi to Recha Jászi, Dunedin, Florida, 16 March 1958, OSzK PC 212/134.

156. On the significance of her contribution to the Smith-controversy, see Alden T. Vaughan, *American Genesis: Captain John Smith and the Founding of Virginia*, The Library of American Biography, ed. Oscar Handlin (Boston, Toronto: Little, Brown, 1975), 190-1.; J. A. Leo Lemay, *The American Dream of Captain John Smith* (Charlottesville and London: University of Virginia, 1991), 7-8 and 13.

157. Her obituaries in *The New York Times* and *The New York Herald Tribune*, 24 December 1959, mentioned only "short illness" and briefly listed her achievements as an educator, feminist politican and historian.

158. Laura Polanyi Striker and Bradford Smith, "The Rehabilitation of Captain John Smith," *Journal of Southern History* vol. 28 (1962): 474-81.

Selected Bibliography

Primary Sources

Archival Sources:

Polányi hagyaték. Országos Széchényi Könyvtár Kézirattár [Polanyi Collection. Manuscript Division, Széchényi National Library], Budapest, font 212.

Polanyi family archives, in the possession of Eva Zeisel, New York.

Michael Polanyi Papers. Special Collections, Joseph Regenstein Library, University of Chicago, Chicago. On microfilm: Mikrofilmtár, Magyar Tudományos Akadémia Könyvtára [Microfilm Archive, Library of the Hungarian Academy of Sciences], Budapest.

Karl Polanyi Archive. Karl Polanyi Institute for Political Economy, Concordia University, Montreal.

A Feministák Egyesülete iratai. Magyar Országos Levéltár [Documents of the Association of Feminists, Hungarian National Archives], Budapest, font 999.

Polányi család fényképei. Magyar Nemzeti Muzeum, Történeti Fényképtár [The Photographs of the Polanyi Family. Hungarian National Museum, Historical Photo Archive], Budapest.

Contemporary Journals and Newspapers:

Huszadik Század 1900-1919

A Nö és a Társadalom 1905-1914

Szabadgondolat 1911-1914

Nyugat 1907-1914

Interviews:

Eva Zeisel, New York, March 1994, March 1995, April 2001.

Jean Richards, New York, March 1994, March 1995, April 2001.

Hilde Striker, New York, March 1995.

Sándor Striker, Budapest, June 1994.

Barbara Striker, Budapest, December 1997.

Kari Polanyi Levitt, Montreal, March 1999.

Ruth Danon, New York, April 2001.

Books and Articles

Alberti, Johanna. *Beyond Suffrage: Feminists in War and Peace, 1914-1928.* London: Macmillan, 1989.

Allen, Ann T. "Spiritual Motherhood: German Feminists and the Kindergarten Movement, 1848-1911." *History of Education Quarterly* 22 no. 3 (Fall 1982): 319-39.

Anderson, Mark M., ed. *Hitler's Exiles: Personal Stories of the Flight from Nazi Germany to America.* New York: New Press, 1998.

Arendt, Hannah. *Rahel Varnhagen: The Life of a Jewish Woman,* trans. Richard and Clara Winston. London: East and West Library, 1957.

_____. "We Refugees." In *Hitler's Exiles: Personal Stories of the Flight from Nazi Germany to America,* ed. Mark M. Anderson, 253-262. New York: New Press, 1998.

Bak, János M. and György Litván, eds. *Socialism and Social Sciences. Selected Writings of Ervin Szabó.* London: Routledge and Kegan Paul, 1982.

Barron, Stephanie, with Sabine Eckmann, eds. *exiles + emigrés: The Flight of European Artists from Hitler*. Los Angeles County Museum of Art, 1997.

Benda, Kálmán. "Review of Bradford Smith, *Captain John Smith, His Life and Legend*." *Századok*, Budapest 88 (1954): 708-9.

Bender, Thomas and Carl E. Schorske, eds. *Budapest and New York: Studies in Metropolitan Transformation, 1870-1930*. New York: Russell Sage Foundation, 1994.

Bentwich, Norman. *The Rescue and Achievement of Refugee Scholars. The Story of Displaced Scholars and Scientists, 1933-1952*. The Hague: Martinus Nijhoff, 1953.

Bibó, István. "Zsidókérdés Magyarországon 1944 után." In *Zsidókérdés, asszimiláció, antiszemitizmus*, ed. Péter Hanák, 135-294. Budapest: Gondolat, 1984.

Biggs, Melissa A. "Spirited Touch." *Metropolis*, November 1994, 39-43.

Bodnar, John. *The Transplanted: A History of Immigrants in Urban America*. Bloomington, Ind.: Indiana University Press, 1985.

Borossa, Julia, ed. with an introduction. *Sándor Ferenczi: Selected Writings*. London: Penguin Books, 1999.

Borsányi, György. *Kun Béla: The Life of a Communist Revolutionary*. Trans. Mario D. Fenyö. Social Science Monographs, Boulder, Co.: distributed by Columbia University Press, 1993.

Borus, Rózsa. *A század nagy tanui*. Budapest: RTV Minerva, 1978.

Boyers, Robert, ed. *The Legacy of the German Refugee Intellectuals*. New York: Schocken, 1972.

Brabant, Eva, Falzeder, Ernst, and Giampieri-Deutsch, Patrizia, eds. *The Correspondence of Sigmund Freud and Sándor Ferenczi*, vol. 1. Cambridge, Mass.: Belknap Press of Harvard University Press, 1993.

Braham, Randolph. *A magyar Holocaust*, vols. 1-2. Budapest:Gondolat, Wilmington: Blackburn International Corporation, 1988. In English: *The Politics of Genocide: The Holocaust in Hungary*. New York: Columbia University Press, 1981.

Burucs, Kornélia. "Nők az egyesületekben." *História*, Budapest 15 no. 2 (1993): 15-18.

Cesarini, David. *Arthur Koestler: The Homeless Mind*. London: Heinemann, 1998.

Cohen, Jean and Arato, Andrew, eds. *Civil Society and Political Theory*. Cambridge, Mass.: MIT Press, 1992.

Congdon, Lee. "The Hungarian Pocahontas: Laura Polanyi Striker." *Virginia Magazine of History and Biography* 86 (1978): 75-80.

_____. *Exile and Social Thought: Hungarian Intellectuals in Germany and Austria, 1919-1933*. Princeton, N.J.: Princeton University Press, 1991.

Conner, Susan P. "Women and Politics." In *French Women and the Age of Enlightenment*, ed. Samia I. Spencer, 49-63. Bloomington, Ind.: Indiana University Press, 1984.

Conquest, Robert. *Inside Stalin's Secret Police: NKVd Politics 1936-39*. Stanford, Calif.: Hoover Institutions Press, Stanford University Press, 1985.

_____. *Stalin and the Kirov Murder*. New York, Oxford:Oxford University Press, 1989.

Crawford, Rex W. "Introduction." In *The Cultural Migration* Franz, L. Neumann, Henri Peyre, Erwin Panowsky, Wolfgang Köhler, and Paul Tillich, 1-3. New York: Barnes and Co., Perpetua edition, 1960.

Csorba, Csilla E. "A kisérletezéstöl az önmegvalósitásig: magyar nö-fotográfusok a századfordulón." In *Szerep és alkotás*, ed. Nagy, Beáta and Margit M. Sárdi, 101-116. Debrecen: Csokonai, 1997.

Czjek, Éva, Erzsébet Vezér, and György Litván. "From Central Europe, Three Friends Remember." In *Karl Polanyi in Vienna: The Contemporary Significance of The Great Transfrormation*, eds. Kenneth McRobbia and Kari Polanyi Levitt, 281-287. Montreal, New York, London: Black Rose Books, 2000.

Dalos, György. *A cselekvés szerelmese*. Budapest: Kossuth, 1984.

_____. "The Fidelity of Equals: Ilona Duczynska and Karl Polanyi." In *The Life and Work of Karl Polanyi*, ed. Kari Polanyi-Levitt, 38-42. Montreal, New York: Black Rose Books, 1990.

Daniels, Roger. "American Refugee Policy in Historical Perspective." In *The Muses Flee Hitler:*

Cultural Transfer and Adaptation, 1930-1945, ed. Jarrell C. Jackman and Carla M. Borden, 61-77. Washington D. C.: Smithonian Institution Press, 1983.

_____. *Coming to America: A History of Immigration and Ethnicity in American Life*. New York: HarperCollins, 1990.

Davidoff, Leonore and Hall, Catherine. *Family Fortunes: Men and Women of the English Middle Class 1780-1850*. London: Hutchinson, 1987.

Davidowicz, Lucy, ed. *The Golden Tradition: Jewish Life and Thought in Eastern Europe*. New York: Holt, Rinehart and Winston, 1967.

Davie, Maurice R. *Refugees in America: Report of the Committee for the Study of Recent Immigration from Europe*. New York, London: Harper and Brothers, 1947.

Déry, Tibor. *Itélet nincs*. Budapest: Magvetö and Szépirodalmi, 1979.

Duczynska, Ilona. "Polányi Károly (1886-1964)." *Századok*, Budapest 105 no. 1 (1971): 89-95.

_____ "'I first met Karl Polanyi in 1920...'," in McRobbie, Kenneth and Kari Polanyi Levitt, eds. *Karl Polanyi in Vienna: The Contemporary Significance of The Great Transfrormation*. Montreal, New York, London: Black Rose Books, 2000.

Edmondson, Linda. *Feminism in Russia, 1900-1917*. Stanford, Calif.: Stanford University Press, 1984.

Eidelberg, Martin. Catalogue essay. In *Eva Zeisel, Designer for Industry*. Le Château Dufresne, Inc. Musée des Arts Décoratifs de Montréal, distributed by University of Chicago Press and, in Canada, Macmillan of Canada, 1984.

Einhorn, Barbara. *Cinderella Goes to Market: Citizenship, Gender, and Women's Movements in East Central Europe*. London, New York: Verso, 1993.

Evans, Richard. *Comrades and Sisters: Feminism, Socialism, and Pacifism in Europe 1870-1945*. Brighton, Sussex: Wheatseaf Books; New York: St. Martin's Press, 1987.

Feingold, Henry L. *The Politics of Rescue: The Roosevelt Administration and the Holocaust, 1938-1945*. New Brunswick, N. J.: Rutgers University Press, 1970.

Fejtö, Ferenc, with the collaboration of Gyula Zeke. *Hongrois et Juifs: Histoire millénaire d'un couple singulier (1000-1997)*. Paris: Ballard, 1997. In Hungarian: *Magyarság, zsidóság*. Budapest: História, MTA Történettudományi Intézet, 2000.

_____. "A zsidók és a modern magyar kultura." *História*, Budapest, 22 no. 8 (August 2000): 14-16.

Fekete, Éva and Éva Karádi, eds. *Lukács György levelezése*. Budapest: Magvetö, 1981.

_____, eds. *György Lukács: His Life in Pictures and Documents*. Budapest: Corvina, 1981.

Ferenczi, Sándor. "Pszichoanalizis és pedagógia." In *Lelki problémák a pszichoanalizis tükrében: Válogatás Ferenczi Sándor müveiböl*, ed. Linczényi, Adorján, 41-49. Budapest: Magvetö, 1982.

Fermi, Laura. *Illustrious Immigrants: The Intellectual Migration from Europe, 1930-41*. Chicago: University of Chicago Press, 1968, revised edition 1971.

Fishwick, Marshall W. "Was John Smith a Liar?" *American Heritage* 9 (October) 1958: 28-33, 110-11.

Fleming, Donald, and Bernard Bailyn, eds. *The Intellectual Migration: Europe and America, 1930-1960*. Cambridge, Mass.: The Belknap Press of Harvard University Press, 1969.

Fraisse, Geneviève, and Michelle Perrot, eds. *A History of Women in the West, vol. 4, Emerging Feminism from Revolution to World War*. Cambridge, Mass., London, England: The Belknap Press of Harvard University Press, 1993.

Frevert, Ute. *Women in German History: From Bourgeois Emancipation to Sexual Liberation*, trans. Stuart McKinnon-Evans. Oxford, Hamburg, New York: Berg, 1989.

Friedman, Saul S. *No Haven for the Oppressed: United States Policy Toward Jewish Refugees, 1938-1945*. Detroit: Wayne State University Press, 1973.

Fry, Varian. *Surrender on Demand*. Reprint. Boulder, Co.: Johnson Books, 1997.

Gábor, Éva, ed. *Mannheim Károly levelezése 1911-1946*. Budapest: Argumentum, MTA Lukács Archivum, 1996.

Gay, Peter. "Weimar Culture: The Outsider as Insider." In *The Intellectual Migration: Europe and America, 1930-1960*, eds. Donald Fleming and Bernard Bailyn, 11-93. Cambridge, Mass.: The Belknap Press of Harvard University Press, 1969.

_____. *My German Question: Growing Up in Nazi Berlin*. New Haven, Conn.: Yale University Press, 1998.

Gerö, András and János Poór, eds. *Budapest: A History from Its Beginnings to 1998*. Social Science Monographs, Boulder, Co. Distributed by Columbia University Press, 1997.

Gluck, Mary. *Georg Lukacs and His Generation, 1910-1918*. Cambridge, Mass.: Cambridge University Press, 1985.

Goodman, Dena. "Enlightenment Salons: The Convergence of Female and Philosophic Ambitions." *Eighteenth Century Studies* 1989: 329-360.

_____."Public Sphere and Private Life: Toward a Synthesis of Current Historiographical Approaches to the Old Regime." *History and Theory* 31 no. 6 (1992): 1-20.

Gunst, Péter. "Marczali Henrik (1856-1940)." In Henrik Marczali, *Világtörténelem - Magyar történelem*. Történetirók Tára. Budapest: MTA Történettudományi Intézet, Gondolat, 1982.

Gyáni, Gábor. *Hétköznapi Budapest. Nagyvárosi élet a századfordulón*. Budapest: Városháza, 1995.

_____. *Az utca és a szalon*. Budapest: Uj Mandátum, 1999.

_____, and György Kövér. *Magyarország társadalomtörténete a reformkortól a második világháboruig*. Budapest: Osiris, 1998.

Haberer, Erich. *Jews and revolution in nineteenth-century Russia*. Cambridge, New York: Cambridge University Press, 1995.

Habermas, Jürgen. *The Structural Transformation of the Public Sphere: An Inquiry into a Category of Bourgeois Society*. Trans. Thomas Burger with Frederick Lawrence. Cambridge, Mass.: Cambridge University Press, 1989. In Hungarian: *A társadalmi nyilvánosság szerkezetváltozása*, transl. Zoltán Endreffy. Budapest: Gondolat, 1971.

Halasz, Nicholas. *Captain Dreyfus: The Story of a Mass Hysteria*. New York: Simon and Schuster, 1955.

Hanák, Péter. *Magyarország a Monarchiában*. Budapest: Gondolat, 1975.

_____. "Problems of Jewish Assimilation in Austria-Hungary in the Nineteenth and Twentieth Centuries." In *The Power of the Past: Essays for Eric Hobsbawm*, eds. Pat Thane, Geoffrey Crossick, and Roderick Floud, 235-50. Cambridge, New York: Cambridge University Press, 1984.

_____. *A Kert és a Műhely*. Budapest: Gondolat, 1988. In English: *The Garden and the Workshop. Essays on the Cultural History of Vienna and Budapest*. Princeton, N.J. Princeton University Press, 1998.

_____. *Ragaszkodás az Utópiához*. Budapest: Liget, no date.

_____, ed. *Magyarország története 7, 1890-1918*. Budapest: Akadémiai, 1978.

_____, ed. *Zsidókérdés, asszimiláció, antiszemitizmus*. Budapest: Gondolat, 1984.

_____, ed. *The Corvina History of Hungary, from Earliest Times until The Present Day*. Budapest: Corvina, 1991.

Harper, Paul V., ed., with the assistance of Donald Thompson. *The Russia I Believe In: The Memoirs of Samuel N. Harper, 1902-1941*. Chicago, Ill.: Chicago University Press, 1945.

Hatvany, Lajos. *Urak és emberek*. Budapest: Szépirodalmi, 1980.

Hewitt, Nancy. *Women's Activism and Social Change: Rochester, New York, 1822-1872*. Ithaca, N.Y.: Cornell University Press, 1984.

Hine, Thomas. "Lines of the Times." *Inquirer* 26 November 1995, 27.

Horváth, Zoltán. *A magyar századforduló*. Budapest: Gondolat, 1961.

Hufton, Olwen. *The Prospect Before Her: A History of Women in Western Europe*. London: HarperCollins, 1995.

Hughes, H. Stuart. *The Sea Change: The Migration of Social Thought, 1930-1965*. New York: Harper&Row, 1975.

Isenberg, Sheila. *A Hero of Our Own: The Story of Varian Fry*. New York: Random House, 2001.

Jackman, Jarrell C., and Borden, Carla M., eds. *The Muses Flee Hitler: Cultural Transfer and Adaptation, 1930-1945*. Washington, D.C.: Smithonian Institution Press, 1983.

Jászi, Oszkár. "Emlékiratok (1953-55)" in György Litván and János F. Varga, eds., *Jászi Oszkár publicisztikája* (Budapest: Magvető, 1982)

_____. *Magyar kálvária - magyar föltámadás.* Vienna: Bécsi Magyar Kiadó, 1920. Reprint, Budapest: Magyar Hirlap Könyvek, 1989.

_____. *The Dissolution of the Habsburg Monarchy.* Chicago and London: University of Chicago Press, 1929.

Jemnitz, János and György Litván. *Szerette az igazságot.* Budapest: Gondolat, 1977.

Kádár, Judit. "'A legerotikusabb magyar irónő': Erdős Renée."In *Szerep és alkotás*, ed. Nagy Beáta and Margit M. Sárdi, 117-124. Debrecen: Csokonai, 1997.

Kaplan, Marion A. *The Making of the Jewish Middle Class: Women, Family and Identity in Imperial Germany.* New York: Oxford University Press, 1994.

Karády, Viktor. "A numerus clausus és a zsidó értelmiség." In *Iskolarendszer és felekezeti egyenlötlenségek Magyarországon (1867-1945).* Budapest: Replika, 1997.

_____. "Egyetemi antiszemitizmus és érvényesülési kényszerpályák: Magyar zsidó diákság a nyugat-európai föiskolákon a *numerus clausus* alatt." In *Iskolarendszer és felekezeti egyenlötlenségek Magyarországon (1867-1945).* Budapest: Replika, 1997.

Károlyi, Mihály. *Hit illuziók nélkül*, trans. György Litván. Budapest: Európa, 1977.

Kárpáti, Endre. "Madzsar József moszkvai leveleiböl." *Századok*, Budapest 105 no. 1 (1971): 105-134.

Katus, László. "Magyarország gazdasági fejlödése (1890-1914)." In *Magyarország története 7, 1890-1918*, ed. Péter Hanák, 263-401. Budapest: Akadémiai, 1978.

Kende, Zsigmond. *A Galilei Kör megalakulása.* Budapest: Akadémiai, 1974.

Kent, Donald Peterson. *The Refugee Intellectual: The Americanization of the Immigrants of 1933-1941.* New York: Columbia University Press, 1953.

Kettering, Karen L. and Knoxville Museum of Art, *Eva Zeisel: The playful search for beauty*, published in conjunction with an exhibition held at the Knoxville Museum of Art. (Knoxville, Tenessee:

2004).

Key, Ellen, with an introduction of Havelock Ellis. *Rahel Varnhagen: A Portrait*, trans. Arthur G. Chater. New York and London: G. P. Putnam's Sons, 1913. Reprint: Westport, Conn.: Hyperion Press, 1976.

Klier, John Doyle. *Imperial Russia's Jewish Question, 1855-1881*. Cambridge, New York: Cambridge University Press, 1995.

Koestler, Arthur. *Scum of the Earth*. London: Jonathan Cape, 1941. The Danube edition. London: Hutchinson, 1968.

_____. *Arrow in the Blue*. London: W. Collins and H. Hamilton, 1954.

_____. *The Invisible Writing, The Second Volume of an Autobiography: 1932-40*. New York: First Stein and Day Editions, 1984.

_____, Ignazio Silone, André Gide, Richard Wright, Louis Fischer, and Stephen Spender. *The God that Failed: Six Studies in Communism*. London: Hamish Hamilton, 1950.

Kontler, László. *Millennium in Central Europe: A History of Hungary*. Budapest: Atlantisz, 1999.

Kovács, Mária M. "The Politics of Emancipation in Hungary." In *Women in History - Women's History: Central and Eastern European Perspectives*. CEU History Department Working Paper Series 1., eds., Andrea Pető and Mark Pittaway, 81-85. Budapest: Central European University, 1994.

Kövér, György. *Iparosodás Agrárországban*. Budapest: Gondolat, 1982.

Krohn, Claus-Dieter. *Intellectuals in Exile: Refugee Scholars and the New School for Social Research*, trans. Rita and Robert Kimber. Amherst, Mass.: The University of Mass. Press, 1993.

Kropf, Lewis L. "Captain John Smith of Virginia." *Notes and Queries* 9, 7th series (1890): 1-2, 41-3, 102-4, 161-2, 223-4, 281-2.

Lackó, Mihály. *Halál Párizsban, a történész Grünwald Béla müvei és betegségei*. Budapest: Magvető, 1986.

Lackó, Miklós. *Válságok - választások*. Budapest: Gondolat, 1975.

_____. *Sziget és külvilág*. Budapest: MTA Történettudományi Intézete, 1996.

Landes, Joan B. "The Public and the Private Sphere: A Feminist Reconsideration." In *Feminists Read Habermas: Gendering the Subject of Discourse*, ed. Johanna Meehan, 91-116. New York and London: Routledge, 1995.

Lanouette, William with Bela Silard. *Genius in the Shadows: A Biography of Leo Szilard, The Man Behind the Bomb*. New York: C. Scribner's Sons, Toronto: Maxwell Macmillan Canada, New York: Maxwell Macmillan International, 1992.

Laqueur, Walter. *Generation Exodus. The Fate of Young Jewish Refugees from Nazi Germany*. Hanover, N. H.: University Press of New England for Brandeis University Press, 2001.

Lazarsfeld, Paul. "An Episode in the History of Social Research: A Memoir." In *The Intellectual Migration: Europe and America, 1930-1960*, eds. Donald Fleming and Bernard Bailyn, 270-337. Cambridge, Mass.: The Belknap Press of Harvard University Press, 1969.

Lehmann, Hartmut, and James J. Sheehan, eds. *An Interrupted Past: German-Speaking Refugee Historians in the U.S. after 1933*. Cambridge, Mass.: Cambridge University Press, 1991.

Lemay, J. A. Leo. *The American Dream of Captain John Smith*. Charlottesville, London: University of Virginia, 1991.

Lengyel, György. *Vállalkozók, kereskedök, bankárok. A magyar gazdasági elit a 19. században és a 20. század elsö felében*. Budapest: Akadémiai, 1989.

Lessard, Susannah. "Profiles: The Present Moment." *New Yorker*, 13 April 1987: 36-59.

Lesznai, Anna. *Kezdetben volt a kert...* Budapest: Szépirodalmi, 1966.

Linczényi, Adorján. *Lelki problémák a pszichoanalizis tükrében: Válogatás Ferenczi Sándor müveiböl*. Budapest: Magvetö, 1982.

Litván, György. "Bevezetés." *A szociológia elsö magyar mühelye: a Huszadik Század köre*, vols. 1-2. Budapest: Gondolat, 1973.

_____. *Magyar gondolat - szabad gondolat*. Budapest: Magvetö, 1978.

_____. *Szabó Ervin, a szocializmus moralistája*. Budapest: Századvég, 1993.

_____. "Introduction: Oscar Jászi (1875-1957)." In *Oszkár Jászi, 1875-1957, Homage to Danubia. States and Societies in East Central Europe.* Lanham, Md.: Rowman & Littlefield, 1995.

_____. *Októberek üzenete.* Budapest: Osiris, 1996.

_____. "Egy barátság dokumentumai: Károlyi Mihály és Jászi Oszkár levelezéséböl." In *Októberek üzenete.* Budapest: Osiris, 1996.

_____, ed. *Károlyi Mihály levelezése, 1905-1920* vol. 1. Budapest: Akadémiai, 1978.

_____, ed. *Oszkár Jászi, 1875-1957, Homage to Danubia. States and Societies in East Central Europe.* Lanham, Md.: Rowman & Littlefield, 1995.

_____, and László Szücs, eds. *A szociológia elsö magyar mühelye: a Huszadik Század köre* vols. 1-2. Budapest: Gondolat, 1973.

_____, and László Szücs, eds. *Szabó Ervin levelezése* vol.1. Budapest: Kossuth, 1977.

_____, and János F. Varga, eds. *Jászi Oszkár publicisztikája.* Budapest: Magvetö, 1982.

_____, eds. *Jászi Oszkár válogatott levelei.* Budapest: Magvetö, 1991.

Lixl-Purcell, Andreas, ed. *Women of Exile: German-Jewish Autobiographies since 1933.* New York, Westport, Conn.: Greenwood Press, 1988.

Luft, David S. *Robert Musil and the Crisis of European Culture 1880-1942.* Berkeley, Los Angeles, London: University of California Press, 1980.

Lukacs, John. *Budapest 1900: A Historical Portrait of a City and Its Culture.* New York: Weidenfeld & Nicolson, 1988.

Magyar Statisztikai Évkönyv, Uj folyam 18 (1910). Budapest: Magyar Királyi Statisztikai Hivatal, 1911.

Mah, Harold. "Phantasies of the Public Sphere: Rethinking the Habermas of Historians." *Journal of Modern History* 72 (March 2000): 153-182.

Marczali, Henrik. "Emlékeim." *Nyugat* 22 (1929) no. 2, 569-76, no. 3, 29-35, 96-112, 225-34, 295-302, 352-68, no. 4, 416-24, 477-84, 709-721.

Marczali, Henrik. *Világtörténelem - Magyar történelem.* Történetirók Tára, ed. Péter Gunst. Budapest: MTA Történettudományi Intézet, Gondolat, 1982.

Marino, Andy. *A Quiet American: The Secret War of Varian Fry*. New York: St. Martin's Press, 1999.

McCabe, Cynthia Jaffee. "Wanted by the Gestapo: Saved by America - Varian Fry and the Emergency Rescue Committee." In *The Muses Flee Hitler: Cultural Transfer and Adaptation, 1930-1945*, ed. Jarrell C. Jackman and Carla M. Borden, 79-91. Washington D. C.: Smithonian Institution Press, 1983.

McCagg, William Jr. *Jewish Nobles and Geniuses*. Bloomington, Ind.: Indiana University Press, 1971, reprint 1986.

_____. "Vienna and Budapest Around 1900: The Problem of Jewish Influence." In *Hungary and European Civilization*, ed. György Ránki, 241-263. Bloomington, Ind.: Indiana University Press, 1986.

_____. "The Role of the Magyar Nobility in Modern Jewish History." *East European Quarterly* 20 no. 1 (Spring 1986): 41-53.

McQuaig, Linda. *All You Can Eat: Greed, Lust and the New Capitalism*. Toronto, London, New York: Viking by Penguin Books, 2001.

McRobbie, Kenneth. "Ilona Duczynska: Sovereign Revolutionary." In *Karl Polanyi in Vienna: The Contemporary Significance of The Great Transfrormation*, eds. Kenneth McRobbie and Kari Polanyi Levitt, 255-264. Montreal, New York, London: Black Rose Books, 2000.

_____, ed. *Humanity, Society, and Commitment: On Karl Polanyi*. Montreal, New York: Black Rose Books, 1994.

_____, and Kari Polanyi Levitt, eds. *Karl Polanyi in Vienna: The Contemporary Significance of The Great Transfrormation*. Montreal, New York, London: Black Rose Books, 2000.

Meager, William. "Acclaiming an American Hero." Review of Captain John Smith, His Life and Legend, by Bradford Smith. *Christian Science Monitor*. 1 October 1953, 11.

Meehan, Johanna, ed. *Feminists Read Habermas: Gendering the Subject of Discourse*. New York and London: Routledge, 1995.

Minczeles, Henri. *Vilna, Wilno, Vilnius: la Jérusalem de Lituanie*. Paris: Editions La Découverte, 1993.

Nagy, Beáta and Margit M. Sárdi, eds. *Szerep és alkotás*. Debrecen: Csokonai, 1997.

Nagy, Endre J. "After Brotherhood's Golden Age: Karl and Michael Polanyi." In *Humanity, Society, and Commitment: On Karl Polanyi*, ed. Kenneth McRobbie, 80-99. Montreal, New York: Black Rose Books, 1994.

Nelken, Halina. *And Yet, I Am Here*. Amherst, Mass.: University of Mass. Press, 1999.

Neumann, Franz L., Henri Peyre, Erwin Panowsky, Wolfgang Köhler, and Paul Tillich. *The Cultural Migration*. New York: Barnes and Co., Perpetua edition, 1960.

Offen, Karen, Ruth Roach Pierson, and Jane Rendall, eds. *Writing Women's History*. Bloomington, Ind.: Indiana University Press, 1991.

Olger, Hertha. *Alfred Adler: The Man and his Work*. Third, revised and enlarged edition. London: Sidgwick and Jackson, 1963.

Orlov, Alexander. *The Secret History of Stalin's Crimes*. New York: Random House, 1953.

Pachter, Henry. "On Being an Exile: An Old-Timer's Personal and Political Memoir." In *The Legacy of the German Refugee Intellectuals*, ed. Robert Boyers, 12-51. New York: Schocken, 1972.

Paletschek, Sylvia, and Bianka Pietrow-Ennker (eds.), *Women's Emancipation Movements in the 19th Century: A European Perspective*. Stanford, Calif.: Stanford University Press, 2004.

Perlman, Robert. *Bridging Three Worlds: Hungarian-Jewish Americans, 1848-1914*. Amherst, Mass.: University of Mass. Press, 1991.

Pető, Andrea and Mark Pittaway, eds. *Women in History - Women's History: Central and Eastern European Perspectives*. CEU History Department Working Paper Series 1. Budapest: Central European University, 1994.

Pichler, Franz. "Captain John Smith in the Light of Styrian Sources." *Virginia Magazine of History and Biography* 65 no. 3 (July 1957): 332-54.

Plant, Richard. "Being Gay, Becoming Jewish." In *Hitler's Exiles: Personal Stories of the Flight from Nazi Germany to America*, ed. Mark M. Anderson, 311-316. New York: New Press, 1998.

Polanyi, Karl, H. Arensberg, and H. Pearson, eds. *Trade and Market in the Early Empires*. New York: The Free Press, 1957.

Polanyi, Michael. *USSR Economics: Fundamental Data, System, and Spirit*. Manchester: University of Manchester Press, 1936.

_____. "Jewish Problems." *Political Quarterly* 1943: 33-45.

Polanyi, Thomas. "Letter to Éva Gábor, editor-in-chief, *Polanyiana*." *Polanyiana* 8 nos. 1-2 (1999): 85-86.

Polanyi Levitt, Kari, ed. *The Life and Work of Karl Polanyi*. Montreal, New York: Black Rose Books, 1990.

Puskás, Julianna. Ties That Bind, Ties That Divide: 100 years of Hungarian Experience in the United States. New York, London: Holmes&Meier, 2000.

Quack, Sibylle, ed. *Between Sorrow and Strength: Women Refugees of the Nazi Period*. Washington, D.C.: German Historical Institute and Cambridge University Press, 1995.

Ránki, György, ed. *Hungary and European Civilization*. Bloomington, Ind.: Indiana University Press, 1986.

Ránki, Vera. *The Politics of Inclusion and Exclusion: Jews and Nationalism in Hungary*, with a foreword by Randolph Braham. New York, London: Holmes and Meier, 1999.

Rau, L. *Jerusalem in Lithuania: Illustrated and Documented*, 3 vols. New York: Vilno Album Committee, 1974.

Rendall, Jane. "Women and the Public Sphere." *Gender and History* 11 no. 3 (November 1999)

Rosenblit, Marsha. *The Jews of Vienna 1867-1914: Assimilation and Identity*. Albany, N.Y.: State University of New York Press, 1983.

Rupp, Leila J. *Worlds of Women: The Making of an International Women's Movement*. Princeton, N. J.: Princeton University Press, 1997.

Ryan, Mary. *Cradle of the Middle Class: The Family of Oneida County, New York, 1790-1865*.

Cambridge, England: Cambridge University Press, 1981.

Sánta, Gábor. "Schneider Fáni (Lux Terka Budapestje)." In *Szerep és alkotás*, ed. Beáta Nagy and Margit M. Sárdi, 93-100. Debrecen: Csokonai, 1997.

Schiffer, Felix. "Vorgartenstrasse 203: Extracts from a Memoir." In *Karl Polanyi in Vienna: The Contemporary Significance of The Great Transfrormation*, eds. Kenneth McRobbia and Kari Polanyi Levitt, 328-346. Montreal, New York, London: Black Rose Books, 2000.

Sinkó, Ervin. *Egy regény regénye: Moszkvai naplójegyzetek 1935-1937*. Ujvidék: Forum, Budapest: Magvetö, 1988.

Smith, Bradford. *Captain John Smith: His Life and Legend*. New York: Lippincott, 1953.

Smith, Ellen Hart. "The Many Lives of Capt. John Smith." Review of Captain John Smith, His Life and Legend, by Bradford Smith. *New York Herald Tribune Book Review* 4 October 1953, 4.

Solomon, Peter H., Jr. *Soviet Criminal Justice under Stalin*. Cambridge, England, New York: Cambridge University Press, 1996.

Spencer, Samia I., ed. *French Women and the Age of Enlightenment*. Bloomington, Ind.: Indiana University Press, 1984.

Sperber, Manès. *All Our Yesterdays*, vol 2, *The Unheeded Warning, 1918-1933*, trans. Harry Zohn. New York, London: Holmes & Meier, 1994.

Steen, Karen E. "The Playful Search for Beauty." *Metropolis*, January 2001, 85-87.

Stites, Richard. *Revolutionary Dreams: Utopian Vision and Experimental Life in the Russian Revolution*. New York, Oxford: Oxford University Press, 1989.

Strauss, Herbert. *In the Eye of the Storm*. New York: Fordham University Press, 1999.

Strauss, Lotte. *Over the Green Hill: A German Jewish Memoir, 1913-1943*. New York: Fordham University Press, 1999.

Strickerné, Pollacsek, Laura. *Néhány szó a nöröl s nönevelésröl*. 1906. Reprint in the Széchény National Library. In *Irástudó nemzedékek: A Polányi család dokumentumai*. vol. 7, Archivumi füzetek, ed. Erzsébet Vezér, 49-60. Budapest: MTA Filozófiai Intézet Lukács Archivum, 1986.

_____. "III. Károly gazdaságpolitikájáról hazánkban." Reprint from *Közgazdasági Szemle*, 1-55. Budapest: Pesti Könyvnyomda, 1909.

Striker, Barbara. "Re: Judit Szapor, 'Laura Polányi, 1882-1959: Narratives of a Life.'" *Polanyiana* 8, nos. 1-2 (1999): 83-4.

_____. "'This is the voice of Radio Schutzbund.'" In *Karl Polanyi in Vienna: The Contemporary Significance of The Great Transfrormation*, eds. Kenneth McRobbie and Kari Polanyi Levitt, 272-74. Montreal, New York, London: Black Rose Books, 2000.

Striker, Laura Polanyi. "Captain John Smith's Hungary and Transylvania." In *Captain John Smith: His Life and Legend*, Bradford Smith, 311-42, New York: Lippincott, 1953.

_____. "Captain John Smith in Seventeenth Century Literature." In *The Life of John Smith English Soldier*, Henry Wharton, 3-31. Chapel Hill: University of North CArolina Press, 1957.

_____. "The Hungarian Historian, Lewis L. Kropf, on Captain John Smith's *True Travels*: A Reappraisal." *Virginia Magazine of History and Biography* 66 no. 1 (1958): 22-43.

_____, and Bradford Smith. "The Rehabilitation of Captain John Smith." *Journal of Southern History* 28 (1962): 474-81.

Szapor, Judit. "Les associations féministes en Hongrie, XIX-XXe siècle." *Pénelope* no. 11 (Fall 1984): 169-73.

_____. "Egy szabad egyetemért: a Társadalomtudományok Szabad Iskolája." *Medvetánc* 1985/86 no. 4-1: 125-158.

_____. "Laura Polányi, 1882-1969: Narratives of a Life." *Polanyiana* 6, no. 2 (1997): 43-54.

_____. "Sisters or Foes: Women's Emancipation and Women's Movements in Hungary." In *Women's Emancipation Movements in the 19th Century: A European Perspective*, ed. Paletschek, Sylvia and Pietrow-Ennker, Bianka. Stanford University Press, 2004, 189-205.

_____. "'Mit akarnak a radikális asszonyok?' Nöi politikusok az 1918-as demokratikus forradalomban." In *Magyar nök a politikában*, ed. Beáta Nagy. Debrecen: Csokonai, forthcoming.

Szegvári, Katalin N. *Numerus clausus intézkedések az ellenforradalmi Magyarországon.* Budapest:

   Akadémiai, 1988.

_____ and Andor Ladányi. *Nök az egyetemeken: küzdelmek a nök egyetemi tanulmányaiért.*

   Budapest: Fövárosi Pedagógiai Könyvtár, 1976.

Szerb, Antal. "Az elsö amerikai Erdélyben." *Magyar Nemzet,* 12 September 1940, 9.

_____. "Captain John Smith in Transylvania." *Hungarian Quarterly* 6 (1940): 734-41.

_____. *Magyar irodalomtörténet.* Fifth edition. Budapest: Magvetö, 1972.

Szilard, Leo. "Reminiscences." In *The Intellectual Migration: Europe and America, 1930-1960,* eds.

   Donald Fleming and Bernard Bailyn, 94-151. Cambridge, Mass.: The Belknap Press of Harvard

   University Press, 1969.

Thane, Pat, Geoffrey Crossick, and Roderick Floud, eds. *The Power of the Past: Essays for Eric*

   Hobsbawm. Cambridge, New York: Cambridge University Press, 1984.

Trotsky, Leon. *My Life: An Attempt at an Autobiography,* with an introduction by Joseph Hansen.

   London: Penguin Books, 1975.

Vágó, Márta. *József Attila.* Budapest: Szépirodalmi, 1975.

Vaughan, Alden T. *American Genesis: Captain John Smith and the Founding of Virginia.* The Library

   of American Biography, ed. Oscar Handlin. Boston, Toronto: Little, Brown, 1975.

Vezér, Erzsébet. *Kaffka Margit.* Budapest: Szépirodalmi, 1976.

_____. *Lesznai Anna élete.* Budapest: Kossuth, 1979.

_____. "The Polanyi Family." In *The Life and Work of Karl Polanyi,* ed. Kari Polanyi-Levitt, 18-25.

   Montreal, New York: Black Rose Books, 1990.

_____, ed. *Irástudó nemzedékek: A Polányi család dokumentumai.* vol. 7, *Archivumi füzetek.*

   Budapest: MTA Filozófiai Intézet Lukács Archivum, 1986.

Vörös, Károly. *Egy világváros születése.* Budapest: Kossuth, 1973.

_____. "Birth of Budapest: Building a Metropolis, 1873-1918." In *Budapest: A History from Its*

Beginnings to 1998, eds. András Gerö and János Poór, 103-38. Social Science Monographs, Boulder, Co., Distributed by Columbia University Press, 1997.

_____,ed. *Budapest története*, vol. 4. Budapest: Akadémiai, 1978.

Weiner, Charles. "A New Site for the Seminar: The Refugees and American Physics in the Thirties." In *The Intellectual Migration: Europe and America, 1930-1960*, eds. Donald Fleming and Bernard Bailyn, 190-234. Cambridge, Mass.: The Belknap Press of Harvard University Press, 1969.

Weissberg, Alexander. *The Accused*, trans. Edward Fitzgerald, with a preface by Arthur Koestler. New York: Simon and Shuster, 1951.

Weisskopf, Victor. *The Joy of Insight: Passions of a Physicist*. New York: Basic Books, A Division of Harper Collins Publishers, 1991.

Wharton, Henry. *The Life of John Smith English Soldier*. Trans. Laura Polanyi Striker. Chapel Hill: University of North Carolina Press, 1957.

Wiltsher, Anne. *Most Dangerous Women: Feminist Peace Campaigners of the Great War*. London, Boston and Henley: Pandora, 1985.

Wistrich, Robert S. *The Jews of Vienna in the Age of Franz Joseph*. Littman Library by Oxford University Press, 1989.

Wyman, David. S. *Paper Walls: America and the Refugee Crisis, 1938-1941*. Amherst, Mass.: University of Massachusetts Press, 1968. Revised edition New York: Pantheon Books, 1985.

_____. *The Abandonment of the Jews: America and the Holocaust, 1941-1945*. New York: Pantheon Books, 1984.

Young, Lucie. "Still Ahead of the Curve." *New York Times*, 14 August 1997, section C, 1, 6.

Zeisel, Eva. Memoirs. Unpublished manuscript.

Zeisel, Hans. "In Memoriam." In *The Life and Work of Karl Polanyi*, ed. Kari Polanyi-Levitt, 241-44. Montreal, New York: Black Rose Books, 1990.

Zimmermann, Susan. "Frauenbestrebungen und Frauenbewegungen in Ungarn. Zur

Organisationsgeschichte der Jahre 1848-1918." In *Szerep és alkotás*, ed. Beáta Nagy and Margit M. Sárdi, 171-204. Debrecen: Csokonai, 1997.

Zuccotti, Susan, *The Italians and the Holocaust: Persecution, Rescue, and Survival*. New York: Basic Books, 1987.

Zweig, Stefan. *The World of Yesterday: An Autobiography*. London: Cassell, 1987.

Fig. 1.Three generations of Polanyi women: Laura, Eva,and Cecile, at their
last reunion, winter of 1937 Budapest.

Fig. 2. The Pollacsek ancestors: Zsofia and Adolf Pollacsek, around 1850.

Fig. 3. A. Wohl, rabbinical scholar and assimilationist.

Fig. 4. The Pollacseks' living room around the turn of the century;
Cecile with the portrait of the children..

Fig. 5. Andrássy út, representative of the capitalist splendour
of the Hungarian capital, in 1899. The Pollacsek apartment occupied
most of the third floor of the building on the left.

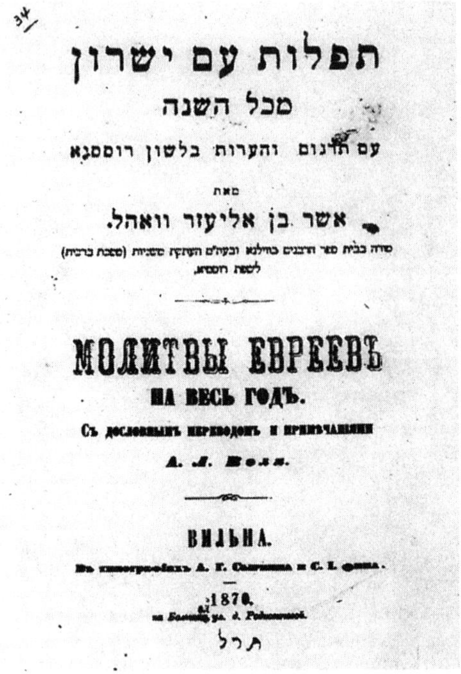

תפלות עם ישרון
מכל השנה
עם דינום והערות בלשון רוסיא
מאת
אשר בן אליעזר וואהל.
סדור בבית פאר וחדבנים כהולפא ובקהלים העוצקן הסביות (שבת ברכית)
לשנה חרסא.

МОЛИТВЫ ЕВРЕЕВЪ
НА ВЕСЬ ГОДЪ.
Съ дословнымъ переводомъ и примѣчаніями
А. Л. Воль.

ВИЛЬНА.
Въ типографіяхъ А. Г. Сыркина и С. Л. фина.
1870.
на Большой ул. д. Романовской.
תרל

Fig. 6. The title page of A. Wohl's Prayer of the
Jews for the Whole Year, Vilna, 1870.

Fig. 7. Mihály Pollacsek (on the right) with his brother Károly
in the early 1900s.

Fig. 8. The salon at the beginning of the 20th century. In the centre, in her trademark reclining position, Cecile. To her right, Mihály Pollacsek. Sitting on the far right, Ervin Szabó and Oszkár Jászi.

Fig. 9. Young Laura (in the middle) with the Klatschko girls at the Klatschkos' summer house at Hinterbrühl, near Vienna, around 1900.

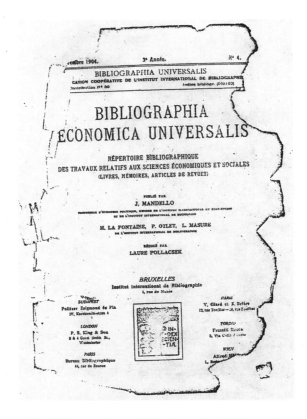

Fig. 10.Title page for the 1904 edition of the Bibliographia
Economica Universalis, edited by "Laure Pollacsek."

Fig. 11. Portrait of Laura from the early 1900s.

Fig. 12. Laura and Sándor Stricker shortly after the birth
of their first child.

Fig. 13. The young wife and mother in the
summer of 1907.

Fig. 14. Laura with Michael and Eva, in impeccably tailored, matching outfits, around 1909.

Fig. 15. Laura and her children in the garden of her kindergarten under 86 Andrássy út, in 1911. Attesting to Laura's progressive pedagogical ideas, the picture was sent as a postcard to her friend, Recha Rundt in Vienna.

Fig. 16. "Aunt Mausi" teaching, 1911. Eva is on the right. Note the gym outfits and bare feet of the children.

Fig. 17. The classroom of the kindergarten. In the first row to the left is Eva Stricker, behind her in the last row is young Arthur Koestler.

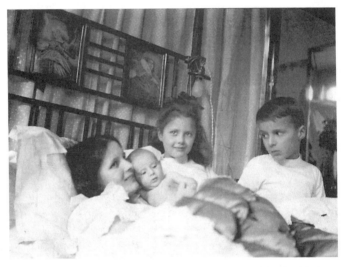

Fig. 18. An intimate portrait of Laura with Michael and Eva, shortly after the birth of their brother George Otto in 1912.

Fig. 19. Karl Polanyi on leave in Vienna, with the Stricker children around 1915. In the back: Sophie and Cecile.

Fig. 20. The family during World War I: Egon Szécsi, Sophie, Cecile, Adolf, Médi Vedres, and (in uniform) Karl and Michael Polanyi.

Fig. 21. At home on the Danube: Sándor and Laura with (from left) Gina Stricker, Eva and Michael Stricker, and unidentified children.

Fig. 22. Laura, the only Polanyi sibling remaining in Hungary, with her husband and youngest son around 1920.

Fig. 23. Portrait of the young artist: Eva in the garden during the early 1920s.

Fig. 24. Alexander Weissberg and Eva in the Soviet
Union, early 1930s.

Fig. 25. Laura in front of a Lenin monument, somewhere in the Soviet Union.

Fig. 26. Laura, back from the Soviet Union.

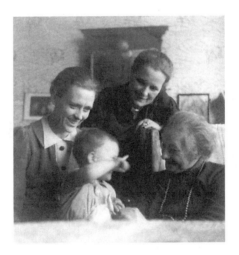

Fig. 27. Last visit: Cecile with Laura, Hilde, and
Michelle Stricker in Budapest, end of 1938.

Fig. 28. Family reunion in uncertain times: Michael, Adolf, and
Laura Polanyi in England, spring of 1939.

Fig. 29.Laura in her New York apartment in the early
1950s, posing under Cecile's portrait. Laura's inscription
on the back: "The thoughtful mother and her pretty little
daughter."

Fig. 30 The last reunion of the four surviving Polanyi siblings in New York in 1954: Michael, Adolf, and Karl, with Laura lovingly looking on.

Fig. 31. One of the last pictures of Laura.